Praise for *Taking Stock*

'Tremendous … We all need to take stock, and this is the ideal starting point. I learnt a lot from this book and laughed a lot too.'
  ROSAMUND YOUNG, author of *The Secret Life of Cows*

'No cow could ever hope for a better appreciation of its truly unique worth.'
  BETTY FUSSELL, author of *Eat, Live, Love, Die* and *Raising Steaks: The Life and Times of American Beef*

'An epic story told with warmth, wit and humanity. Will make us feel differently about these long-suffering animals.'
  GRAHAM HARVEY, author of *Grass-Fed Nation*

Praise for *Liquid Gold*

'A great book. Painstakingly researched, but humorous, sensitive and full of wisdom. I'm on the verge of getting some bees as a consequence of reading the book.'

CHRIS STEWART, author of *Driving Over Lemons*

'A light-hearted account of midlife, a yearning for adventure, the plight of bees, the quest for "liquid gold" and, above all, friendship.'

Sunday Telegraph

'*Liquid Gold* is a book that ignites joy and warmth through a layered and honest appraisal of bee-keeping. Roger Morgan-Grenville deftly brings to the fore the fascinating life of bees but he also presents in touching and amusing anecdotes the mind-bending complexities and frustrations of getting honey from them. But like any well-told story from time immemorial, he weaves throughout a silken thread, a personal narrative that is at once self-effacing, honest and very human. In this book you will not only meet the wonder of bees but the human behind the words.'

MARY COLWELL, author of *Curlew Moon*

'Beekeeping builds from lark to revelation in this carefully observed story of midlife friendship. Filled with humour and surprising insight, *Liquid Gold* is as richly rewarding as its name-sake. Highly recommended.'

THOR HANSON, author of *Buzz: The Nature and Necessity of Bees*

'Behind the self-deprecating humour, Morgan-Grenville's child-like passion for beekeeping lights up every page. His bees are a conduit to a connection with nature that lends fresh meaning to his life. His bee-keeping, meanwhile, proves both a means of escape from the grim state of the world and a positive way of doing something about it. We could probably all do with some of that.'

DIXE WILLS, *BBC Countryfile magazine*

'Peppered with fascinating facts about bees, *Liquid Gold* is a compelling and entertaining insight into the life of the beekeeper. But it's much more than that. It's the story of a life at a cross-roads when a series of random events sets the author off on a different, and more satisfying, path. It's a tale of friendship and fulfilment, stings and setbacks, successes and failures and finding meaning in midlife.'

WI Life

'[A] delightfully told story ... Wryly humorous with fascinating facts about bees, it charts the author's own mid-life story and the joys of making discoveries.'

Choice magazine

'The reader will learn plenty about bees and beekeeping from this book, although it is about as far from a manual as pos-sible. *Liquid Gold* is a well observed delve into the hobbyist's desire to find what is important in life, no matter their age or preparedness.'

The Irish News

'[A] delightful exploration of the world of bees and their honey ... a hymn to the life-enhancing connection with the nat-ural world that helped Morgan-Grenville reconcile himself to the fading of the light that is middle age.'

Country & Town House magazine

'Both humorous and emotionally affecting ... Morgan-Grenville's wry and thoughtful tale demonstrates why an item many take for granted should, in fact, be regarded as liquid gold.'

Publishers Weekly

Praise for *Shearwater*

'This charming and impassioned book meanders, shearwater-like, across a lifetime and a world, a rich tribute to an extraordinary bird drawn through tender memoir and dauntless travel.'

HORATIO CLARE, author of *A Single Swallow* and *Heavy Light*

'*Shearwater* is sheer delight, a luminous portrait of a magical seabird which spans the watery globe'

Daily Mail

'This is wonderful: written with light and love. A tonic for these times.'

STEPHEN RUTT, author of *The Seafarers: A Journey Among Birds*

'What I love about Roger Morgan-Grenville's writing is the sheer humanness of it ... There are environmental issues and pure natural history in here, but the overall feel of the book is simple, humble wonder. Roger was lucky to have a grandmother who knew how to gently foster a live-wire mind. She loved birds, she loved Roger, and the combination guided him to her way of thinking as he grew older – and this odyssey for shearwaters is the result. Bravo – a truly lovely book.'

MARY COLWELL, author of *Curlew Moon*

'*Shearwater* is a delightful and informative account of a lifelong passion for seabirds, as the author travels around the globe in pursuit of these enigmatic creatures.'

STEPHEN MOSS, naturalist and author of *The Swallow: A Biography*

'A memoir lit by wry humour and vivid prose ... his evocation of the Hebrides is as true as the fresh-caught mackerel fried in oatmeal his grandmother used to cook for him.'

BRIAN JACKMAN, author of *Wild About Britain*

'This is a book that birders will enjoy because it is stitched together around a fairly amazing bird, but if you've never heard of shearwaters you will still get a lot out of this book if you are interested in nature, in adventures, in foreign parts, in landscapes or in people ... a very good read.'

MARK AVERY

'A great read'

birdwatching.co.uk

'[A] lovely blend of natural history and memoir ... Morgan-Grenville beautifully blends science, memories, and wonder in this striking homage to an amazing bird.'

Booklist

'A captivating mix of memoir, travel and ornithological obsession ... A book not just for seabirders or island-addicts, but for all who have ever gazed longingly out to sea and pondered vast possibilities and connections.'

BBC Wildlife magazine

'Morgan-Grenville is a delightful writer ... his writerly tone here is perfect: serious, but not hysterical or preachy, with a gleam of hope evident.'

10,000birds.com

'A beautiful mix of memoir and natural history ... entirely infectious.'

Scottish Field

By the same author

Across a Waking Land (Icon, 2023)

Shearwater: A Bird, An Ocean, And a Long Way Home (Icon, 2021)

Liquid Gold: Bees and the Pursuit of Midlife Honey (Icon, 2020)

Unlimited Overs (Quiller, 2019)

Not Out of the Woods (Bikeshed Books, 2018)

Not Out First Ball (Benefactum Press, 2013)

Taking Stock

Taking Stock

A Journey Among Cows

Roger Morgan-Grenville

ICON

First published in the UK and USA in 2022
by Icon Books Ltd, Omnibus Business Centre,
39–41 North Road, London N7 9DP
email: info@iconbooks.com
www.iconbooks.com

This edition published in the UK in 2023 by Icon Books Ltd

ISBN: 978-178578-952-6

Text copyright © 2022 Roger Morgan-Grenville

British Library Cataloguing in Publication Data.
A catalogue record for this book is available from the British
Library.

Typeset in Sabon by Marie Doherty

Printed and bound in Great Britain by
Clays Ltd, Elcograf S.p.A.

CONTENTS

ABOUT THE AUTHOR

Roger Morgan-Grenville was a soldier in the Royal Green Jackets from 1978–86, serving all over the world. In 1984–85, he led the first expedition that successfully retraced Sir Ernest Shackleton's escape across the sub-Antarctic island of South Georgia. After leaving the British army, he worked in, and then ran, a small family company importing and selling kitchenware. In 2007–08, he helped to set up the charity Help for Heroes, and in 2020 he was a founding member of the conservation charity, Curlew Action. He jointly set up a roving cricket team in 1986 (The Winchester Hunters) and lives in West Sussex. This is his sixth book. His earlier titles, *Liquid Gold* and *Shearwater*, are also published by Icon.

DEDICATION

This book is dedicated to every livestock farmer in the world who puts excellence ahead of speed, welfare ahead of profit and biodiversity ahead of tidiness.

And, particularly, to John and Emma who patiently walked me through their world for the best part of eighteen months, and still gave me digestive biscuits every time I turned up.

GRATITUDE

There is a long list of acknowledgements at the back of the book, but I am obviously profoundly grateful to Caroline, Tom and Alex for their patience, encouragement and love while I was writing it.

PROLOGUE
The Everywhere Cow

The Market Cross, Chichester

....

'God does not play dice'
ALBERT EINSTEIN

....

Come in from the fields for a time. Our modern cow story begins right in the heart of a busy city.

By the market cross a teenage boy polishes off his burger, before putting the packaging in a bin and carefully wiping his mouth on the sleeve of his sweatshirt before sauntering happily away towards the cathedral.

A few yards from him, a small group of girls sit on the stone bench and, draining off their fruit smoothies, they laugh at a limping seagull.

Nearby, turning right out of West Street and into South Street, a bus passes, its hissing air-brakes momentarily masking the sound of its tyres running across the urban tarmac.

Just behind them, the safety company is doing its annual inspection of the fire extinguishers in the Dolphin and Anchor, just as the barman removes the drying towels from the handles on the pumps in preparation for what he hopes will be the evening rush.

A few yards into East Street, an undergraduate removes his £30 from the tray of the cashpoint at Barclays, the light catching briefly on his glasses as he turns into the sunshine to walk back to his flat to complete his overdue essay on feedback loops.

You might not think so, but cows are virtually everywhere, even in those tyres, that tarmac, that cash, those glasses, that fire extinguisher. If the evening rush in that pub creates hangovers, then it is even highly likely that a cow will be involved in the cure.

Vanishingly little that you do with your life, or buy, or use, or move around in, doesn't have a cow involved at some point, often many points.

Halfway through a quiet Thursday afternoon in the little cathedral city of Chichester, the unseen signature of the cow is everywhere, as it is in every village, town and city in the country.

You will find it in every aisle of the supermarket: on the meat counter and the dairy section, of course, in the tempting artisan Brie and the tasteless processed slices of factory cheese. It is present in the chewing gum in the dispenser by the checkout, in the powdered supplements and the packaging of the unappetising curry meal for two. The clean shirt that you put on to go shopping went through a pre-wash that was assisted by a cow, and the granite sideboard you picked it up from this morning was clean partly because a cow was involved in the cleaning agent.

If you stopped to count the number of times it appears in the pharmacy in East Street, you would be there for hours, days perhaps: shaving cream, lipstick, soap, sunscreens, dental floss, shampoos, cough syrups, bubble baths and moisturising creams would simply be the tip of a vast iceberg of bovine derivatives that have worked their way into the supply chain.

In the sweet shop, it's the gum in those chewy sweets, the nougat, the marshmallows and the little white bits in some of those chocolate chip cookies. It's in the sophisticated scented candles of the gift shop next door, and the soles and uppers of the beautiful Italian shoes that are reduced from £140 to £90 in the shoe shop just up from the jewellers.

Down in the garden centre, you will find it in the fertiliser, manure and bonemeal, and much else besides; it's in your left hand when you take out your wallet, and your right when you pay for your purchases with that £20 note. As you head across the ring road to the DIY store, it'll be waiting for you in the plywood adhesives, the rust inhibitors, the greases, the lubricants.

If you walk far enough down North Street, you can just about make out the roofs of St Richard's Hospital. Every department there relies, to some extent, on a by-product of a cow, whether it is heparin in the anticoagulants used to treat post-operative patients, the adrenal glands in the steroids that are prescribed, or the tiny quantities of pancreas within the insulin given to diabetics. Anti-adhesion bandages, injectable collagen, tissue sealants – even in the treatment of varicose veins, a tiny bit of the cow will be there to help you out when you need it. She is, indeed, an animal of gifts.

Even the fact that you don't have, and never will have, smallpox – a disease, let's not forget, that killed around 30% of everyone who caught it – is basically down to a cow called Blossom. After all, where do you think the word 'vaccine' came from?*

Ten thousand years after Neolithic man first domesticated cattle, and whether we know it or not, the cow is almost as tightly woven into our daily lives as the air that we breathe: one billion of them,† one for every seven and a half of us, and they are in every country of the world except Greenland and The Vatican. You will find them grazing just about everywhere, from the beautiful pastures of the Sussex Weald to the dusty plains of Ethiopia, and from the forest clearings in Borneo to the windswept prairies of Canada. A third of all the cows on earth live in India, which comes as a surprise to some, and you can make that into a half if you add Brazil, neither of them countries you would naturally associate with ideal grazing conditions.[1] Rather less than 1% of them live in Britain, even though it has some of the most reliable rain, and best grassland on earth.

In support of our species, and for millennia, cattle have also carried loads for us, pulled our carts and dragged our ploughs. They have been asked to go to war with us, and to

....

* From *vacca*, the Latin for cow, because of the early use of the cowpox virus in the treatment of its much nastier cousin, smallpox.

† 987,510,000, to be exact (Statista, 2020). But you will find any figure between that and 1.5 billion, depending on where you look. For consistency, I have used the Statista figure throughout.

fight, and charge and buck for our entertainment. Often, they have provided rudimentary central heating to families deliberately choosing to live above the rising heat from their bodies. Many of our words for money and property, *pecuniary* and *chattel*, for example, are derived from the cow's status as a signal of wealth, even transferable wealth. They are venerated in Hinduism, Jainism and Zoroastrianism, have played walk-on parts in many other religions, and are seen as a measure of wealth by cultures like the Kenyan Maasai and the Mundari in South Sudan. We even send them as gifts.

But here's the rub.

They may be ten times as much practical help to us as other, more feted, domesticated animals, but their lot instead is to be frequently mocked rather than respected. After all, no one ever called a cow 'man's best friend', or used the term as a compliment. In the pecking order of our respect for domesticated animals, the cow is probably in fourth place after the dog, horse and cat, and just above sheep, goat and chicken. In the last 100 years, the average productivity of a cow has doubled, while its average life expectancy has halved, which is good if you are a shareholder of a soya shipping business in Brazil, less so if you are called Daisy and just want to live out in the meadow.

We worry about the methane from their wind, even though there were probably greater numbers of large ruminants burping their way around the countryside three centuries ago than there are cattle now; we read reports about slurry pits leaching into watercourses, and we note with alarm the huge distances that cattle feed has to travel these days to reach them, and the rainforests that are cleared for their grazing, or for crops that they will consume thousands of miles away. The cow has become the unwitting battleground over which we fight our battles on diet, lifestyle, biodiversity loss, land and water use, and animal ethics. At the same time, for all that they give us – and it is a great deal – we ask very many of them to lead lives of indentured slavery in grassless, sunless sheds and joyless barns. Evolved to graze the grasslands, summer and winter, many of them instead lead entirely indoor lives, and are then blamed for the fossil fuel emissions that result from a global supply chain that is bringing largely unsuitable food substitutes halfway across the world to grow them faster than mere biology could.

Let's not conveniently invent a mythical past when the grass was greener, the world kinder and everything for the cow was perfect, but something significant seems to have happened in the last half century or so, something that has created a giant one-way gap of understanding between people and cattle. It is as if we have stopped making any serious connection between the beast grazing in the field and the milk we drink, the beef we eat, let alone the shoes we wear. Maybe it is a conscious distancing from a concept (in this case the inevitable death that precedes meat) that makes us feel uncomfortable; maybe our busy lives are just too full of gifts already to remember that the cow should rightfully be considered one of them. Or maybe, when we first wandered off into the towns and cities and left our cattle behind in their pastures out beyond the ring road, we left our manners on the grass right there with them, the deadlines and challenges of our utterly connected urban lives just leaving no space for a creature we'd rather not know too much about. When our own species slaughters 34,000 of theirs each hour,[2] you might start to think that this is a strange oversight.

In a part of the world where we pay around half the relative amount on food that we did 30 years ago, and where that food travels ever further, and from ever more industrial processes to be on our plates, it is hardly surprising that we have become disconnected from its origins. At a time when around 11% of our planet's 7.7 billion people go hungry,[3] and yet over twice that amount are overweight or obese,[4] it should not come as a shock to us that we have persuaded ourselves that food is an issue for people brighter than us, no more than one of the routine obligations of the busy day, and not the still point of our turning world that it arguably should be. As the argument rages, it is quite easy to overlook that the British Isles is probably the most suitable place on earth to raise cattle, in terms of its grass-friendly climate and geology, its plentiful water supply and its relative soil equilibrium. But, with a world expected to double its demand for meat over the first half of this century,[5] not even the most committed steak eater can pretend that things don't need to change.

We live in the most de-natured corner of a determinedly de-natured world, within which the cow finds itself marked up as biodiversity villain rather than the ecosystem engineer it should be. For some reason, farming bores us. After all, agriculture these days accounts for under 1% of Britain's GDP, and we are paying fifteen times the annual budget of our farming and countryside ministry (Defra*) just on a little-wanted railway

---

* Department for Environment, Food and Rural Affairs.

line upgrade from London to Birmingham.[6] Back in 1925, there were over a million agricultural workers against a sixth of that now,[7] so the chances of you knowing and understanding someone who works on the land are vastly reduced. When a senior Treasury adviser argues in his bizarre submission to the National Food Strategy that 'Britain doesn't need farmers' and that the food sector 'isn't critically important to the UK',[8] you can start to understand the issue, if not the solution. Unlike most countries, we are a pliant people of almost limitless faith who have been happy to entrust 90% of our food supply into just eight boardrooms,[9] so you could be forgiven for thinking that we don't really care – certainly not about having any semblance of control.

Then again, when the *Oxford Junior Dictionary* disposes of words like *acorn*, *buttercup* and *crocus* in favour of *analogue*, *broadband* and *chatroom*, it is perhaps understandable that our children grow up to replace *cow* with *curry*. The human race tends to comply with Gilbert's theory of belief, a crude version of which is that we come to accept as true what we are most repeatedly told, whatever the evidence against it might be.[10] And like all modern consumers, we generally like to blame everyone but ourselves for the consequences of the decisions we make on our weekly shopping trips. One of the questions which this book examines is what we have been told about cows over the last few years, and what we have therefore ended up believing. Some of it is right, some nearly right, and some plain wrong. Very little of it does the cow any favours.

That cow grazing quietly on that little bit of pasture just

outside town* is a sophisticated, intelligent and highly social animal that has unwittingly done more than just about any other creature to help man in his relentless climb to the top. As John Connell points out: 'It is we who brought them from the wilderness to join our family and walk by our side.'[11] From continent to continent and century to century, for 10,000 years, they have trotted compliantly behind us wherever we go. It's time we celebrated them. There has never been a better time to remind ourselves of their contribution, past and present, and of our responsibility to work out a good future for them.

You might call this their side of the story.

....

* Or *inside* the city limits, in the case of Cambridge, where traditional breeds such as Longhorn, Red Poll and Hereford have been grazing the city's green spaces for centuries, saving the authorities a fortune in mowing bills, conditioning the soil, and making tourists happy. It is a service known as 'pinder'.

PART 1

Then

1. A PREHISTORIC JOURNEY

3.5 billion years ago—20,000 BCE

....

'The chicken is only an egg's way of making another egg'
RICHARD DAWKINS

....

I am not a farmer. I just happen to like cows. They press a button in my soul that other, perhaps better regarded animals simply don't.

My sole contribution to agriculture until recently was the one late, scorched summer in 1976 that I spent doing bale-cart for Jim Bennett on his mixed farm down the road from us in the Rother Valley. Looking back at it, Jim paid me, quite literally, pence,* but he treated me well and, most important, he allowed

....

* Thirty of them for each hour I worked, according to my diary at the time. Agricultural labourers' basic hourly wage was about £1.27; teen-agers took what they were offered.

me to drive the old red Massey Ferguson tractor with its articulated snake of trailers behind it. As a spotty teenager who was an angry confusion of odd attitudes, being paid anything at all to drive around our local lanes towing the winter's hay back to the barn was a glimpse over the wall into the secret garden, and I would probably have done it for free, if he'd asked me to. In a quiet village where I sometimes felt that I amounted to little more than being my father's son, this was a short-term leasehold on manhood. I often took the long route home just on the off-chance of being seen by more people, especially if they included my parents. To be in charge of anything, let alone an agricultural machine of fully 39 horsepower, showed that I had achieved something, and that my playing days were over. More importantly, the cash enabled me to park for a time the rather perilous income stream that flowed from my having spent that summer furtively selling the koi carp from my parents' fish pond while they weren't looking, to people I fondly hoped they would never meet.*

In those days, working on the land was the only possibility in our valley in terms of holiday jobs, and the only casual work that was generally available was seasonal fruit and vegetable picking: strawberries (before the strawberry field was turned into a house and garden), apples (before the trees were grubbed up too, to make way for new homes), and backbreaking Brussels sprouts on the coastal plains in the January

* With cruel irony, one of them eventually did meet my father, introduced to him by the vicar after the harvest festival at our parish church. 'Wonderful fish you have,' was all he needed to say to bring my world crashing down.

frost. Nothing that I experienced in nine subsequent years of serving in the Army all over the world came close, in toughness, to my routine 30-mile round trip through the dark and freezing fog on an underpowered motorbike, sandwiching eight hours of leaning over sodden yet frosted sprout plants, being paid piece rate in competition with scarily robust women who had done it all their lives, and who made it abundantly clear that I was an idiot, and in the way.

Everything else has gone, but 40 years on, those wretched sprouts are still grown in the same bloody field. To this day, a shard of misery enters my body whenever I see a Brussels sprout.

I think my first awareness of cows was triggered by the tiny plastic black and white ones which populated the fields of My Little Town, a primitive German set of wooden houses, combined with Dinky cars that were five times the size of the livestock, in all of whose company I would pass hour after aimless hour once my older sister had gone off to primary school and I was waiting for her to return. My first sustained experience of cows, however, came during our holidays at my grandmother's Hebridean croft, with the docile and shaggy Highland cattle that wandered right up to the dry stone walls of her garden, and sometimes, to her fury, right through them and on into her vegetable patch. To an impressionable boy who had not yet learned what he liked in life, let alone what he actually wanted to do with the years ahead of him, those Highland cattle were a compelling metaphor for a wildness and solidity that I missed down south, but which nonetheless filled me with happiness and excitement.

Bit by bit, and breed by breed, cows became an enduring fascination for me. Also, as a boy who enjoyed making lists, I found that I could add different breeds of cow to the rich diversity of things that I already counted up in my little notebooks: birds, planes, trains and castles, for a start. I must have been an irritating passenger in the family car as we drove around Europe on our holidays, shouting out 'Charolais' or 'Évolène' every time we drove past a field.

'It will pass,' said my mother. But it didn't.

Evolution is, of course, not a planned journey with a clear direction of travel, but a gradual change in characteristics from one generation to the next brought about by the innate need to maximise the chances for subsequent generations, and the connection between a simple, ancient bacterium and our modern cow is a long and tortuous one. For the first three billion years or so, it is also extremely boring, as the bacteria bit lasts a lot longer than we might like it to.

The potted history of bovine evolution begins in earnest a quarter of a billion years ago, when the cow's ancestors, along with those of all other mammals including humans, were cynodonts, 'advanced mammal-like reptiles of the middle and late Triassic that were dog-like predators',[1] rather than the dinosaurs that we would secretly like them to have been. So let's say that we need to go back around 300 million years to when we and cows shared common ancestors. It was a time when the world was covered by warm, shallow seas, and the climate was generally humid and mostly unchanging from season to season. Gradually, changes in jaw structure and function led to differentiations in what these creatures went on to become, changes that we can at least keep track of, since bones, unlike skin and hair, fossilise. By 50 million years ago, the cow's ancestors had become *Artiodactyla*, animals with short legs and a set of teeth that suggests that they lived on herbage rather than meat. With a brain cavity that was about the size of a walnut, you can draw any unkind conclusions you choose about their mental capacities.

If their minuscule brains were actively involved in anything other than eating, which on the face of it seems rather unlikely, they were probably taken up in trying to avoid becoming a meal for one of the resident predators of the time. And as that time went by, they divided and sub-divided, first into camels and ruminants, and then further into deer, giraffe and bovines. But we can guess with some assurance that they left behind a genetic trail that led inexorably to the ruminants.

The first recognisable ruminants probably evolved around 50 million years ago and lived in forests. They would have been much smaller than the modern cow, and most likely omnivorous, 'not unlike the primitive chevrotain, a type of small deer known as the mouse-deer, which still inhabits the rainforests of Malaysia'.[2] It would have been at this point that they developed the two-way digestive system that allowed recently eaten food to come back up for a second go in the mouth, before going back down into the 'fermentation vat' below. This chewing of the cud has defined ruminants ever since, and is what uniquely allows them, but not competitors, to feed off what a fifth of the world is carpeted with, namely grass. It almost certainly evolved to allow what was a prey animal to graze swiftly in the relative danger of the forest clearings, and then get back to the safety of the deep forest to process the food at its leisure. Indeed, it is sometimes easy to overlook that these were once forest animals.

Around 750,000 years ago, one branch of the cynodont's descendants evolved into what we now know as the aurochs, ancestor of all our cattle, and a herbivore that we would probably recognise today. It originated in what is now India, and its fossilised signature appears to us tantalisingly all over the Eurasian landmass, deprived of traces of its soft tissue but still able to articulate the journey it has taken, and passing on the occasional hint of its role as an ecological engineer that will be one of the abiding themes in this story.

So with what other animals would those early ruminants have been sharing their grazing lands, say, 50,000 years ago? If we narrow our search down to the small herd of aurochs in the Fertile Crescent of the Middle East from which cows most likely descended, they might have been seeing dwarf elephants no taller than a modern deer, wild horses, Merck's rhinos and hippos 'the size of a large pig'.[3] And in the interests of avoiding becoming someone else's meal, they would have been alert to the presence of predators such as man himself, spotted hyenas and steppe lions.[4] As it worked its slow way westwards, the aurochs probably became a more and more substantial meal for a carnivore, as it grew ever larger.

From the very start, the aurochs had a use to the earth far beyond its status as the occasional meal for a predator, described nicely by its official biographer:

Grazing and browsing with their front end, trampling with heavy weight and sharp hooves with the middle, relieving themselves from their rear end, and at the end of their lives dying and becoming carcasses. All vitally important features for a multitude of species, from butterflies and microbes to fungi, birds, beetles, reptiles, plants and trees. Among the grass eaters, the aurochs with its great eating and cellulose-processing capacity, its herd behaviour and its abilities to reproduce, was the most important keystone species. The ecological value of bullshit has defined the natural heritage of Europe for thousands of years.[5]

As we shall see, in the face of great transformation and many millennia later, nothing has really changed in terms of that ecological value.

The strangest thing of all would not have been the variety of animals around the aurochs that would be unrecognisable to us today, but the speed and intensity at which they headed for extinction in the next 30 or 40 millennia – and the bigger they were, the quicker they went. As with the dinosaurs, so with the megafauna. In North America alone, it is thought that three-quarters of the continent's large herbivores disappeared in just a 10,000-year period, around the time man was domesticating cattle elsewhere. These days, we call that period the 'Near Time', and we are led to believe that the rapid extinctions came about through a chance coming together of localised climate change and all the normal human-driven challenges: hunting, fires, and possibly infections.* (Rather pleasingly, a recent study

* We will see in Chapter 5 what a disease like rinderpest can do to a population.

has also come up with the argument that, fundamentally, the thicker your species is, the more it will thrive, on the basis that big brains need more food, which leads to lower population densities.[6] Philosophically, this raises intriguing questions for the future of mankind, or it might prove that we have been thick all along, and just plain lucky.) As with the ocean-going seabirds in our current era, it turned out that man arrived, and increased, at a rate that simply didn't allow their local competitors to adapt in time, including learning the useful and often overlooked quality of fear.

Whatever the causes of it all, the aurochs would once have been no more than a medium-sized resident of its ecosystem; by 10,000 years ago, it was one of the largest animals left in the northern hemisphere. Fast forward another hundred years or so from now, and the cow will likely be the largest animal on earth.

The inconvenient and inelegant truth is that if you were a large animal, and man didn't have a continuous and profitable use for you, you were in all likelihood heading for extinction. Granted, if you happened to live on an inaccessible island, you would maybe have lasted a little bit longer: the Wrangel Island woolly mammoth, stranded by rising sea levels, hung on in there right up to 1500 BCE, sticking two elephantine fingers up at the problems of its tiny available gene pool.* Other than

....

* As if to confirm the point, the modern and flightless Inaccessible Island rail survives and thrives on its little corner of the South Atlantic simply because man hasn't yet contrived to introduce rats there. The hint is in the name.

that, it was fundamentally one-way traffic for between 750 and 1,000 of our biggest animal species. 'Ours is a dwarf and remnant fauna,' as George Monbiot puts it, 'and, as its size and abundance decline, so do our expectations, imperceptibly eroding to match the limitations of the present.'[7] As our story progresses, opinion may divide on whether the survival of cattle has always been to their benefit, but in evolutionary terms they have certainly utilised mankind just as much as we have utilised them. So it is for sheep, goats, pigs, dogs and even corn.

The wider bovine family evolved into its different types by travelling vast distances, and across land bridges, into other continental land masses. In 1879 in Altamira, Spain, a series of cave paintings of what was quite clearly a primitive cow were discovered, telling us not only that the aurochs were around a very long time ago, but that they were also clearly on man's radar, as why else would he or she bother to engrave their likenesses onto a limestone slab all over south-west Europe? Although humans were still some time away from domesticating them, they obviously formed an important part of the fauna that they hunted. Representing in art the things that we are about to eat is one of the more esoteric of our contributions to global culture, something that resonates through the centuries into the thousands of sensually illustrated cookbooks today. From Lascaux to Lawson,* from longing to lust, food has happily always stirred in us some emotion deeper and more visceral than just eating the stuff.

....

* Nigella Lawson, of course.

Between the 'glacial maximum' of the last Ice Age (25,000 BCE) and 10,000 BCE, it seems that a series of overlapping processes drew Palaeolithic man into the twin activities of domestication and cultivation that eventually led to what we know as agriculture and its bedfellow, settled living. Far from happening only in one place, this process was going on in at least six distinct areas, from the Yangtze Delta in China to the Mexican plains, all involving our forebears at slightly different stages of development. To get an idea of what life was like on the eve of our era as farmers, we can reasonably safely say that it was 20 degrees Celsius colder than now, with a sea level 100 feet below current levels, and that we had already developed quite sophisticated clothing, tools and art. Life also tended to be conducted in the coastal regions, where experience had suggested the prey was both more abundant and rather less likely to eat you. Pleasingly, it is also likely that we had already domesticated the wolf, and developed beer, long before the last Ice Age glaciers retreated, meaning that the practice of walking my old dog down to the pub of an evening is probably a whole lot older than I thought.

From the outset, the forerunners of cattle were herd animals, drawing life, safety and comfort from being part of a group, and exhibiting every sign of mental agony when deprived of it. Even the Great Hall at Altamira has depictions of twenty or more aurochs grazing together. This matters throughout our story. Within the herd, a prey animal doesn't have to waste energy on being ever on the lookout for trouble and, as 19th-century anthropologist Francis Galton put it, it receives 'a maximum security at the cost of a minimum of restlessness'. And with herds came the structures and hier-archies that we can still see, for example, in dairy farms today where the same dominant female leads the other cows in every day for milking.

Even though aurochs* were widespread, it was possibly just one small population of them† in the Middle East that became the ancestors of the vast majority of domestic cattle on earth, when Neolithic man in that area started to iden-tify the possible benefits of keeping a useful animal close and handy, particularly one that could convert one protein source that humans couldn't deal with, grass, into two that they could, meat and milk. This was a pivotal development and we are fairly certain it took place between 10,000 and 12,000 years ago.

From this point onwards, cows were inextricably linked to mankind, whether they liked it or not.

＝

It is late summer and I am leaning over a gate with my friend, John, staring into a field of cows, his cows.

Under the slanting rays of the evening sun, they seem to exude a sheen of well-being, and I tell him so.

'Do you think so?' he asks, looking happy with the compliment.

....

* The original plural of aurochs was aurochsen, from which, with some help from the old German languages, we arrive at the word 'oxen'.
† Some researchers say that the herd concerned was as small as 80 head. Others put the numbers at more like 1,000.

The noise of long tongues wrapping themselves around clumps of grass and tearing them out fills the comfortable silence. Committed grazing is a noisier activity than you might think. It will take me a number of months before I work out that it is also just one stage in a natural cycle of huge and benevolent complexity. Eat, move, repeat is what most of their lives consist of. Eat, move, repeat. It's kind of what I did as a boy.

'What's the key to what you do?' I ask after a while. 'I mean, what makes your animals special to the people who buy them?'

He thinks about it for a moment. 'Well, I suppose that it's to create the healthiest, best-looking, best-mannered cattle that I possibly can, and then send them off to improve the bloodline on other farms.'

'How do you do that?'

The white on the bellies of the last of the summer's swallows catches the horizontal sun, as they tirelessly pluck insects from the sky to sustain them on their coming flights to Africa.

'Grass management,' he says with a faint smile, 'plus what's in this book.' He opens up a dirty old blue hardback notebook, small enough to have come out of the side pocket of his trousers, and shows it to me. Lines of handwritten numbers, names and dates fill each page, together with the sort of grubby off-green stains that you would tend to associate with a life spent among cattle. He hands it to me, and I notice that it smells of farming.

'That's everything I've done for the last ten years, I suppose. It's a record of every calf we've ever reared, who the mother was, who the bull was, what date the calf was born and what its registered number is. Even where it eventually went,' he adds, as I look at the lines of neat simplicity. It is a monument to a decade's work.

'So tell me about this one.' I point at a nearby bull calf who has broken off from the main body of the herd and is grazing quietly near us at the gate. A large yellow tag in its right ear announces it as 1025, a number that, along with its details and a sample of its DNA, will be currently sitting in a record office somewhere up in Cumbria, along with those of the 9 million or so other cattle currently alive in Britain.

'Him? He's probably one of the best of this season's lot.' Then, without referring to his book at all, he adds: 'That's his mother over on the left, and you saw his father, Tiger, in the first field we went to. He was the larger of those three bulls we saw there.'

Tiger has done a good job for the farm in the short time he has been in action. Generally, calves that are sired by Tiger prove to be highly desirable. By now, 1025 is grazing his way back towards his mother, so we can only see him from the back end. When I ask John what makes a good calf, he suggests that we climb over the gate so that he can show me in person.

'He has to grow well,' he says, slapping the rump of the closest animal appreciatively, 'which probably means that, like this one, he is larger than the others of his age at any stage. He needs good legs, and a level, wide back, especially on a beef animal like this. I tend to look for a wide muzzle, for grazing efficiency, and for jaws that meet together well, not overshooting or undershooting, so that they don't get teeth problems later. Eventually, I want to see his weight in thickness and not in height. Ideally, he has good hooves, where the two parts aren't forever going to cross over each other and cause vet's bills.'

'And what's down the line for him? What's the plan for 1025?'

John thinks about it for a bit. 'If I'm lucky, and if he's lucky, and everything goes well, he'll go off to somewhere new next spring and perhaps start a bloodline of his own. Maybe Cornwall, maybe Cumbria, maybe Croatia. People will start coming to look at him in a week or so, or ask me to send them images of him from every angle. Then, if they like him, they'll make me an offer, and that will be that.'

'And if not? If he doesn't measure up?'

He doesn't answer, just turns his head northwards up the line of the road to Guildford and the abattoir. Breeding cattle is no business for the sentimental.

'And grass management?' I ask, curious as to the prominence that he had accorded it.

'We're organic,' he explains. 'Which means that we can't just dump additives onto fields to make them grow stuff quicker. The way we graze our 27 fields isn't so very different to how someone might have done a few centuries ago. Sometimes grazed, sometimes growing, sometimes cut for hay and silage* and sometimes just resting. The cows know when it is time to move on, and I know where to move them.'

Twenty-seven fields in 270 acres of low-lying flatlands, that's what land the farm consists of. And in between the fields

....

* Silage is grass cut shorter, greener and earlier in the season than hay, and then preserved through fermentation.

are the headlands* and wide ancient hedges, punctuated by tall oaks and ashes, that make each field a discrete entity and give it its distinctive character. And within the hedges and border-lines runs a network of small puddles and streams that trickle, chuckle and pour through culverts and descend down to the infant River Rother which, in turn, makes its way to the Arun and then the sea.

'It's a funny old thing, looking at these guys,' he says, after a pause. 'They reckon that every cow on earth is descended from one herd of around a couple of hundred aurochs in the Fertile Crescent about 10,000 years ago. Every single one.'

He is wrong, but not by much.

....

* A headland is traditionally the area at each end of a field where the machinery would be turned round.

2. MANKIND'S WORST-
EVER DECISION

20,000 BCE–5,000 BCE

....

'Extinction is the rule. Survival is the exception'
CARL SAGAN

....

On the way back to the farmhouse that evening, John paints a word picture of the aurochs, and gives me a tiny potted history that connects the Palaeolithic then with the pastoral now.

He is passionate and, in some recess of my mind, I remember a mild-mannered English teacher one day illuminating the poetry of Tennyson for the class with a passion so manifestly genuine, and so all-consuming, that it was almost impossible not to be hooked, even if you hated poetry, and hated English. As then, so now, I have unwittingly stumbled onto one end of John's emotional rainbow, and have discovered the crock of gold that lies there. In a world where many people I know merely tolerate their jobs, often just mouthing the right words in the right order to the right people until one day the music stops and they are free to go, I find only love.

After a while, he says, 'Stop me if I'm boring you', but I am fully absorbed. This is partly because getting to understand what makes another human being tick is one of the great unsung privileges of friendship; and partly because, in our virtual world of branding, management speak and the cynical quick buck, what could be less virtual than someone who has spent three decades getting incrementally better at just raising fine, happy animals?

He detects my enthusiasm and adds a sober postscript. 'The trouble is no one really wants to do it any more. I'm struggling to get everything done on the farm, and have been advertising on and off for a couple of years for some temporary help. It turns out that part-time farm labouring is not at all what people want these days. And it's not as though I'm getting any younger.'

He looks lean and fit to me, out there in the evening sun, but I take his point.

As we bump back down the track towards the farmhouse, he points out the three hand-reared Border Leicester sheep in a small field by the garden. The sheep are a sideline, but they are also part of what is probably the biggest flock of that breed left in the country. On the surface, it all looks like a little slice of paradise, but I already understand that this isn't how it actually is. The reality of livestock farming is just as much fallen fences, lame animals, mucking out, infections, paperwork, TB checks, worry, winter feeding, compliance, and cold, wet nights lambing, not to mention the sheer, routine loneliness. And that is before the gentlemen in face masks turned up at two o'clock one morning and revved their Subaru Forester to its limits in their attempt to break free the quad bike from its anchorage, and then threw a crowbar through the dark in John's general direction for good measure when he challenged them. Or before the endless changes in what is required from, or offered to, farmers by successive governments and supra-governments. I have enough friends in the business to know that, by any yard-stick, farming on your own can be as tough a career as there is. The scenery and the wildlife are just fringe benefits.

And yet there is something utterly beguiling about the sim-plicity of his search for excellence, about the way that I can imagine his life marching to the beat of a drum that has been sounding since before the time of the Bible. Besides, I have spent half a lifetime wanting to lean against gates and look at cows. Sometimes I feel that, along with eating digestive biscuits, this is what I have been put on earth to do.

When we turn into the yard, I look up at the neatly stacked bales of winter silage and try to frame my next question as casually as I can.

'That part-time labouring job. When are you interviewing?'

It turns out, for the time being at least, that the one thing wrong with my life is that it doesn't have enough cows in it.

⇌

If you can bear to ignore the ethnobotanist T.P. McKenna's attractive theory that man's interest in domesticating the aurochs was first pricked by the discovery of magic mushrooms in its dung, which personally I can't, there were probably three main reasons why we headed in that general direction: keeping a food source conveniently close by, using the by-products to keep warm, clothed and shod, and having something around that had the strength to pull and carry things that we didn't have the strength or inclination to pull and carry ourselves. Furthermore, whatever animal you ended up domesticating had to fulfil half a dozen conditions: fast growth and reproduction, no high jumpers or fast flight reactions, a robust digestion, a trusting disposition and a pack instinct.[1] Basically, the animal in question had to be able to be stripped of its aggression and fear without losing its social instincts; it had to be able to be bred in captivity and, finally, it had to grow fast on a food source that didn't compete with man's. Fundamentally, that is what sheep, goats, horses, pigs, dogs and chickens all did as well, but none of them to such a comprehensive degree as the cow.*

It would be wrong to look at the domestication of cattle as an isolated event in an isolated location, or to think that, even now, we know or agree on exactly how it happened. Prompted perhaps by the decline in availability of natural foods in their locality, our forebears all over the place were simply making the best use of the things they found around them, and then gradually using the best of them, and discarding the worst. That's the irritating thing about evolution: you can't give anything precise

---

* There is an outside chance that every domesticated pig comes from precisely the same region, and same timescale, as every domesticated cow. If you don't love that possibility, you should.

dates, or handy chapters. So, at the same time as they were domesticating beets for leaves, wheat for something they could turn into bread, and flax for something (linen) that was more comfortable to wear than animal skins, they naturally turned their attention to animals. And, if you wanted to guess why the powerhouse of Europe and Western Asia eventually ended up colonising most of the rest of the world, you might need to look no further than the fact that thirteen of the fourteen domesticated large animals on earth* were originally found only in Eurasia.†

How man actually did the domestication, and how long it took him, is still a matter for hot scientific debate and speculation. With dogs, which were probably domesticated a good deal earlier than the aurochs, it is thought that it could all have started by bringing back to the settlement the offspring of wolves killed in the hunt for amusement, and the same could apply to the aurochs. Alternatively it may be that such species were attracted towards human settlement and duly captured, or that they were set on what is known as a 'directed pathway' for some very specific purpose, such as riding in the case of the horse. Or that, as seems to be the case for the cow, it was simply a matter at the beginning of maintaining live prey, like having a few lobsters in a tank in an upmarket seafood restaurant. What is important is that it was done, and that, almost as soon as it

....

* The 'big five' (sheep, goats, cows, pigs and horses) are joined by Arabian and Bactrian camels, donkeys, reindeer, water buffalo, yak, Bali cattle, and mithan. Only the llama came from somewhere else.

† For much more on this fascinating theme, read Jared Diamond's *Guns, Germs and Steel*.

was done, restless Neolithic man began to head out from the Fertile Crescent to take his new lifestyle around to share with the rest of the world.* And the chances were that, wherever he was, he had a good go at domesticating each of the local fauna to his purposes, until he had comprehensively proved with each of them that it wasn't going to work.

Herding, which is what this was, was a sort of halfway house between hunter-gathering and full-blown agriculture, and cattle immediately would have presented man with a few challenges on his travels that were distinct from those of the smaller and more pliable sheep. First, sheep tended to be genetically predisposed to 'heft' themselves to a particular area (in the Lake District the Herdwick ones still do) and stay still, while cows behave like boisterous schoolchildren on a museum visit, and generally want to be wherever they aren't. Secondly, there is some evidence that even back at the beginning of farming, man had taught his domesticated wolves to round up sheep as a substitute for them actually hunting them,[2] whereas a cow would generally have had none of that.

Various advances in technology then set in motion the gradual transition from nomadic hunter to settled farmer, not least the innovations in stone-making technology, particularly polishing, that led to stones being used as hoes and rudimentary scythes, and not just axes and arrowheads for the hunt.

....

* Modern academic research suggests that there might have been, in fact, two (and possibly three) independent domestication events, rather than just the one in the Fertile Crescent, and that they could have been up to 4,000 years earlier, close to the first burst of warmth after the last Ice Age.

Slowly but surely, man gathered animals around him, used his knowledge of fire to clear the forests for them to graze more widely, and, equally slowly but surely, he developed the concept of property and of being settled. Probably more than any other thing, the cow enabled him to make the change from a life of perpetually going *to* somewhere to that of coming *from* somewhere, in the sense of belonging, on the back of which most of the ups and downs of our civilised lives have since ridden. Up in those rudimentary fields had already sprung weeds that became wheat, oats and barley, up from the ground rose fruit and nut trees that man now actually had time to wait for the fruits from, and which he duly plundered. Even our alphabet, which emerged out of the Fertile Crescent roughly the same time as cattle did, starts with the letter 'A', 'representing an ox-head turned upside down'.[3] Our knowledge of this period of history may be patchy, but it is quite clear that cattle have been our species' constant companion ever since. And that this changed everything, for us just as much as for the cows.

One of the many effects of humans settling down into fixed communities turned out also to be the single biggest thing that ever happened to our planet, certainly since ten square miles of meteor struck the Yucatan Peninsula in Mexico 66 million years ago. Through ridding themselves of the need to wait until the first child could walk unaided before they had the next, and the next, our species set in train the population explosion that has governed everything, ever since, and created the one giant problem of our modern lives that even spectacularly clever people have no answer for.

Indeed, the conversion of our ancestors from hunter-gatherers to food producers, which was more a collision of thousands of events and movements than any particular invention or discovery, is quite possibly the worst thing that ever happened to us. From that point on, we were fated to work hours that we weren't used to, eat food that we weren't suited to, fight wars we weren't equipped to, work under hierarchies we hadn't needed before, and breed killer germs that would otherwise have evaporated into the deep blue yonder. Fifteen thousand years ago, your hunter-gathering ancestor's gut saw around 150 health-giving food types a week; right now, it's lucky if it sees twenty.[4] It must have been with a hilarious lack of irony that people eventually started to refer to this as the 'ascent of man'. Some of them still do.

Simultaneously, our gradual development as food producers has led to our restless habit of changing everything around us that we see as not helpful to our species. It is a habit that 'distinguishes man from all other animals in that he, instead of adapting himself increasingly to his environment, has undertaken to subdue the environment to his purposes'.[5] In other words, what we criticise ourselves for doing in the 21st century, we have in fact been doing since the dawn of the Neolithic age.

There was one final huge change that this new agrarian life brought in its wake. Through creating food priorities, and the need to police them, from the surpluses that it produced, it inadvertently allowed the stronger males to dominate the physically weaker females, in a way that they never had as pastoralists and hunter-gatherers. And, with the occasional cultural exception such as the Irish Celts and the Vikings from the frozen north, it was how it was going to be from then on until the dawn of practical feminism. Women may have gained a measure of economic freedom through being in charge of the milk cow but, from that point on, it was hard to argue that it wasn't a man's world.

In a way, the cow had the easier part of it. But only in a way.

Up until the domestication events, the aurochs had always been something of a mob-grazer, a term that, because it will appear over and over in our story, bears a little deeper explanation. Fundamentally, mob-grazing describes a form of short-duration, high-density grazing in which the grazer instinctively knows when to move on, and when to move back in again.* It is one of the ultimate circles of virtue in the natural world, because the flipside of mob-grazing is the benefits that the grassland receives in turn from the grazers, which is the trampling effect of many hooves (for breaking up and aerating the soil), the growth-promoting effect of the way that the grass is eaten, and the fertilising dung that is left on the ground when the cattle move on. Co-evolution means that both sides have adapted to the perfect interval between visits. Perhaps the greatest mob-grazers of our times were the bison on the grasslands of the 19th-century Midwest United States, all 60 million of them,

---

* Also known as pulse grazing, rational grazing, short-duration grazing and controlled grazing. It was a concept reintroduced to the world in the 1950s by French biochemist André Voisin, in his book *Grass Productivity*, as if you needed reminding.

until they were killed off between 1800 and 1900, the evolutionary blink of an eye.*

Where previously he had travelled around in tight and unencumbered family groups, now man had the responsibility of accompanying animals, which meant that, when he got to somewhere that pleased him, he stayed put as much as possible, becoming, in the process, agrarian. Besides, travelling with a group of animals to keep fed, and to protect from marauding predators, was a rather riskier business than being in one place. As we have seen, this state of knowing where the next meal was to come from, rather than having to continually go out and chase it, set the scene for a population explosion that has multiplied humanity from an estimated 4 million in 10,000 BCE to 7.7 billion now.† Just how well this agrarian life has suited us, or the other 8.7 million species with whom we share our blue and green planet, has recently become rather less of a foregone conclusion than it was in the days when all of us, rather than just a select few, truly believed that we were God's chosen people. The select few drone on to this day, but generally we tend to ignore them.

....

* The locals had form. The passenger pigeon went from being the most abundant bird on the planet to extinction in 50 years, the 'victim of the fallacy that no amount of exploitation could endanger a creature so abundant' (Audubon). The last one, called Martha, died in Cincinnati Zoo aged 29, in 1914.

† An increase of around 200,000%, for what it's worth. During the same time, interestingly, the number of cattle on earth has increased by 125,000,000%. One day, if they haven't already, someone will do some academic research that links a species' usefulness to human beings to the steepness of its population growth.

While we wouldn't necessarily recognise the early agrarians' primitive little territories as the farms we know today, they gave time for the animals to slowly acquire characteristics of their own, suitable for whichever locality they found themselves in: for example, the Indian (or Indicine) cow became hardier and more drought-resistant than its western cousins. Thus, bit by bit, what had once been an aurochs split into a number of different, but still closely related animals. Even at that early stage, its human masters were also starting to genetically adapt their herds to their own purposes, by deliberately breeding their future stock from the less aggressive cattle, for example, and the ones that gave the biggest yield of milk, or had the smallest horns.*

You may be starting to drift off, but don't. You are just a genetic hair's breadth from entering the story yourself. Me too. And, if it's possible, it gets even more exciting.

꠲

Like all the best job interviews, it is remarkably short and unspecific.

'Sounds good,' says John, when I offer my services to the farm that sunlit evening. 'When do you feel like working?' No previous employer has so taken my own feelings into account at interview, still less been so refreshingly uninterested in any detail of my past, let alone a CV which, anyway, I don't possess.

---

* Ironic, as what would become the Texas Longhorn in the 1600s and 1700s evolved back towards having those long horns as a device for protecting their young from predators.

He thinks about the possible pinch points in his upcoming workload for a moment or two, and then suggests a start date a week or so later.

'Bring some gloves,' he adds mysteriously as I start to drive away. 'And some tea. I'll provide overalls.'

And so it is, on a misty Friday morning in mid-September, I make my optimistic way to John's farm to start my fourth career, armed only with a couple of cheese and pickle sandwiches, a flask of tea and a quiet determination to squeeze myself somewhere into that hundred-million-year story of the aurochs' descendants.

Obviously, I forget the gloves.

For the next eighteen months, I always forget the gloves.

3. FROM THE BIBLE
TO BEEF SHORTHORN

5000 BCE–1750 CE

....

'Progress is man's ability to complicate simplicity'
THOR HEYERDAHL

....

Early autumn, and it is tipping with rain.

The fact that it so regularly tips with rain in these islands is a major reason why our fields are so suited to grazing ruminants. The British Isles have what is probably the best natural grazing on the planet.

Back here in the 21st century, I am quickly learning that there is a great deal to absorb if I want to be half-useful in my new role. Clad in my uniform of green overalls and borrowed industrial gloves, I start to find my way around the patchwork of fields, paths, hedgerows and tiny waterways that make up the 270 acres of the farm, and to understand how each barn, outbuilding and bit of machinery has its own specific role in the work we do. I find out about the different groupings of cows in the different pastures, the calves still with their mothers, last year's heifers dotted around elsewhere, and the three resident bulls, Tiger, Saturn and Dancer, in robust isolation down by the edge of the village. One by one, I learn about the farm's 27 neighbours, and how each reacts to us.

All the fields have their names, of course, tokens of routine conversational currency that I have to quickly absorb. Most of these have been in place since before recent memory, which means that no one knows exactly how they became what they are, or who did it. It is easy to see how some of them got their titles – the Warren, Eleven Acre, Orchard Meadow and Church Field, for example – while some evolved over the years to reflect some change or other, such as Long Meadow turning into Brickyards. A few just hint at some centuries-old moment of caprice or whimsy, possibly the humouring of an enthusiastic or difficult child, and each time I trudge through them, it intrigues me to imagine how Pieces, or Silence, got their names.

The fields have their characters, too. This can depend on many things, from gradient to drainage, geology to shade and history, to name but a few. Some would make your heart soar with the bounty of it all; some sulk in dark corners of infertility, others still rise and fall between the two from season to season, and year to year. There are footpaths everywhere, which subtly add to the pressures. Ninety-nine out of a hundred walkers are ones with whom sharing the farmland is a privilege in itself, but the other 1%, who might leave a gate open that should be shut, or carelessly let their dog onto a sheep's throat, have an effect out of all proportion to their numbers. Curiously, the rights of the dog walker trump the rights of the new-born livestock every time.

I learn of the short cuts between fields at opposite ends of the farm, of the dark corners of sheds where small tools are stored, and of the careful, unhurried routines within which the work is done. Miles of fences and dozens of gates that to a visitor would simply be an unregarded component of an agreeable view, become the vital architecture of how we keep the livestock to where it is meant to be. Artificial though a farm may be, I quickly understand that it is an ecosystem of unimaginable complexity where the livestock are just a small part of a far wider circle of life, where loose ropes of birds rise and fall on the breeze, and a billion insects go about their work in the stagnant pools and the rotten boughs of the fallen oaks.

Back home, even my dog has to adapt to my new lifestyle. Having normally had my undivided attention on our morning walks, he now finds himself not only going out an hour earlier than usual but then, for the thirteen minutes between 5.45 and 5.58am, losing me entirely to my portable headphones and *Farming Today*, a BBC radio programme to which, incidentally, it takes me a further six months to find a single farmer who actively admits to listening. Before these days, the dog and I would constantly point things out to each other on our walks – principally wildlife that one wanted to draw the other's attention towards.

In an effort to be more helpful about the farm, I begin to absorb information, making no allowance as to whether it's relevant. It kicks off with basic terminology, but a few weeks in, if you asked me the current market prices for store cattle in Carlisle or Exeter, I could not only tell you, but would also insist that you were explicit about whether you meant continental-sired, native-sired or Holstein Friesian. *The Times* on the breakfast table gives way to *Farmers Weekly*, and my bedside reading material metamorphoses from novels and wildlife books to the *American Red Angus Magazine* (published ten times a year, at $100 including airmail) and various pamphlets from the Beef Association. My wife Caroline notices that I am even more boring than normal, and she holds a pleading hand up to me over breakfast as I regale her with the inner protocols of TB testing regimes.

Farming is generally quite a repetitive activity, and the arrival of someone new and interested is a not unwelcome interlude; it prompts John to hand over a veritable library of out-of-print cattle books to me each Friday evening, with which I can further my education. From histories of selective breeding to accounts of the Nguni cattle of the Zulu people, I start making up for 50 wasted years by trying to appreciate what a life around cows boils down to.

And, like all new ventures in a life, I have an entirely fresh vocabulary to come to terms with. I have entered a world where people routinely speak of 'store cattle' and of 'suckler herds', of 'herbal leys' and 'marbling'.* If I want to do anything other

....

* Obviously you know. But, on the tiny off-chance you don't, store cattle are growing animals up to about two years old that are bought and finished; a suckler herd is a beef herd where the calves stay with the cows; herbal leys are complex 'seed mixture[s] of grasses, legumes and herbs', which bring benefits to both the grazers and the soil condition; and marbling means the intra-muscular fat that, for many, defines good beef.

than nod in a confused way, then I need to go back to school. Thus, the pile of books on my bedside table grows higher and higher, just as I am rarely seen out in public without my rolled-up copy of the *Farmers Guardian*. (*Farmers Weekly*, so I am told by another farmer, is for 'posh boys' from down south who studied at Cirencester, whereas *Farmers Guardian* is for northerners who like to drone on endlessly about machinery and market prices. Traditionalists lament the passing of *Farmer and Stockbreeder*, and edgy people with car stickers seem to buy *Country Smallholding*.)

Above all, I become powerfully aware that my time here is just a frame frozen in the long story of an animal that has been grazing its way across these very pastures for millennia, no more than a polite clearing of the throat in the journey of their evolution.

⇋

The direct ancestor of calf number 1025 had arrived in north-western Europe by about 5000 BCE, and it had made the journey either round the Mediterranean coast or up the Danube Valley. Either way, by that date, there would have been cattle pretty close to the ones we know today, grazing around the North Sea,* and it is alongside these, *Bos taurus*

---

* I have knowingly oversimplified this. There is some evidence from recent DNA-based research that British cattle, for example, have had some Spanish input somewhere along the line, and probably some from the local wild stock, as well as what came north from out of the Fertile Crescent. And, by the same token, the Tibetan yak shares DNA with the American bison. Joyfully, nothing in science is simple.

to give the Latin name, that we will be walking our inquisitive way in this story. And we shouldn't be over-surprised that the genetics of all our modern cattle point to one tiny area in the Middle East; after all, the genetics of every single apple you have ever eaten come from the side of a specific hill in Kazakhstan's Tien Shan mountains, spread gently and gradually westwards in the apple cores of the Silk Road traders who were eating them, and the dung of the horses on whom they rode.[1] Nothing stands still, and all history is movement.

Who knows when the first cattle made their way on skin or leather rafts across the deep marshlands that made up the English Channel at the time? But cross they did, probably around 4000 BCE and maybe only 30 of them at first, and they spread quickly to the four corners of the island once they had arrived. Of the two stepping-off points for Neolithic traffic into Britain (Brittany and the Pas de Calais), it is likely that they came over on the shorter transit of the latter, along with the axe-heads and beakers that were part of man's newfound habit of acquiring things. We don't know much, but what we do know is that domesticated cattle were pulling ploughs in South Street, Wiltshire by about 3500 BCE,[2] and were present at Skara Brae in Orkney in about 3100 BCE, which suggests that they had moved relatively quickly throughout the islands.[3] Ironically, as a nation that obsesses about invasive species more than most, we often overlook that our own arrival on these shores, together with the cattle, sheep and goats that we brought along with us, makes the latter invasions of rabbits, rats and rhododendrons pale into insignificance. No species on earth has been more invasive than *Homo sapiens*. Just ask Neanderthal man.

Evidence suggests that these cattle were small beasts (maybe 300 kg and 1.2 metres high at the shoulder) and we already know from the current White Park herds, a breed that we will revisit later, that there would not have needed to be many to achieve sufficient genetic diversity. There would be no distinction between beef and dairy breeds back then, and Neolithic man would largely have been keeping them for their milk, and only then eating them when they died. Population modelling allows us to estimate that 100 years or so after that first group came over, there might have been 2,000 cattle in all,[4] possibly in 50 or 60 small groups, and that they started at that early stage making the little adaptations to the areas in which they found themselves. Large, small, shaggy, smooth, and every muted colourway from black to white, these were the true precursors of all the breeds we know today. From that point out, they just developed along suitably local lines, and this process eventually went on to produce a high-water mark of around 1,311 breeds of cattle, of which around a sixth are now extinct.[5]

If we were to fast-forward and try to piece together what life for a cow in Britain would have been like at the heart of the Bronze Age, say 1000 BCE, we would have to start with the weather, which was going through one of its 300- or 400-year periods of intense wet and cold.* Not a mini ice age,

* Possibly instigated by the eruption of the Icelandic volcano Hekla.

but enough to move populations downhill, and southwards. Cattle herds are growing in number, possibly as a reaction to successive failures of the surrounding crops, and as a cow you are probably owned by one of the upper class, such as it was, and leased to one of the minions to be looked after. Your life progresses, much as it does now, to the rhythms of the seasons, whereby you are brought in to over-winter within the settlement before calving and then being turned out to the local grasslands in spring. One uncomfortable ritual which you may well be faced with at this season (Beltane, as it was known) is to be driven through fire on your way out to the fields, so as to be cleansed of the vermin that may have infested you in the damp winter. Once you are out there, you will notice around you relatively new field divisions, hedges or dry stone walls depending on where you are, and you will look back at a settlement that is steadily growing in size and population.

When and if the humans speak to you, it will be in Celtic, a language that has drifted northwards up the Atlantic coast of Europe during the previous millennia. You are one of two prevailing currencies (the other being slaves) – 'six heifers equating to one slave, or three milk cows'[6] – and you are likely to be more highly valued as a female than as a male. As the season rolls towards Samhain (late October), you probably start to keep your head down, as this is generally the time for feasting, and there is a likelihood that you will be on the menu, particularly if your owner is trying to impress someone. If you are out of luck, you will probably be boiled in a bronze cauldron in the main house of the settlement, and then fed on bronze plates to people who will be getting drunk and aggressive on beer, and will eventually throw up on the floor.* If you were having a particularly bad day, you might be sacrificed and have your blood drunk by the presiding druid, who would then spend the night inside your hide.

And so it continued for centuries without much change. A thousand years later, around the time Julius Caesar made his first speculative invasion of Britain in 55 BCE, your life as a cow wouldn't have been a whole lot better, or a whole lot different. The weather was less miserable than it had been for your Neolithic forebears, although you wouldn't have thought so from Caesar's complaints about the endless fogs. Your principal use is now as a draft animal, particularly for ploughing and, in the hundred or so generations that have passed, your size has varied considerably up and down, quite often dependent on how thick and difficult the soil was. So, for example, in the sandy soils of Norfolk, you were much smaller than in the thick clays to the west. Humans are finding more and more ways of utilising you, from stretching your hide across the base of their coracles, to trading you throughout what has now become a relatively sophisticated market system. They still have their feasts, but nowadays you are more likely to be spit-roasted than boiled, and the beer has oftentimes been replaced by wine that the Romans have brought with them. If Caesar had ventured far to the west, he might well have seen something that looked remarkably like today's Ruby Red Devon. We only

------

* This pen picture owes much to Barry Cunliffe's magisterial book *Britain Begins*, which is recommended reading for anyone with an interest in how the nation developed.

know what we know from bones, and from the occasional historical account, but there is no question that, from this point on, sharp variations between the different cattle emerged, that would swiftly lead to the many regional breeds that we will formally meet again in Chapter 13.

Elsewhere, aurochs start to emerge regularly from the pages of written history, here in a hunt in the Nile Valley swamps, there as part of the planned defence of a Spanish village against Hannibal's brother, another time on the altar of a druidical sacrifice, and again as a wild resident of the vast forests of what is now southern Germany. 'They are a little below the size of an elephant', said Julius Caesar with enthusiastic exaggeration, 2,000 years ago. 'Their speed and strength are extraordinary, and they spare neither man nor beast.' For admirers of continuity, there is a pleasing chance that the white cows that Romans favoured for their sacrifices, and with which Caesar would have been familiar, have their direct descendants in the White Park cattle in England today.[7] Indeed, they were probably here before Stonehenge was built, and when there was still a land bridge to the European continent. A hundred years later, Pliny the Elder, who generally but not always got things right, let his imagination run riot in the matter of the aurochs' defence mechanism: 'It has to depend upon its flight,' he said, 'and, while in the act of flying, it sends forth its excrements, sometimes to a distance of three *jugera*,* the contact of which

....

* About 30 metres!

burns those who pursue the animal, just like a kind of fire.'
Curiously, we will meet this phenomenon again a thousand or
so years later.

Around the time of Christ, the old pure aurochs themselves began to disappear from the scene, their evolutionary
job having been done as far as our story is concerned. Once
our forebears discovered that the aurochs was a good animal
to hunt, and that it traded a good number of benefits for not
very much risk, there was no going back, and it steadily began
to disappear from wherever it found itself near a human. Unlike
the cows who had descended from them, aurochs by that stage
tended to be forest and wetland grazers, which probably made
them easy to hunt, and kept them out of competition with
the local cattle.[8] First they vanished from the Mediterranean
coast, next from the area of the North Sea (600 BCE) and then
from everywhere outside a limited zone around the Baltic Sea.
There is plenty of evidence that *Homo sapiens* had already been
causing local aurochs extinctions for about 9,000 years at this
point. Finally, a century after Columbus had introduced the first
cattle to the Americas, and in the heart of Poland's Jaktorów
Forest, the last ones died out under the attempted protection
of the bishops of Kraków. The year was 1627, and that they
had made it so far into the modern era says much for the work
that was done to conserve them.

Thus it is that the aurochs' slightly unfortunate contribution to the history of science is that it was the first recorded
creature on earth to become extinct (to be followed about
50 years later by the much put-upon dodo). In fact, finding
yourself near a human for any length of time seems to have

been a failsafe way to reduce your own species' population. Unless, of course, you were already domesticated, in which case the polar opposite applied. Cosying up to man was a sure route to breeding success, if not to a comfortable or a dignified lifestyle. Either way, with our Saxon forebears clearing more and more space for farms, villages and towns, there was proportionately less and less space for the aurochs to graze their way around Britain, and extinction was probably an inevitability.

In a footnote not entirely unrelated to the disturbing ideas of racial purity that were making their way around their country at the time, two German brothers called Heck started a process in the 1920s that is still continuing to this day, albeit rather more innocently, to try to recreate the aurochs for the modern world, on the basis, they asserted, that nothing is actually extinct so long as its genes are present in some population, somewhere. Pause that general thought there, for we shall return to it in due course, but a century of effort thus far has merely proved that it is just about as difficult to breed wildness back into a domesticated animal as it is to domesticate a wild one, before you even start to get into the genetics of it. Without having a particularly accurate idea of what the aurochs actually looked like, the Hecks used a process that involved imagining which breeds might conform most closely to their vision of the aurochs, and then 'breeding back' into them. Using a mix of Corsican, Grey, Highland, Podolian, Angeln and Lowland cattle, they failed in their first objective, but at least produced their own variety of Heck cattle which are still used to this day as a curious-looking and bad-tempered conservation breed in

Germany and beyond.* Such was their sense of purity, that the Nazis were even driven to draft a Reich Landscape Law in 1941, 'banishing exotic plants from pure German landscapes'.[9]

Finally, with an ironic nod to the history that he almost certainly didn't understand at the time, Hermann Goering seized another Polish forest, the Białowieża, to 'help restore the true German ecosystems degraded by the assaults of civilisation'[10] and create the largest hunting reserve in the world. Among the first animals planned for reintroduction there was the aurochs, and you don't even want to know what happened to the park's human residents before the whole project inevitably failed; suffice it to say that you can trace some of the roots of the Holocaust to the selective clearance of its 20,000 or so people. Heck cattle survive to this day, even if not to universal enthusiasm. Mercifully, the Nazis don't.

Thus the aurochs left in its place a basic long-horned cow of the sort that Anglo-Saxon man would have tended, and which very slowly started to develop small regional differences and characteristics, a process that continued until supermarkets influenced the development of just a handful of super-productive breeds, like the Holstein Friesian or the Limousin. For at least a thousand years after the Romans left, most cattle were in the hands of peasant farmers, who grew what they needed and needed what they grew; what little trade there was tended to be in livestock, and what crime there was tended to involve its illicit removal, in one way or another.

---

* Most notably at the rewilding park of Oostvaardersplassen in the Netherlands.

Peaceful in its ignorance, the humble cow was something of a fulcrum around which the heavy work, the manuring and the trading of the farm got done.

Over the succeeding centuries, the size of herds gradually increased, in line with the farmers' ability to look after ever greater numbers of stock, with the indirect consequence that settlements became hamlets, which became villages, which then became towns, all relying on the meat and milk that came from the animals in the fields around them. By the time of the Domesday Book (1086), cattle had enabled activities like ploughing to become relatively sophisticated, and far quicker than before, with cow numbers much influenced by the heaviness of the local soil. After a fall in the number of cattle in the early Dark Ages, the numbers rose steadily, and the archaeological evidence of most deaths taking place at 24–30 months suggests that the Saxons knew a thing or two about prime beef even back then.[11]

According to the Domesday Book, England had about 81,000 ploughs and 648,000 oxen*[12] to draw them – which, with calves and milk cows uncounted, allows us to estimate that there were around a million head of cattle back then, by no means a small number, and far more per capita than there are now. In the agrarian year-cycle, livestock for meat tended to be slaughtered in November or December, both to save the cost of providing forage for them over the winter, and to keep the meat in some kind of acceptable condition in the colder days that followed. The meat was often treated with spices, not, as

* Male cattle specifically bred for heavy draft work.

the old wives' tale goes, to disguise the smell of putrefaction, but because they 'were a demonstration of wealth, and people liked the taste'.[13] Of one thing we may be sure: not one part of the cow went to waste; underground, salted or smoked up the chimney, just about every last bit would make its way into the food chain or some other use.

As early as the 13th century, there are records of farmers sending their cattle and sheep up the old droving roads to major market towns like London or Norwich, showing that, even then, there was a relatively sophisticated trade in livestock going on around the country, and that it wasn't all just local. The further north you came from, the more likely it was that your drove would be disrupted by bandits, the border reivers, who would relieve you of your stock and, occasionally, your life along with it. Many of the roads and long-distance footpaths that we use today started life as drovers' routes, wide and unpaved thoroughfares that connected the main cattle areas with the main market towns. Over the centuries, the verges of these routes became full of nutritious herbal vegetation, which the cattle could graze on and encourage as they made their slow way by.[14]

A classic illustration of the droving life could have been found in Scotland where, for example, a black Highland cow would be reared out in the islands, fed in the mainland glens, fattened in lowland pastures and then driven south to Edinburgh, York or London to be eaten. The practice grew over the centuries, with highly respected drovers enabling a vibrant livestock trade to be carried out wherever it was needed; so much so that by the late 18th century, somewhere around

100,000 cattle and 750,000 sheep would arrive each year just into London's Smithfield market,[15] and it was only with the arrival of the railway train that the profession fell into disuse. When you finally got to eat your cow back then, it would inevitably have had a great number of miles in its legs.

Up until selective cattle breeding started in earnest in the 18th century,* most cows within a given area looked pretty similar, getting smaller and smaller in relation to the aurochs (just as man had shrunk since his pre-agrarian days), until suddenly putting on a big growth spurt in the last hundred years. (It is not for nothing that US abattoirs have had to be largely redesigned and rebuilt to handle huge cows in the last 30 years.)

All in all, though, the life of the average cow, if such a thing existed, was not so very different from the life of the Neolithic forebear that we met two and a half millennia earlier on. The really significant changes wouldn't come until the agricultural revolution and the 250 years immediately afterwards.

For now, at least for the purposes of our story, we can agree what a cow is.† On the phylogenetic tree of life, it is first cousin of the horse, second cousin of the hedgehog, and our own seventh or eighth cousin.

---

* Something that is covered in more detail in Chapter 4.

† Technically, the term 'cattle' covers all bovines, regardless of age, sex or purpose. Oxen tend to be working animals, whereas cows (exclusively female) are kept purely for meat, milk and breeding.

Also, we can think whatever we like to think, but we share about 80% of our genetic coding with them, which makes them pretty close.

On John's farm, the breed we work with is the Red Angus, a colour adaptation of the better known black Aberdeen Angus.

It had been back in another barn, in another country, in another century when, in 1842, Hugh Watson from Angus had finally succeeded in breeding what is now regarded as the founder of the Angus breed, a bull called Old Jock. From the loins of Old Jock, in an exercise that combined careful breeding with cute marketing know-how, eventually sprang the ancestors of every one of the millions of cattle who go under that breed these days, a third of a million in the USA alone. The Aberdeen Angus, the sturdy beast whose name has now become synonymous with high-quality beef all around the world, is generally pure black in colour, but there is a recessive gene that produces a red animal that is remarkably similar in colour to the South Devons.

At some stage in the 18th century, the black Scottish cattle were considered too light in build to provide oxen powerful enough to be useful on a farm, so some were crossed with larger English Longhorns, who happened to be red. The black colour remained the dominant one (like Old Jock) and it was only through subsequent interbreeding that the recessive red version became predictable, just as the horns disappeared.[16] Over the years, the red version, which reflects more of the sunlight back into the sky and is therefore better in the heat, had been popular in Australia and Latin America but not really in Britain, or in the United States, where the black silhouette of the Angus is a powerful brand logo for great beef. Besides, Hugh Watson had arbitrarily decided all those years ago that black was the correct colour for the breed, which is how things tended to work in those days.

And yet it was from an American breeder of 'reds' that John and Emma first brought over the embryos that were implanted into, and then carried by, the last of their old South Devons.

The work of the farm is primarily to breed bulls, either to keep for the future, to sell to other Angus herds or, as likely as not, to introduce desired changes and a bit of hybrid vigour* into herds of different breeds.

I quickly gather that, although cows are instinctively gentle and patient animals, they have their limits. Any creature with good musculature, quick reactions and seven times my own weight is not to be messed with, and I learn through experience which end kicks (the back), at what angle (a 90-degree arc from behind to alongside), where on the body (kneecaps seem a favourite), and how hard (as hard as she likes). If a cow really means business, she will come at you with her head. From being comically anxious the first time I am in a field alone with Tiger or one of the other bulls, always checking the quickest route out of the field, I start to relax, but only because I begin to trust the animals, and understand the triggers. On average,

....

* The phenomenon whereby crossbred animals can show a higher genetic potential for, say, growth than either of the purebred parents. (*Practical Cattle Farming*, Kat Bazeley and Alastair Hayton.)

the UK's 9.8 million cows kill four or five people a year, most of them farm workers. There is some evidence that the continental breeds like Limousin and Charolais are rowdier, that dairy bulls are the most dangerous, and that walking through the middle of a field of cows and new-born calves is best avoided, whether it is a footpath or not, particularly with dogs.*

The farm is an ecosystem, and we all have to understand our place in it.

* If you like that kind of thing, the website killercows.co.uk, a forum that believes the issue of cow attacks isn't taken seriously enough, has plenty of incidents for you to browse through in its 'horror stories' section.

4. FROM BAKEWELL TO BISMARCK, NORTH DAKOTA

1750 CE—Now

....

'Progress is not inevitable.
It's up to us to create it.'
ANONYMOUS

'Technology, which is presented as the only way to
solve these problems, in fact proves incapable of
seeing the mysterious network between things and so
sometimes solves one problem only to create others.'
POPE FRANCIS, ENCYCLICAL ON
OUR COMMON HOME: LAUDATO SI

....

O n the afternoon of February 9th, 2019, a little piece of history was made in a packed barn on a ranch in North Dakota, a few miles south of the state capital, Bismarck.

After about four and a half minutes of frantic to-ing and fro-ing between the Stetson-hatted bidders and the Stetson-hatted auctioneers, the hammer went down at a world record $1.51 million for lot number 1, namely a thirteen month-old Black Angus bull called SAV America. The often incomprehensible bidding was punctuated throughout by references to his provenance ('American owned and American made'; 'still the best country in the world'), and the buyer was given a rousing standing ovation once he had won the auction. 'Throw your hands in the air for Charles', said the auctioneer, with understandable enthusiasm, and throw their hands they did. Especially, it is tempting to think, the gentleman who had unsuccessfully bid $1.505 million himself a few seconds before.

For all that his record-breaking bid might have cost him, Charles Herbster didn't even get to put his new bull in a trailer and drive it the 671 miles back south down the I-29N to his own Nebraskan centre of operations and, in fact, he only got 80% of the rights to him. No, SAV America stayed firmly put, quietly grazing behind the auction hall, his role in life to be a presumably very well insured participant in what is in reality a giant embryo transplant programme.* What the Schaff Angus Valley herd offers, according to its surprisingly modest website, is a disciplined programme 'with a worldwide reputation for

....

* Charles Herbster, I should point out, is no ordinary cattle farmer. As you might expect, a man who pays $1.5 million for a bull has very deep agribusiness interests, and he also sat as a key adviser to President Trump on agriculture. He is currently standing as the Republican governor of Nebraska.

consistent, reliable quality Angus genetics with built-in reliability'. Getting 'reliability' in twice in the space of eight words probably sheds some light on the unique selling proposition behind SAV America's extraordinary value.

From the standpoint of my alien culture, there may be a certain amount to smile at in the stereotypes of this Dakotan vignette, but men as smart as Charles Herbster don't part with that kind of money for fun, or even to get a headline. Just one look at the compact hugeness of the bull in the ring, and just one scan of his genealogy, would tell even a layman that this animal was something beyond special, maybe as near perfect a stud as man has ever bred for a line of beef cattle. And this is not so much about farming in the here and now, as it is about rib-eye steaks in fine restaurants some time in the future, in a country whose per capita annual consumption of beef (36 kg[1]) dwarfs most others outside South America. And it's all a far cry from the labours of Robert Bakewell, back in mid-18th-century Leicestershire, and the dawn of selective breeding.

Back then it was all about husbandry and experimentation. These days, it involves test tubes, digital timers and some very deep pockets indeed.

But first, for two reasons, we need to go back to 1760.

On the face of it, what Robert Bakewell did all those years ago was not overly complicated: he was simply the man who first consistently took random chance out of cattle and sheep breeding, or at least the first man who made a big noise about it. That he did this a full hundred years before Charles

Darwin published his *Origin of Species*, and the same length of time before, in what is now the Czech Republic, Gregor Mendel pioneered the science of genetics through his experiments on the seven heritable traits of peas, was undoubtedly ground-breaking.

By way of background, there were two factors working strongly in favour of Britain's cattle culture, one permanent, and one temporary. The lasting one was, and still is, that the climate of the country is just about perfect for raising grass-fed livestock, with moderate seasonal differences and plenty of rain. The one that was getting going at the time of Bakewell was the industrial revolution, whose twin effects were to create an ever-growing market for beef and milk, and an ever-growing need for the by-products such as leather and tallow. In a way, cattle turned the country's vast store of inedible grass into much of the energy that powered the growth of the British Empire.

Bakewell had been sent off by his father as a young man to do the Grand Tour of Europe, but it was a Grand Tour with a difference. He didn't seek out, as everyone else did, the crumbling stoneworks of the Acropolis or the soaring archangel statues of Raphael, but the tiny fields of the hill farms of France and, particularly, the flat polders of Holland. By the time he took over the 440-acre family farm in Leicestershire in 1760, his brain was full of the new science of breeding, and of how to convert it into cash. Doing no more than separating males and females to avoid 'accidents', and then concentrating on animals with the characteristics he wanted, and culling those with what he thought were undesirable traits, he steadily improved the gene pool. So much so, in fact, that he was one of the first farmers to send his own stud bulls and rams out to do their work in distant herds, improving the bloodlines, the genetic diversity and Bakewell's personal fortune as they did so, and the first to specialise certain beasts for certain functions (e.g. the Leicester Longhorn for beef). Bakewell was also enlightened enough to understand how influential the environment was for the condition of his livestock, and experimented with irrigating individual fields and liberally applying rotted-down dung. He even built his cattle barns on raised platforms, which kept them clean and reduced 'disease, and [eliminated] the expense of strewing absorbent straw across dirt floors'.[2]

Up until the mid-18th century, cows and bulls of the same herd tended to be left to get on with it in the same field all year, with results that were predictably varied in timing and quality. The genius of Bakewell, aside from the talent for self-publicity that ensures that his is the only name we generally still mention in this context 250 years later, was deliberately to inbreed (known as 'in-and-in' breeding) the best characteristics from close relatives, and then to rent out, rather than sell, the results to neighbouring farmers. The former ensured that he knew more or less what he was going to get, and the latter that he had, in effect, a self-licking lollipop of an income for life. The fact that the in-breeding often produced animals with terrible physical problems was, as is so often the case in pioneering science, just acceptable collateral damage (by the time he died, the average weight of one of his beef cows had doubled from under 400 pounds to over 800). His stud fees were, even by North Dakota standards today, stupendous: by 1789, he was letting out rams at 80 to 90 guineas* a go (about £20,000 in today's money), and the farm was bringing in £4,000 (£3.5 million) a year just from this side of its activities. The secret, as far as these early selective breeders were concerned, was simply to produce the animal that would 'make themselves the soonest fat'.[3] Much as it might be today, in fact, at any Nebraskan feedlot.

Bakewell's professional achievements were matched in part by his colourful character. Managing to be declared bankrupt when you are letting rams out at the equivalent of £20,000 a go is one thing, but wriggling out of the bankruptcy because four of the five commissioners investigating you are personal friends, one is too ill to travel and two are bankrupt themselves is quite another. He was a legendary entertainer and, while not above buying and then showing neighbours' 'outstandingly ugly' beasts alongside his own at shows to make his look all the better, he was generous with his time and advice to those who came to seek it. By the time he died in 1795, other farmers from Northumberland to Norfolk, Somerset to the Sussex Downs were doing as he did, and there was no question that the selective breeding genie would ever again be squeezed back into its sanitised bottle.

As this process gradually found its way around all the local breeds of the country, one thing was starting to become abundantly clear. It was just not possible to produce a cow that was equally good at producing milk as it was meat, as the criteria for

....

* A guinea was 21 shillings, or £1.05, and was generally used at auctions, where the seller got the pound and the auctioneer got the rest. Far away days, indeed.

the two are very different. Whereas the traditional Shorthorn had been for centuries an acceptable compromise between the two, and therefore to some extent the nation's go-to cow, increasingly farmers wanted the highest-yielding cow in their chosen sector, and for their local terrain, in the fastest possible time, particularly as the horse had by then largely taken over the draft duties from oxen, so brute strength was no longer a prerequisite. Thus, from that point on, most farmers, and most breeds, specialised in one or the other but not both, and if you take a look at a pedigree dairy cow from behind, and then a pedigree beef cow, you will very soon see why.

The second, brief, reason we need to go back to the late 18th century is the passing of the Enclosure Act of 1773, which drove the final nail in the coffin of commoners' rights of access and privilege after 500 years of gradual erosion. Indirectly, it probably also started to do for the future of the bovine as a draft animal. Just as we cannot separate our livestock from our farms, so we cannot separate our farms, how we farm and, ultimately, our relationship with food, from the vexed issue of land ownership. The United Kingdom has just shy of 60 million acres of land, over half of which is now in the hands of less than 0.5% of the population.[4] This has had the effect of distancing the vast majority of the population from the production of their food, and has required, and enabled, the growth of an extremely powerful food industry. Just as it is hard to exaggerate the effect that this would later have on our food systems, and therefore our cattle, so it is tempting to dismiss activist and ecologist Satish Kumar's words to me, when I asked him the question, as mere idealism. 'Everyone needs an acre, maybe two', he told me, in the gentle tones of a man who had once walked 8,000 miles for peace, 'to grow fruit and vegetables, have a cow, and be rooted in the soil.' Satish has been watching this issue closely for 60 years, and he knows cause and effect when he sees it. He even pointed out the similarity between the number of acres we had, and the number of people (both 60 million). You don't need to be a revolutionary firebrand to say that the way our land is owned can easily act as a permanent 'keep out' sign to young potential farmers of modest means.

By the end of the Second World War, cows had largely given up sex, or rather, been asked to. A short trot through the history of the modern cow will obviously miss out much detail, but two important dates should divert us briefly: April 20th, 1868 when Louis Pasteur discovered that, if you heat something up enough,* you destroy its ability to pass on harmful pathogens; and sometime in 1790 when John Hunter, by impregnating a draper's wife with her own husband's sperm, seems to have the most compelling claim to have invented artificial insemination (AI). Taken together, pasteurisation and AI have proved enormously influential developments for humans, but the latter is incomparably more important from the standpoint of the cow. These days, AI is the linchpin of just about every modern cattle farm, especially the dairy ones.

Another development, from the Victorian era, was the notion that the answer to raising ever more livestock lay in

....

* 63°C for 30 minutes, or 72°C for 15 seconds, as a rule. To 'enjoy' milk free of all its vitamins, enzymes and taste (UHT), try 20 minutes at 115°C.

intensive and artificial systems that put production above all else, known by its detractors as factory farming. It is hard to establish when this first started, or where the exact borderline with other systems lies, but its best example is in the 87,000 'feedlots'* currently operating in the USA,[5] in which young cattle that have reached a certain weight (say 300 kg) are moved from the range into open-air factories, grouped intensively, and then fed on corn, barley, alfalfa and other grains and by-products in order to rapidly accelerate their growth. 'Here', comments an enthusiast, as if describing a holiday camp, 'cattle typically spend four to six months, during which time they have room to move around and eat at feed bunks containing a carefully balanced diet, and where vets, nutritionists and cattlemen work together to look after each animal.'† Others are not so charitable.

Often now seen as the cheap and profitable solution to feeding a hungry planet, factory farming has also led to biodiversity loss, climate change, water pollution, disease and a return of just seventeen calories of meat for every hundred calories of edible crops fed to the animals.[6] And that is before you take any account of the animal's welfare or, for that matter, the bizarre phenomenon of a third of all agricultural land being used to grow food for animals that could eat the grass under their feet. At its best, this system does what it says on the tin, which is to accelerate production of a particular commodity; at its

....

* More correctly known as Concentrated Animal Feeding Operations (CAFO).

† Pennsylvania Beef Council, funnily enough.

worst, it is a hidden world of abuse, pollution and, as we will see in Chapter 7, a growing antibiotic resistance nightmare. Either way, it is not something on which meat-eaters can tenably remain neutral, and it is perhaps the first glimpse we get of the true cost of the current scale of our crowded world's meat habit.

From the middle of the last century onwards, depriving the bull of what he might reasonably think of as his *droit de seigneur* has enabled breeders to be more adventurous, more planned, safer and altogether more precise with their programmes. It has also allowed the breeder to easily bring in fresh genes from a whole range of different bulls from other countries or even continents, in the name of hybrid vigour, thus avoiding the risks of inbreeding without diminishing the bloodline. Almost the biggest benefit that AI has visited upon farmers is that every cow in a particular herd can be inseminated on the same day, by the same vet on the same cost-effective call, and thus give birth to calves at roughly the same, predictable time. This cheapens the whole process and, even if it takes the raw natural instinct out of it, allows the farmer to plan accurately for what is inevitably a challenging season of their year. Finally, the advent of 'sex-sorted' semen can provide for gender accuracy these days that is consistently above 90%, which allows dairy breeders to avoid the sight of unwanted Friesian bullocks wandering around their yards, trying as hard as possible to look as if they are interested in milk. In an already tough world, being a surprise bull calf on a dairy farm is a rough call indeed. Constant refinement of AI is the route map by which breeders eventually arrived at the $1.51 million SAV America, although beef cattle are more likely than dairy ones to arrive at conception by traditional intercourse.

Broadly speaking, 55% of the UK's 9.8 million cattle* are now for dairy purposes, and 45% for beef, with numbers for the former relatively steady, and the latter dropping by about 2.5% a year, under the tacit encouragement of the government.[7] Nearly ten million inheritors of the aurochs, busily converting stuff that we can't eat into things we can, everywhere from Wick to West Cornwall, and a good proportion of them beginning life in a straw inside a test tube.

These days, there are exactly 200 official breeds of cattle in Britain on Defra's coding schedule, from the Aberdeen Angus (AA) to the Zebu (ZE), by way of the ultra-traditional Jersey and the intriguingly exotic, such as the Norwegian Red Cross or the Baltata Romaneasca, all the way from Romania. However, those black and white cattle grazing quietly in a field near you right now (Holstein Friesian, in one form or another) make up over a third of all numbers on account of the sheer volume, if not the quality, of their milk, and a just under a third of the rest are Limousin, which do roughly the same service for beef. In other words, substantially over half the cows in Britain are from just 1% of the available breeds. This possibly helps explain two things, both of which we will explore later on: why most cows in Britain seem to look roughly the same, and why it was felt necessary, in 1973, for the Rare Breeds Survival Trust to be established.

....

* A figure that is well down, incidentally, on the recorded peak of 15.2 million beasts in 1974.

One by one, the breeds that we now have to call 'rare' or 'heritage' because of their depleted numbers, found themselves shoehorned out of mainstream farming because they couldn't measure up to the absolute returns needed by a relentlessly pressurised farming community. Out went the little Dexter (too troublesome), the Alderney (milk too creamy), the Lincoln Red (insufficient beef yield) and the Dairy Shorthorn (superseded), and in came animals that could simply chalk up a higher return on capital employed. Over a relatively short period, the cow had gone from being a faithful reflection of the local *terroir* on which its breed had developed to an animal that often needed endless expensive and artificial inputs just to stay productive, which, in turn, demanded bigger and bigger herd sizes to justify the expenditure. In a sense, the mainstream cow had become an embodiment of the paradox of Theseus' ship, in the sense that the basic framework was the same, but everything inside was altered beyond recognition. Ironically, many of these old breeds are currently making successful comebacks in the hands of forward-thinking farmers who are looking to the past for lessons that can release them from the vicious circle of 'more', a subject for a later chapter.

These days, technology is front-and-centre of the 'cow business'. Mostly, this is very positive for both the cow and us, with, for example, genomics that accelerate desirable trends, breeding decisions that are informed as much by science as by feel, and a restless search for climate change mitigation measures. As we will see, when technology leads us astray, as in antibiotic misuse, it is generally the fault of a small number of humans searching for ever more profit, rather than the technology itself.

So the storyline that runs all the way from Robert Bakewell in 18th-century Leicestershire to that auction hall in North Dakota in 2019 is one of relentless endeavour generally in pursuit of two mutually incompatible ends, at least in one animal: the cow that will give a reliable ten tons of milk in a year, or one that will produce 300 kilos of boneless, trimmed meat. In other words, an animal that has been genetically supercharged to produce about double the commodity that evolution suggests it should, in half the time that it normally gets to do it.

Apart, perhaps, from the wolf, no animal has been asked to undergo so much change on man's behalf as the cow.

⇌

Out there on the ground, it's all a bit more complicated than a neat history lesson.

John and Emma, my employers, run one of the 192,000 farms left in the UK,* a figure that is some 70% less than it was at the end of the Second World War.[8] If you discount part-timers like me, agricultural employment during the period 1945–2020 has dropped from just under a million to just over 180,000,[9] to the extent that the whole industry sometimes seems to reflect the declining importance that the wider population attaches to food production. After all, when the percentage of the workforce engaged in farming has declined from 15% (1850) to 0.5% (now), it is perhaps not surprising that we don't understand agriculture like we did, when a great many of us were imbued with the routine rhythms of it all. The

....

* Around 75,000 of which involve beef cattle.

advances in productivity have been extraordinary, enabling far more food to be produced from the same acreage of land with about a sixth of the people.

'How did you get into all this?' I ask John while we are manhandling 40 bags of organic feed supplement off a pallet and into a nearby loose box. What I have actually been wanting to ask all morning is 'Why do cows moo?',* but I don't, as it sounds childish and I feel that I should have known the answer all my life.

'I suppose we got into it a bit genetically, too', he says, stretching his back after throwing the last of the bags down. 'Since we both come from farming families. But how we got into actual breeding is a bit more complicated.'

Over the course of the next hour or so of driving around the farm attending to the myriad little jobs that need doing, righting troughs, securing loose fenceposts, replacing the odd salt lick, he paints a picture of a family with cattle in its blood, of a childhood spent helping out with the milking, a gap year spent on ranches in Australia, an early career in the African bush and finally a gradual centripetal attraction back to Hampshire, and to the farm where it had all started.

'Almost as soon as we took over from my parents in the early nineties, we were forced to do a complete rethink, when they drove the new trunk road through a chunk of our land, a chunk that also happened to be most suitable for crops. At that point, we had to give up any idea that we could be a mixed

....

* One of six reasons, so it is generally thought, which are: finding their friends, finding their calves, a pre-sex chat-up line, a signal of hunger, a plea to be milked, and an indication of stress.

farm, abandoning the crops and the dairy, and deciding to concentrate instead on breeding South Devons.'

From the start, John's idea of how he wanted to achieve excellence with this relatively uncommon beef breed had rather more in common with Robert Bakewell than it did with the Schaff Angus Valley project.

'We didn't want to create the biggest cow, or the heaviest', he explains, remembering aloud as he did so a neighbouring farmer's comment to the effect that he wanted cows that looked *over* the gate, and not just *through* it. 'We just wanted to improve the breed as the brilliant "grass converters" they are until we were a centre of excellence that other farms could trust. Actually, if anything we tended to produce smaller cows rather than bigger, which butchers might not like, but breeders can favour as they generally lead to less traumatic births. The weight thing can be a bit of a vanity versus sanity argument in this business. One large headline cow breaking a local auction record just might hide a couple of previous cows that have died in childbirth back on the farm.'

Farming in Britain has always been a series of switchback rides, each one seemingly more extreme as successive metropolitan governments get ever further divorced from the human realities of agriculture, and it wasn't too long before the next one came along in the form of the BSE* crisis of 1996. Almost

....

* Bovine spongiform encephalopathy, BSE, more commonly known as 'mad cow disease', an infection thought to be caused by feeding cattle meat-and-bone meal, and whose variant version occasionally jumped to humans in the form of Creutzfeldt-Jakob disease. More on this in Chapter 7.

overnight, anything to do with cattle was twice as complicated as before, and on top of that, beef couldn't go into the food chain if it was any older than 30 months. They struggled through it, and then through the foot and mouth disease outbreaks of 2001 and 2007, always keeping focused on being as good as they could in their chosen breed, and always running the farm to standards that they trusted would give them the maximum chance of not being hit by the next outbreak, whatever it happened to be. John pointed out that, while some disease prevention was down to pure luck, much of it was simply about good husbandry and hygiene. The closer to naturally that a cow is allowed to live its life, the less you find yourself staring down the barrel of infections like TB.

'We had always had a few Red Anguses around the place', he goes on. 'But then in 2015 we made what for us was the huge decision of giving up on the South Devons, and breeding the Angus full-time.'

'Why would you do that?' I ask. 'I mean, when the world knows you for your Devons?'

'We just had a cold, hard look at the relative size of the two markets. We had taken a small breed as far as we could, and we thought it was time to get into a breed with worldwide reach before we got too decrepit.' He looked genuinely rueful as he told of the day the last of the Devons left the farm.

'When you give up a breed', he adds, 'it's not just selling off a few cows, it's saying goodbye to the whole wide network of your fellow breeders. You've stayed on their farms, drunk whisky with them deep into the night at shows and maybe, from time to time, even judged their cattle. They've done the same for you. They're as much family as Auntie May once was.' He looks skyward, in a way that suggests Auntie May had disappeared at roughly the same time as the Devons, and was possibly not as deeply mourned as they.

By this time, we have arrived back at the last of the many gates on the farm, and are taking the opportunity to lean against it and observe the evening sky gently closing down the view into the fields beyond.

'Bacteria to aurochs to Bakewell to this, then?', I remark, trying to pull those 120 million years of evolution together in my mind. I feel that I am just beginning to understand the arc of development that has delivered the cows I see in front of me.

'Sorry, to what?' His mind is elsewhere, possibly with the five heifers that we need to separate out the next morning for their onward journey to new owners. Or on the contents of the top shelf of the oven in his farmhouse a few hundred yards away.

'It really doesn't matter,' I say.

'You know, we were approached by the Angus Steak Houses to see if we wanted to be a supplier the other day', he says, after a comfortable pause. 'We decided that it wasn't for us, though it was nice to be asked.'

And then, out of nowhere: 'This has all been about beef so far. I think you need to go and learn about milk before you go much further.'

The history lesson is over.

PART 2

Now

5. THE MIRACLE OF MILK

For a while, he just sits there stirring sugar into his tea, and looking out at the fields beyond the window with a far-away look in his old eyes.

'Well, I'm buggered if I know', he says, after the longest pause, in answer to a question about where farming was headed. 'They're just going to get bigger and bigger, I suppose.'

Robert Bridger had been born into a farming family in the little West Sussex village of Easebourne 82 years ago, and he had rarely left it. At one point in his childhood, his parents looked after a flock of sheep that had been moved over from Kent so that they didn't fall too easily into German hands if and when they invaded.

He remembers the endless arguments between his father and the Kent farmer over the price, arguments that would only finally get sorted out on the last ten yards of platform at the railway station before the departure of the 4.00pm to Pulborough.

'I went to Australia briefly to join my older brother, but I couldn't take the weather. One day, I picked up a spanner, and burned all the skin off the palm of my hand where the metal had been frying in the sun all day. I'd had enough. That was my signal to go back to Sussex on the next Ten Pound Pom ship* I could find.'

'I started work on this farm when I was sixteen, and just out of school. Mainly Shorthorns, we had, then. We had six little herds of them round the village, and I looked after the ones here. Ten of them. If you got five gallons a day out of one of them, you had a good cow. Not like the Friesians these days, who'll do double that. I suppose the whole farm had 150 or 160 cows on it. No more than that, for sure. And there were nine or ten of us working on the farm back then. Twenty-four

----

* Ten Pound Pom. Colloquial term for the British citizens who emigrated to Australia on the Assisted Passage Migration Scheme after the Second World War.

shillings a week if you were a cowman; nineteen shillings a week if you were me.'

'That was plenty', he adds. 'I could spend it in the Holly Tree Inn, and I had more milk to drink than I knew what to do with.' If nothing else, it was an improvement on sixpence a skin that he used to get as a kid for trapping the occasional mole. 'Besides', he goes on, 'there wasn't a whole lot of things to spend it on.'

Midhurst had a railway station back then in the days before the Beeching axe fell, and he explains how all the milk from the farm needed to be down there by seven in the morning.

'That was before the Milk Marketing Board* had us set up. After that, we just had tables on the road outside each dairy, high enough up so that the churns could be dragged easily into the truck that had been sent. So long as I got my milk there on time, I wouldn't get into trouble.'

I remember the ones on our road in my childhood, too: one for each little farm.

The MMB doubled as the 'Man from the AI' in those days. 'But the Shorthorn breeders wouldn't sell them semen, as they wanted the closed shop for themselves. We put the better cows to a Friesian bull, and the not so good ones to an Angus or a Hereford. That was the trick.'

I ask him whether the actual milking was hard work.

'Not really', he says. 'Certainly not when you think of all the other things we had to do round the farm.' He tells me how

....

* Originally formed in 1933, the MMB was legally obliged to buy every gallon of milk from each English dairy at an agreed price. It finally died in 1994, from the wounds inflicted on it in a twenty-year campaign by the European Commission.

he would carry the pails of milk up to the top of the cooler and pour them in, delighting in watching the fresh white liquid spiral down into the tank below.

'None of this "three years and you're done" back then', he goes on. 'So long as she went on having calves, she could go on giving milk. A dozen years was normal, and then the trip to the abattoir in Petersfield for the next bit of her life.' He looks up at me for a moment, to check that I wasn't 'one of those sensitive types' who was going to wilt under the notion of a cow meeting her end. 'Then that was before the abattoirs started closing one by one.'

He had married a nurse when he was 32. 'We'd been courting for a while', he explains. 'And then one day, she just looked at me in the pub one Saturday night and asked: "Who's going to marry you?" Well, I couldn't answer that question, least not in a way that made any sense, so I just said, "You, I suppose." And that was that.'

They settled down to the life of the small tenant farmer, with their cows, some sugar beet and a little bed-and-breakfast to supplement the housekeeping.

'I never borrowed a penny all my life', he says with some pride. 'All those times they tried to make you go with the HP,* but I wasn't having any of it.'

'Everyone could turn their hand to anything back then', he goes on. 'Bricklaying, fence mending, fixing the old International W6 tractors.' When I ask him if it had been a good thing that

---

* Hire purchase.

there wasn't any 'health and safety', as he put it, back then, he mulls it over for a bit.

'Not really', he concluded. 'There's a lot of us still carrying around farmer's lung, and a lot more who eventually died from it. And, looking back, some of the accidents on the farm were just ...' He thinks carefully about a suitable word and then says rather quietly, 'avoidable'. I've lived in the area long enough to remember one in particular, so I understood the pause.

'What do you make of it all now?' I ask. He may have been farming ten years before I was born, but, in reading and listening, he kept remarkably up to date with it all.

'I don't really think I have a view', he offers, with the air of a man who absolutely does. 'These animals out there – all bulling the same day, having AI the same day, giving birth the same day, weaning the same day, and every one of them a heifer. Is it right for the cow? I don't know. Is it right for us? I don't know, either. But I'll tell you one thing: I *do* know that we are asking too much from the land. You only have to dig down a few inches to see that.'

Robert Bridger has taken a lifelong interest in worms, and he of all people knows when they are disappearing.

⇒

With the exception of Finland and Australia, drinking large quantities of milk* is peculiar to the British Isles (and

....

* Around 85% of all milk drunk by humans originates from cattle. For the purposes of this book, that is what is generally meant when using the term 'milk'. (UN Food and Agriculture Organization, 2011)

particularly Ireland), which is why we mind more about it than others. In the USA, they drink about 30% less than us, and in most of mainland Europe, around a half. In fact, fresh milk is digestively unsuitable for well over half the people in the world, whose systems cannot tolerate the lactose that is otherwise removed by the action of enzymes.

There was presumably one of those 'eureka' moments shortly after Neolithic man domesticated cattle, when some enterprising individual, lactose intolerant for sure, looked enviously at a calf suckling and thought: 'I'll have some of that.' Initial results would probably have been gastrically uncomfortable, to put it mildly, but via some long lessons in fermentation, kefir, cheese and yoghurt eventually became mainstream parts of the agrarian diet. At the start of the process, it was just infants who could stomach dairy products; by the end of it, non-human milk was another brick in the wall of mankind's relentless ascent to top animal. A perforated pottery sieve found in Poland and dating back to around 7,000 BCE suggests that this all happened early on in our relationship with cows, and it was followed, crucially, by a genetic mutation among people from what is now the Middle East, Europe and, by extension, America, that enabled the body to accept lactose by producing its own lactase on into adulthood. From that point onwards, each region of the world came up with its own area-specific dairy behaviours: yak butter in the high Tibetan mountains, mares' milk in Russia to make kumiss, reindeer milk for the brutal cold of the Lapland winters.[1]

Archaeologists tend to believe that cheese was first discovered when milk was stored in the stomach of an animal, and had separated into curds and whey. In consequence, the first attempts at it were probably white and tasteless, much like most industrially produced cottage cheese is now, but regional variations like cheddar and Parmesan have been around for well over a thousand years and, each year, more varieties are added to the 1,800 or so already out there. The three basic types of yoghurt – Balkan (hard set), Swiss (thin and creamy) and Greek (cheese-like and long-lasting) – evolved alongside cheese, as did butter, which is made from the creamy fat of the milk. A trip down the dairy aisle of your local supermarket will constantly surprise you with the extensiveness of the product ranges these days, not to mention modern man's exquisite talent for using storytelling as a device for selling things.

'The art of dairying', says ex-dairyman and author Philip Walling, in a passage that explains neatly the subtle complexities of getting the right cow for the right area, 'is to balance the quantity and quality of the milk over a lactation* with the costs of keeping the cow and breeding replacements, the longevity and health of the beast, ease of calving, and resistance to foot troubles.'[2]

The successors of Robert Bakewell, having split the functions of cattle into the two specialisations, went on experimenting at pace. As the populations in the cities grew, the dairy industry first turned its thoughts to how to produce more, and quicker, and then how to get it to the cities as fresh as possible. Indeed, cities themselves contained many town dairies,

---

* A period of about 300 days of the cow giving milk, which precedes the 60-day dry period before the next calving.

'with herds kept in dark cellars and fed chiefly on used brewery grains, bakery waste, and the "cake" left over from oilseeds after the oil had been extracted'.[3] Unsurprisingly, the quality was often rotten. From as early as the 1840s, inventors played around with milking machines that were, by turns, useless at the task and miserably painful for the cow, and it wasn't until 1895 that Alexander Shields of Glasgow patented the 'pulsator', a device that 'regularly broke and re-made the vacuum … mimicking the natural squeezing and releasing involved in hand milking'.[4] Various people criticised it, normally for the wrong reasons, but by the turn of the century, mechanisation of what had so recently been done by armies of dairy maids (and they mainly were maids) had become an unstoppable force. The rotating dairy unit arrived just before the Second World War, until eventually supplanted by the milking robot. Meanwhile, the night train moved centre-stage in the transport of milk into towns, particularly from the West Country into London, just as the inner-city milk herds started dwindling away.

The shock delivered by the Second World War – and there is no shock like that of not knowing where the national food is coming from – changed dairy farming massively, and for ever, in three ways: genetics, food science and technology. First, the arrival of the American high-yielding Holstein into mainly Friesian bloodlines contributed to a quadrupling of average yields from fifteen to 60 litres per cow per day; secondly, a winter diet that had been purely hay for centuries was suddenly supplemented by far more nutritious silage; lastly, the process of milking itself, done by hand since time immemorial, rapidly became automated. This ramping up of intensiveness brought with it success, underpinned by the background guarantee from the Milk Marketing Board that every gallon would be collected and paid for at a known rate; it also increased the herds' health issues, with mastitis, infertility and lameness more prevalent than they had ever been in the previously underworked cows. And while the number of dairy farmers inexorably reduced worldwide, in Britain in particular, things were good.[5] Fundamentally, small herds of differing breeds – Alderney, Jersey, Shorthorn, Ayrshire, for example – grazed away on equally small pastures on more or less unadulterated grasses, clovers and legumes, producing unhomogenised milk. As a child, I have a strong memory of running round the side of the house each morning, after the milkman had been, to fetch the bottles of creamy-topped milk off the step before the blue tits got stuck in.

Then a new trading bloc and three entirely different concepts brought the good times to an end: cholesterol, quotas and supermarkets. From a situation in the 1960s when citizens were being urged to 'Drinka Pinta Milka Day', the growth of milk consumption first plateaued and then reduced as people were less and less convinced about its health benefits; simultaneously, the embarrassment of overproduction (known as 'milk lakes') with the European Union led to a quota system that, at a stroke, made reliance on growth out of the question. And finally, from the comforting embrace of the Milk Marketing Board and its guarantee, the market became dominated by a handful of supermarkets, all with a keen interest in securing the lowest possible price for themselves, and then holding it there. When the music stopped after a century of rapid change, 90% of British dairy farms had disappeared, and the average cow was yielding four times the milk she had been yielding at the beginning, as we saw above. In more than just the imagination, the cow had become an uncomfortable adjunct to our industrial lives, an asset from which to extract the maximum return on capital employed.

For many decades, milk produced in the European Union (EU) was subject to a system of subsidies which meant that farmers were guaranteed that all their milk would be bought from them, and all at a certain price. Weighing against the smaller farmers that it was supposed to protect from the very start, because it paid by the acre, it was a system that could only have been invented by a committee of people with a complete ignorance of agriculture, of trade and of the laws of supply and demand. Replacing the much-derided Milk Marketing Board in the UK in 1994, the system managed to lead simultaneously to lower factory gate prices for the farmers, and higher world prices. The current five-year average price of 28.43 pence per litre[6] is roughly what it was in November 2008, since when both the supermarket price of milk and the input costs of farming have risen substantially, and farmers have consistently sold the commodity at a loss.[7] For a reason that escapes most people, not paying the justified cost of the food we eat has become something of a first-world hobby, and it will be a recurring theme in this story.

This is a book about cattle and not governmental systems, but if you happened to be running a Top Ten chart for disastrous interventions, then vying for the top spot would surely be the EU's Common Agricultural Policy which, aggregating its effects over the years, has contrived to produce illogically priced foods that are closely aligned to the not-so-gradual death of the viable small-scale farmer and a wholesale assault on an entire continent's biodiversity. And all that, some might say, to satisfy the militant farmers of just one of the member states – France.

A few statistics are unavoidable here, if only to understand what we are dealing with. While the number of dairy cattle in the UK has remained reasonably steady at around 2.65 million,[8] the number of dairy farms has declined consistently from around 100,000 to its current level of about 14,000, meaning that the average herd size has increased year on year to around 150 as farmers try to build economies of scale into the business. About 90% of those dairy cattle are the familiar black and white Holstein Friesians, each producing somewhere around 40 litres a day, or about eight times the amount that they might normally produce to support a calf.

Nearly fifteen billion litres of milk are produced each year in the UK,[9] about a fifth of Europe's total yield,[10] of which only just over 10% goes on to become drinking milk. By far the biggest use for it is in cheese-making (37.7%), where 10–15 litres is needed to make one kilogram, followed by butter (29.4%) and then cream (11%). And it is only when you start to follow the trail out from the udder of that single cow on that isolated farm that you begin to get some idea of the scale of the whole thing, and the different ways in which what was essentially a mother's nutrition for her calf has filtered into every corner of our lives. However you look at the statistics, the 3.1 million daily glasses of milk we waste[11] as a nation could reduce the need for dairy cows by 30,000 animals at a stroke if we stopped doing it. You shouldn't be surprised: if you think of global food waste as a country being judged on its emissions, it ranks third-worst, behind only China and the USA.[12] Irritatingly, sometimes life is a whole lot more simple than we like to pretend.

Some modern research tends to support the idea that drinking milk is 'neutral to harmful' for those adults whose diet is fundamentally good but, nevertheless, down the supply chain it still cascades. From farm to cooperative, to wholesaler, to retailer to you. Maybe yours is still delivered by a milkman, a trade that was limping towards extinction by the remorseless power of the weekly supermarket shop until, of all things, Covid-19 reversed the decline; suddenly, what had seemed to be almost quaint became again futuristic, with its battery-powered floats, its lack of crowds and its recyclable glass containers.* Maybe you buy organic dairy products, among other things in the confident (but not always correct) expectation that the cows that produce it live civilised, grass-fed lives. Maybe you buy it from your local supermarket, only vaguely aware that it is one of the battlegrounds over which these giant retailers fight to increase their market share, or maybe you buy it in some other way, from the farm gate, perhaps. One thing is certain: your great-grandmother would hardly recognise what comes out of your milk bottle today as fundamentally the same product that came out of her 1920 bottle at the close of the First World

---

* According to Kantar, the number of UK households using the milkman rose from 527,000 to 716,000 between March and September 2020.

War: pasteurisation, homogenisation and skimming have seen to that. But the chances are that, unless you are an entirely vegan household,* you will go on buying it, or its derivatives, until the cows come home.

So the issue for dairy consumers now seems to be *how* to consume the product rather than *whether* to consume it. The industry has predominantly headed in an industrial direction, where the norm is selectively bred Holstein Friesians in large shed-bound herds, fed entirely on a mix of food that is carried to them, and each producing up to ten tons of low-butterfat milk a year before being 'retired' after only three or four lactations. To be fair, standards of hygiene and welfare are generally high, and I can find no hard evidence that an industrial cow yearns for a meadow that it knows nothing about. This may not be a process for the faint-hearted, but I suspect that it is also no more than we signed up for in our quest for ever cheaper food, and by our capacity to tolerate what critics dub 'white water'. It is also probably no more than the logical end product of a farming subsidy system that has relentlessly encouraged intensive agriculture, low biodiversity and large commercial units.

It doesn't need to be like this, and the fight back is well under way.

⇌

'We're having a repeat of the Corn Laws moment.'

....

* The plant-based milk market (e.g. oat, rice, soy) stood at £230 million in 2019, and was growing at over 13% a year. (Source: Vegan Society)

Surrounded by her mob-grazing dairy herd in mid-Devon, Mary Quicke explains how the completion of the Canadian Pacific railroad in 1885, coupled with the repeal of the Corn Laws 40 years earlier, had been the inspiration for and engine of her world-famous cheese dairy. Mary insists that the best place to talk about cows together is not in an office, but sitting in the middle of a large pasture of 300 of them, and we are striding out through the gridwork of temporary fences to find them.

'When my dad was thinking back to his childhood in the 1920s, he distinctly remembered a conversation with a cobbler, who had himself been a boy in the 1850s. That old man could still remember the horses helping sow the acorns on the land that had been rendered useless for grazing by the effect of that railroad and the lower corn prices that the repeal of the Corn Laws had brought. And, in turn, my dad could still remember the milk buyer from Exeter calling his own father one morning in the late twenties and saying, "I can't take your milk today. Sorry." For a dairy farmer, that is devastating. It was not long after this that they worked out for themselves that they simply had to concentrate on producing what their customers wanted, and not for the wholesalers. It was the only way that they could be in control. It's what we've been trying to do ever since.'

The underlying fragility of the farming profession – through disease, weather, changes in public taste, and the subsidy regime – is a recurring theme of all the conversations I have. Mary Quicke might have added, as one eminent academic recently did,[13] that this is also our Beveridge moment (1936 version). In that year, Sir William Beveridge was tasked by the government of the day to look at the state of the UK's national food security, did so, and was then disbelieved by a government and food industry that told him that a new war was 'highly unlikely'. Knowing how well that went, you might think that one of the most fertile countries on earth producing only around half its own food at an unstable time, as we do today, is both a threat and an opportunity.

Mary sees the whole farming game as far more than the sum of cheese production and cattle management. Beyond that, beyond even her duty to protect the beautiful landscape, it is about the social and ecological 'patchwork', and her belief that the supply of food is a public good.

'Rewilding is all very well', she adds, with a nod to the current craze for it, 'but not everyone has a spare 3,000 acres, or can call upon limitless grants. Besides, someone has to produce stuff for people to eat and drink.'

The Quickes have been farming here since the 1540s, but the recent story of the farm dates back to 1973, when Mary's father first thought about selling his own cheese. Back then, in a system that probably only a British civil servant could have invented, a dairy would buy back at a lower price milk that it had just sold to the Milk Marketing Board, and then would create as much cheese out of it as it had been given permission for, before selling it back to the Board so that it could be sold anonymously on the dairy's behalf, and at a loss.

'It was all block cheddar, back then,' says Mary, who remembers travelling around Liverpool at one point trying to point out to retailer buyers the benefits and excellence of her family's cloth-bound cheese, to persuade them that it wasn't inferior to the plastic-wrapped block cheddar. 'But by 1984, the farm was selling it direct to certain retailers, which probably makes us one of the country's first modern-era artisan cheese-makers. Many of the local dairies thought that we were selling out at the time.' As in so many family businesses, Mary was sent off to learn (in her case at agricultural college), and then to 'make her mistakes' on someone else's farm up in Shropshire. In 1984, she was back in Devon with her husband, and in charge of the whole farm.

Onwards they went, always keeping an eye on the quality, always pushing the name, and gradually building up the herd, which now numbers 600, divided into a summer block and a winter block. And absolutely central to what they did was, and still is, grass management, where a field will be grazed from a stock of 3,000 kilos of grass per hectare until it is down to 1,500 kilos, at which point it will be rested until it is back up to 3,000 again. It is a geographically appropriate version of Allan Savory's famous vision of mob-grazing,[14] which Mary calls 'paddock grazing', in which half the grass is harvested by the cow, and the other half is left to sustain the new growth. If you see someone wandering around a farm pressing a large horizontal disc on a stick into the ground at regular intervals, they are simply measuring the rate of growth of the grass.

'Every now and again, one of our customers emigrated', she goes on, when I ask her how they managed to break into America. 'I suppose they just took the stock lists with them and continued to buy what they had been buying when they were over here. I'd like to say it was more planned than that, but it really wasn't.' Whatever the case, Quicke's cheese is now highly popular in specialist delis in the States.

'It turned out that we were in the vanguard of the artisan cheese movement', she says, 'and more through good luck than intention.' Back in 1984, at the same time as the Quickes were taking their first tentative steps into 'proper' cheese, Randolph Hodgson had set up Neal's Yard Dairy in Covent Garden, London, as a one-man mission to save what was left of British cheeses. Just at the point that Britain was heading full-tilt for a joyless and industrial food culture, and in the face of the overwhelming power of the supermarkets, it was people like Hodgson who turned the tide. Whether it was debunking the myths of compulsory pasteurisation* or persuading cheesemakers to retain the wooden shelves that Whitehall was demanding should be replaced by steel ones, Neal's Yard just went on buying what the best artisans could provide, and then helping them to open new markets all over the world. This is a world of passion, and that is why it mainly thrives. You only have to look at the breadth and depth of the prize-winners at the British Cheese Awards to understand where that passion leads.[†]

We climb over the fence into the crowded field, and choose a clean patch of grass to sit down on. After a couple of minutes, we are surrounded by inquisitive cows and, watching her, it

---

* Stilton, for example, caved in to the pressure in the end, and all of it is now pasteurised. Stichelton, a 'raw milk cheese that is Stilton in all but name', was set up in 2006 to carry the flag.

[†] Although Mary was awarded an MBE (for services to farming) in 2005, I suspect that deep down she is rather prouder of her 'Exceptional Contribution to Cheese' award at the World Cheese Awards in 2015.

strikes me that this 66 year-old farmer has never once lost the passion for what she does, and nor can she afford to.

'This one's mother was getting a bit on the large side, so we brought in a bit of Jersey to bring the next generation down to size a bit', she says of the dark-faced cow that is noisily sniffing her collar. 'Whereas this one's mother was a little bit precious, so we shoved in some robust Montbéliarde. Hence the beautiful brown and white.' This is about as far from the standard Euro-blob Holstein Friesian as you could be, a herd within which the genetics might just as easily come from a high Swiss mountain as a frosty Swedish forest, a quiet French upland as a tiny Channel island. We are surrounded by an extraordinary variety of cattle, an unrepeatable moment in time in a lightly choreographed ballet. With one arm reaching out to a pastoral tradition that goes back millennia, and the other embracing laboratory genetics, this is what Mary believes has to be done to wrest back that control.

Only from her careful supervision of the breeding process right through to the milking regimes, from the microflora on the cloth that binds her cheeses to her precision management of the grass in the fields that run down to the River Creedy, does she believe that she can create, and maintain, the *terroir* that allows her cheese to thrive in a crowded marketplace. She talks with passion about 'grazing the shoulders of the season' so as to get the best spring grass, and the 'unknowable impacts' of the tiny differences that each new season, even each new day, brings.

'At the end of it all', she says, 'it has to be a bit of an exercise in humility. Stuff happens, and you simply have to do the best you can to make sure that you take it in your stride. The one thing we know is that the end product has to be completely consistent.'

In the cheese store, where the bacterial smell reminds me of a French wine cellar, she shows me the 27-kilo wheels of cheddar that are the culmination of everything she does. The cheeses are stacked on trays of four that are rotated each week, and which slowly work their way towards an exit to the marketplace that can be as far as two years away. It is hard not to be moved by the mixture of care and love that stands out in the production of artisan food, and to marvel at its distance from its industrial cousins.

'So why exactly is this a Corn Law repeal moment?' I eventually ask, as we watch the herd start to wind its way towards the yard for its afternoon milking. A barely perceptible shadow passes across her face.

'Brexit means that we have no choice, we have to decide what kind of a food nation we want to be', she answers. 'And to realise absolutely that eating and shopping are both intensely political acts. I'm not sure we have understood that yet.'

On the long drive home, I reflect on that last comment, and know again – as I am reminded a hundred times on this journey – that we are never as powerful as when we are standing in the aisle of a supermarket clutching our wallet, never more likely to change the behaviour of the buyers than when we change our own.

If we don't take responsibility for our own choices, we can't be surprised if others take it for us. As that annoying expression goes, if we do what we have always done, we will surely get what we have always got.

~

On a whim, I call up Robert Bridger again, and ask him if he would like to come with me to visit a highly modernised neighbouring mixed farm with 120 milkers, and cast his professional eye over 60 years of development, and particularly the state of cattle welfare. He has known the current farmer, James Renwick, as a boy and, insofar as his old limbs allow him to, he positively jumps at the chance to come and look round.

'It doesn't smell much of cow', he says suspiciously, as we climb out of the car and into the yard.

James's is a 'freedom farm', where the milking takes place continually throughout the day and night on two individual robotic machines, each one of which cost £120,000 to install, each one able to handle up to 60 cows. Essentially, the cow decides when she would like to be milked (on average three and a half times in a 24-hour period, or 75% more frequently than can generally happen on a busy dairy farm), and is cleaned and treated to a small feed each time she does. When he sees the information screen with its banks of figures (weight of cow, volume of milk, udder function, temperature, etc.), Robert is utterly absorbed. Far from expressing disapproval at the impersonal modernity, he sees immediately by the demeanour of the cows that they are content, and says so, before he is even asked.

'The cow just does what it does best when it is working to its own natural rhythms', explains James. 'And not just the daily timetable of a busy farmer. It's pretty obvious, really.'

'Am I impressed?' Robert asks, when he is watching the teats of the machine aligning themselves carefully with the positions of the individual udders. 'Bloody right I am. They've got good udders, the lot of them, which means something's going right. And they're queueing up for their turn, which they wouldn't be doing if they didn't like it.'

A calm line of cows at the entry gate to each of the robots endorses what he has noticed. Suddenly, he is 30 years younger, and back in the world of cattle behaviour. He wants to know about the silage-hay feed mix, how James stops the young milkless heifers queueing up and confusing the machine, how you deal with a cow that has learned to push open gates of its own volition, once it gets back out into the fields, and how the eternal battle against the antibiotic is being waged, something that has been raging since he was a teenage farm labourer.

'This machine can detect and immediately report the tiniest change of temperature, even in just one of the four udders', says James. 'It means that we can deal with mastitis ahead of when it gets bad, and without drenching antibiotics all over the place. Better health; happier cows, more milk.' He reckons that he is getting 15% more milk per day out of each cow, which, with the investment he has made in the machinery, is perhaps just as well.

It amuses Robert that, after many years out of fashion, rotation of fields is becoming a thing again. 'Everything that goes around, comes around', he says. 'Just like all of a sudden the smart farmers are back-pedalling to smaller beasts. Suddenly, we're not quite as stupid as they all thought we were.'

'Who said we thought you were stupid, Robert?' says James, smiling.

'Oh, not you. You know, the ...' He thinks for a moment, and then lets the sentence pass unfinished, as if specifying exactly who, would spoil a fine afternoon.

The affiliated farmers' relationships with the huge dairy cooperative Arla are generally good, but the wholesaler can only pay the farmer in relation to what they are paid by the supermarkets, which is not a lot. To help change the maths of the farm, and to utilise some of the extra 15% he reckons that he is getting, James has recently set up his first farm-gate milk-vending machine in a small barn by the road up to the farm. There, consumers can buy the real thing 24 hours a day, dispensed by the litre into reusable glass bottles, at around four times the wholesale price. The milk is pasteurised but not homogenised, and a conversation with fellow shoppers confirms that it is a product the like of which most can't ever remember having tasted, even from their childhoods. To add some scale, James also offers bags of potatoes and boxes of eggs, together with locally grown seasonal produce such as asparagus, and he says that the whole operation breaks even at about 100 customers a day. While dwarfed by the 6,000 litres of milk that is waiting to go up to the Arla dairy in Aylesbury, it all adds up to a tiny but incremental taking back of control, and the creation of local customer relationships. Apart from anything, it has allowed another of his children to get involved in the farm in a meaningful and profitable way. It won't solve everything, but it's a start.

But if it's a small start, James is one of a growing number. In West Dorset, I spent a morning at Hollis Mead Organic

Farm, where Oliver Hemsley sells the entire output of his dairy via twenty vending machines spread about the local villages and towns, offering milk, yoghurt, cream, cheese and even kefir. 'Anything that is left', he says, 'is fed back to the calves.' His petite Old British Friesians are a far cry from the Holstein-enhanced standard dairy cow, and are only milked once a day. 'An industrial dairyman would laugh at our small yields', he adds, 'but what we do is about health; health of the cow, health of the consumer and, above all, health of the biodiversity.' Lark song out in the neighbouring fields underscores that last point elegantly, and he talks with enthusiasm about the levels of Omega-3 fatty acids in his milk. I ask him what the key is to a more self-determined future, the aspiration that I heard from Mary Quicke and James Renwick, and that will be echoed from a hundred farmers over the year. How do you stop your farm being like seaweed on a rocky shore, buffeted this way and that by the pricing games of supermarkets and the ever-changing subsidy regimes?

'Creating a brand', he says, without delay. 'Once you have created a good brand, everything changes. They can't touch you.'

A few miles from him, near Bridport, Arthur Crutchley has recently ignored a consultant's advice to the effect that the way to make an 800-cow indoor herd profitable was to increase it to 1,200, by going in the exact opposite direction and halving it to 400, at the same time throwing open the metaphorical barn doors for outdoor summer grazing.

'400 was the number of cows that was right for the available summer grazing within the distance of just over a mile from the farm that a cow is happy to walk', he tells me when I ask him how he reached such a dramatically different figure. 'And 400 was the number of cows that the land we had could just about sustain through the silage, hay, wheat and maize that we could grow on the rest of it for the winter.'

We watch the late autumn sunshine evaporating last night's rain in wisps of cloud that nudge and slide their way up the little wooded valleys.

'We get about £0.28 per litre for our milk, out of which the feed costs per litre are about £0.115, nearly half. So everything we can do to reduce that helps make us a little more profitable.'

Most farmers will tell you that the biggest obstacle to making money is the growing cost of 'inputs', stuff that has to be bought for real money from outside the farm, so the aim of reducing those costs by producing a higher percentage themselves is an entirely logical one which is already paying dividends. It also reduces the farmer's dependency on the 'agribusiness' machine, just as Oliver Hemsley has, and on the financial sector, for the cash borrowings.

Not for the first or last time in this story, someone had worked out that growth is not necessarily all it is cracked up to be, and that to escape from the hole you are in, like Winnie the Pooh once did, sometimes you just need to get smaller. Counterintuitive though such notions may be in our scaled-up, flat-out commercial world, this was to become a recurring theme in the scores of farms I spent time on.

A few hours east, among the Wealden woodlands of West Sussex, Jeremy Way is breaking out, too. He has just finished the transition of his herd (British Friesian, Norwegian Red and

Jersey crosses) to organic, where the extra 10 pence per litre (the 'organic premium') helps to offset the smaller number of cows that the untreated land will sustain. His is a world of new ten-year herbal leys, of fields of red clover and lucerne. Under skies of barn owls and kestrels, and on mob-grazed pastures of growing numbers of dung beetles, he reckons to get nine lactations out of his animals, somewhere around three times the industry norm. And it's not just in milk that he is gaining.

'A couple of years ago', he says, when I ask him how he deals with the meat from unwanted bull calves and barren heifers, 'I might have got £1.50 a kilo from the dealer. Last year, we teamed up with the village shop and I had a queue halfway back to the road with customers paying me £8 a kilo for the same thing. Not only do I get more, but I start to build a long-term relationship with my local community. In the end, we clean ran out.'

I ask him where he wants to be in five years' time.

'Same number of animals', he replies, keen to point out that this is not about overall growth. 'But with less cake and more lucerne, and all the silage off our own ground. Then to have our own customer base who really get what we are trying to do with the organic initiative.'

In other words, to highlight the difference between 'white water' and the rest.

Finally, up in West Oxfordshire, I watch 28 year-old Hallam Duckworth leading his three Austrian Fleckvieh milkers into his micro-dairy. Just three cows, all of them pasture-fed with no concentrate feed being used; just a natural diet of grass, wildflowers and herbs, and the milk shared with unweaned calves. Just 50 or so litres of milk. He is a farmworker who has been given the chance by a local landowner to do what he has always wanted to do, and raise livestock. It won't make him a living on its own, but it will incomparably add to the quality of his working life, if not to the quality of his sleep.

For now, he will sell it all to the locals in branded glass bottles, like James Renwick does, but on the smallest scale of all.

You won't see people like Hallam mentioned in any National Food Strategy, and plenty of industrial food producers might comment that micro-dairies are not part of the solution. But here, in the damp of an August dawn in the Cotswold Hills, a young man and an imaginative landowner are taking the first steps towards solving a giant national problem.

⇌

Back in Midhurst, it is time for Robert Bridger to head home for his tea.

'It's natural, that's what it is', he says, thinking back to what he has seen at James's farm, as we walk to the car. An 82-year-old farmer lost in admiration for the new way of doing things. By the time he saw Tyrone, the muck-vacuuming robot, making its way down the aisle of the barn, and politely waiting for cows to budge so that it could get past, he looked like all his Christmases had come at once.

'He's a fine farmer', he says, when I ask him what he thought of it all during our short drive back to his house, 'and he has fine cows. But then he's not the problem, is he?'

I drive on down the muddy lane in silence, waiting for the answer to the rhetorical question that he has posed. For much of my adult life, there seems to have been an air of prevailing hopelessness about dairy farming, an irrational disconnect between the work involved and the reward available, and a cruel imbalance between who in the supply chain gets what out of it. The further away from the cow you happen to be, it seems, the more likely you are to make a fortune out of what it produces. An industry based on a norm of selling a commodity at a *lower* price than it takes to produce it is, in the long term, going to struggle until it changes.

'Who is, then?' I ask, when the answer never comes. After another long pause, he points at a supermarket online delivery van carefully parking up outside a house by the main road. 'Responsibly sourced', runs the writing on the side of the van. 'Delivered to your kitchen.'

'Them', he says. 'That's what's buggered it all up.'

6. FROM PASTURE TO
PLATE (AND BACK AGAIN)

....

*'What grocery store item is more silent about
its origins than a shrink-wrapped steak?'*
MICHAEL POLLAN, 'POWER STEER'
(ARTICLE IN NEW YORK TIMES, MARCH 2002)

....

In November, we bring our own cows in for the winter, one field at a time.

The timing of this decision is one of the many balancing acts in the cattle farmer's life. Do it too late, and you have ill-fed animals who have trampled the edges of the wet fields into a morass that even a dry spring won't sort out. Do it too early, on the other hand, and you will run the risk of a cold snap at the start of spring finding you with no hay, silage or straw left, and consequently extra costs that might have been avoidable.

Besides, out in the fields cows can largely be left to their own devices; once they are in the barns, they are a running chore that to miss for even a day could bring problems, disaster even. A beef cow produces 25 kg of manure a day which, if you multiply it by the number of our cows, and the number of days in the barn, comes to something around 540 tons of the stuff that has to be cleared over the winter. And they will eat about 600 tons of hay, all of which has to be acquired, stored, collected and dispensed. You don't want them in a minute before you have to.

A handful of the heifers will outwinter in the fields, and there are plenty of herds around the country where all of them will. To do so, it is easier if they are on better drained ground than ours, and for the cows concerned to be on the small side, tough and 'thrifty', a lovely word that describes the ability of some livestock to make a living out of virtually nothing. 'You could leave a Galloway in this small concrete yard all winter', said one farmer I visited, about one such breed, 'and it would still find enough to keep it going.'

'Like I said a few weeks ago, it's about grass management, although it was actually the acorns that decided me in the end this time around', says John, as we follow a group of mothers with their bull calves homewards down a little wooded track. Cows love to eat acorns and, on a heavily wooded farm, they get many opportunities; if they eat too many, they can fall seriously ill from the effects of the tannic acid, even die, and it can pass birth defects to the next generation.[1] This is in sharp contrast to pigs who, a thousand years ago, would have been driven deliberately into these woods and along these hedges in huge numbers in the autumn of each year for pannage,* in which acorns, alongside beechmast and chestnuts, were the leading element of the diet, leaving them completely unaffected. Different animal, different digestion. That thousand-year glimpse backwards should shout out to us about the vital need to reconnect ourselves with the story of our food.

Some noisy jackdaws escort a buzzard off the premises above us. Across the field, a great-spotted woodpecker flies heavily home from one copse to another, a dark shape, who knows what, hanging from its beak.

'Also, this is all natural selection in action', John goes on after a while. 'Generations of cows being used to our old, low and occasionally rickety fences and gates has led inexorably to gentle and biddable cattle, which is what we are known for. It is amazing how often the farms with the high-security fencing seem to coincide with badly behaved and aggressive animals.' This is a factor not to be underestimated when so much of what we do here comes down to asking a 650 kg beast to go where she doesn't much want to.

There is an understated elegance about an experienced cowhand moving cattle from one place to another. It is less about driving, and more a case of allowing the animals to explore somewhere accessible and new, by using the fact that their mob-grazing genetic make-up means that they are always looking to move on. Open the right gates, leaving the other

---

* Pannage may be an ancient term, but it still applies in the New Forest in a delightfully symbiotic fashion in which the pigs are fed for free, and the ponies and cattle are protected from acorn poisoning for another year.

ones closed, and the chances are that they will make their way to where you need them to be with the minimum of interference. There is little noise, no shouting and as little eye contact as possible, so as to reduce stress. In sharp contrast to all those yee-hawing Hollywood cowboys from the old films, skilled drovers respect the fact that cattle are stressed by noise, and like to keep it as quiet as possible. A small length of blue plastic piping tends to be all we need to give a gentle reminder of the direction required, and to instil a little sense of urgency. Time was when John would do all this on a quarter horse, so named because it could turn on a sixpence and beat any other horse over a quarter of a mile, but those days are long gone. These days, it is largely done on foot. Once in the yard and the spacious barns, it becomes a ballet of the gates, as they are continually swung through the angles and back again, so as to segregate the mothers from their calves and to end up with the right animals in the right spaces. Aside from the inevitable jousting between dominant cows trying to establish their fresh positions in the pecking order when groups are newly thrown together, it is generally a peaceful process.

'It's a bit of a game of chess', admits John, 'where you are always trying to think four or five moves ahead. We wean the calves off their mothers at the same time as bringing them in, which means we need to end up with bull calves in one set of enclosures, heifers in another, mothers in a third, and then the older bulls in a fourth.'

'I also like to keep moving them a bit throughout the winter. The change of scene does them good, even if it's just outside in the yard while we change the bedding, and the more we can be a routine part of their lives, the greater the chances that they will be gentle with other humans when and if they move.' I discovered quickly that gentle livestock was one of the towering ambitions of the farm.

Before they get to settle down to a winter of hay, every calf has to pass through the little weighbridge to have its 200-day weaning weight recorded, and its condition assessed and noted. Running repairs are administered to a couple, in the form of antibiotics for foot infections, and then the neighbourhood settles in for two days of constant noise as the cows complain volubly about the broken partnerships. During the morning's work, my friend 1025 crushes me briefly against a gate and then, for good measure, kicks me in the leg, just under the kneecap. For a moment, and not for the last time this winter, we stare at each other across the concrete, each quietly marking the other's card.

After that, they all quickly move on and settle down. Almost overnight, the farm has moved into its winter self.

⸺

Over the last few weeks, every other Saturday evening, I have been gently working my gastronomic way around the anatomy of the cheaper cuts of a beef cow, always grass-fed, always cooked by me: a rolled brisket, a slow-cooked oxtail or shin, or an even slower-cooked stew of topside; and the slight throwing open of the cages of the second Covid lockdown has encouraged Caroline and me to head for our local pub, the Horse Guards, before everything is slammed shut again. By the time I have finished my researches, I have promised myself that I will have sampled all 39 primal cuts,* and much else besides.

'The beef there is all grass-fed', Caroline reminds me, in the slightly weary tones of one who has heard enough about mob-grazing in recent weeks to last her a lifetime. 'So that should make you very happy.'

I have asked John and Emma along, so that we can savour the hoped-for perfection of a prime cut together, and they can explain it from the farmers' point of view as we go along.

The Horse Guards Inn is one of a growing number of pubs and restaurants for whom the provenance and flavour of each one of their ingredients is inextricably linked. Indeed, a long and changing list of suppliers is up on one of the blackboards for all to see: scallops from Rye Bay, garlic from the Isle of Wight, goat from three fields away and beef from Rother Valley Organics about ten miles to the west.

'Fast-food burgers are about growing the beef to suit the product', chef and owner Sam explains when I ask the difference. 'Here, all we are doing is buying the natural product and allowing it to speak for itself. We sell it on with as few changes as possible. A great steak shouldn't be an everyday thing. It

....

* **Front end**: Neck, chuck roll, Denver muscle, underblade muscle, underblade fillet, forerib, rib-eye, blade, feather, LMC, Baby LMC, clod flat muscle, clod shin muscle, shoulder brisket muscle, fore shin, needle, flat brisket, brisket cap muscle, forequarter flank. **Back end**: strip loin, fillet, rump cap, prime rump, rump bistro, muscle, silverside, salmon cut, topside, tender top, heel muscle, hind shin, prime hind shin, thick flank, centre cut, rump tail, thin flank, flank skirt, goose skirt, inside skirt. (AHDB Meat Education Programme)

should be an occasional treat that improves your world, one that also respects the animal that provided it.'

For Sam, it is simple: dining out is an important event that should be simply wrapped in the joy of taste. This is what he has been doing, the passion he has been building, since he was a twenty year-old sous-chef in Wandsworth. Most British beef ends up in retail shops, with foreign beef largely going to the catering industry,[2] so he is bucking the trend a bit. People like Sam are the alchemists who turn artisan ingredients into memorable plates of food.

I am nervous, as this is my first steak for three years, after a well-meaning host had insisted that I chose the $70 'Signature USDA* prime dry-aged, bone-in 28-ounce rib-eye' at Smith & Wollensky's steakhouse in Chicago.† He was paying, so I felt I had little option. He told me that he came here each night of the five-day trade show, and that the experience energised him for the next day. To say that it defeated me is like saying that the 1916 Somme offensive was a slight waste of men and resources. Within five minutes I was sweating profusely, and it went downhill from there. All around me, outsized steaks, no doubt tender and delicious and perhaps the inheritors of a bull like SAV America, made their elevated and hurried way between the tables on chargers held by brash waiters; all

....

* US Department of Agriculture.

† In terms of outsized steaks, it turns out that this one wasn't even on the dance floor: the 72 oz (2 kilo) 'Big Texan' is generally considered the daddy of them all. If you get through it in an hour or less, you get it for free. Or you ask yourself all over again how the hell man became top animal.

around me, the diners of the Midwest polished them off, while my plate remained resolutely charged, at best fiddled with and rearranged so as to create the illusion of activity and enjoyment. The truth was that the sheer volume of meat was sending apocalyptic signals to my stomach that it was under sustained attack. After a while, and to my shame, I made some pathetic excuse and ran out of the restaurant and into the kindly sub-zero fogs of the banks of the North Chicago River, so that I could conceal from polite society what happened next. I swore many things at the time, but one of them was never to eat a steak again in my life.

In contrast, the eight-ounce sirloin that Sam brings to me has come from towards the back of the top of a Belted Galloway that has grazed in fields in nearby Rogate, and in whose farmhouse I had once been patched up as a young boy after a bike crash while trying to take a corner too fast. The meat has come from between the ribs and the fillet, the area below where a farmworker might affectionately pat a cow moving from one pen to another. Among the 'big four' cuts (sirloin, rib-eye, fillet and rump), the sirloin is sometimes seen as the compromise cut between the extreme tenderness of the fillet, which comes from a little-used muscle and might be hung for just 21 days, and the extreme flavour of the rump, which has walked every step of the way with its late owner, and may hang for nearer 35. It was not, as the old story goes, knighted by some delighted but deluded monarch, but named from the French for 'above the loin'.

Emma looks over at me as I am about to make the first incision.

'Maybe just stop and think about it for one minute', she says quietly. 'This is what we used to tell our children. What's on your plate is the end chapter of maybe a five-year story, not just a plate of food. It's the sum total of all the grazing and browsing, the moving from field to field, the grasses, wildflowers, coppicing, sucker shoots and hedges, the walking, standing and running, the winter hay and silage, the water, the rain and sun, sleet and snow; it's the result of decision-making and health checks, the passporting and breeding decisions. It's the journeys here and there, the minerals peculiar to its own farm, and the water that flows through it. No piece of meat from anywhere else on earth will ever taste exactly like it. Please treasure it.'

For someone who doesn't make speeches, this is a speech. But then, this is a woman who has spent the best part of 30 years preparing cows for a moment like this. It isn't her beef, but, in this business, blood is thicker than water; I have been on the farm for four months, and my respect is due, and expected.

And I do treasure it, every last scrap of it. Less than a third of the size and weight of its Chicago predecessor, it is something that I can savour, as Emma demands, slice by slice, gloriously, and from beginning to end. I find that, if I stop and think a bit about the taste, then I can also stop and think a bit about the animal that has provided it; if I close my eyes and let the flavour run across the roof of my mouth, I can just about make out the salt grasses of Hayling Island where the Galloway had recently finished its grazing life.

It is almost too good to be true, certainly too good to be adulterated by the glob of mustard I put on my plate, by force of habit, just after it arrived. So on a whim, as the waitress clears our plates, I decide to trace it back to its pastures and try to understand its journey a little better.

When I get home, I go to check on that prescient comment of Aldo Leopold back in the 1940s that I half-remember, to the effect that 'there is a value in any experience that reminds us of our dependency on the soil-plant-animal-man food chain, and the fundamental organisation of the biota'.*

In other words, to celebrate eating as more than a necessary inconvenience in our busy lives.

Curiously, it is the last steak that I am to eat for over half a year. Not because I don't want one, but because there are so many other cuts to find out about, and I have made a promise to myself to eat beef no more than once a fortnight.

⸺

A word on beef, the 'flesh of a cow, bull or ox, used as food'.[3]

Let us say that a particular cow weighs 600 kg, known as liveweight, at the time of its slaughter.

Opinions differ slightly, but let us then say that 50% of that is usable meat, while 50% is bones and other stuff.

Of that 50%, or around 300 kilos, known as carcass, let's assume that a further 120 kg will eventually be discarded, and around 180 kg go on to be fully butchered. Maybe 20% of that (36 kilos) is what are traditionally known as 'prime cuts' – the

---

* Biota, a word not commonly used now, but meaning the plant and animal life of an area.

sirloin, fillet, T-bone and rump – and the balance is, to put it crudely, everything else.

As a gross generalisation, the higher up and further back you go on the cow, the more financially valuable the meat, which obviously means that by the time you get to the shins on the front legs, you are in the territory of a budget meal, or in need of an imaginative chef, or both.* In between, you have all the topside, featherblade, rib, brisket, neck, skirt, flank and mince that should, but too often doesn't, make up so much of the display in your local butchers. As another generalisation, the more work the muscle that you are eating has done, the longer and slower it needs to be cooked, but the more flavour it potentially has. Equally, the less you paid for it, the more carefully you should probably cook it, which may well explain why some of the very best restaurants serve some of the very cheapest cuts, and, ironically, some of the least ambitious ones only serve expensive steak. Prime beef, as opposed to prime cuts, is generally regarded as coming from a cow aged 12–30 months, but this tends to be a label for the guidance of wise men, and the strict adherence of fools.

It sometimes comes as a surprise to those who relish the freshest of food that most beef, especially good beef, is aged for somewhere between fourteen and 40 days, in an essential process in which microbes and enzymes break down the connective tissues within the muscle, and so improve both tenderness and

---

* The finest meal I ate in the researching of this book was a beef ragù made out of £4 of shin, and which easily fed six of us. The recipe, which is my son's, is in the Appendix.

flavour. In 'dry ageing', which takes place hanging off a hook in a cold room and is generally regarded as the superior process, the flavour intensifies as the weight of the meat slowly reduces, sometimes by up to a third. 'Wet ageing' takes place in a sealed bag, and has the advantage (for the butcher or supermarket) of maintaining the original weight and, for the consumer, of keeping the distinctive red colour. Show-offs in the most expensive steakhouses have some of their beef aged for 100 days or more, although I never found a butcher who was remotely convinced that the extra time fulfilled any useful purpose beyond its own marketing storyline.

Since the days of Ulysses, for whom only the fattiest possible cuts were good enough to be sacrificed to his annoying gods, our enthusiasm for fat on our beef has fluctuated along the lines of what country, or what century, we happen to be in. Here, in the third decade of the 21st century, as a rough guide, the nearer you are to Europe's old gastronomic heartland, France, the less fatty your beef is likely to be, and the more you will be going for flavour, which helps explain the dominance of the Charolais and Limousin breeds there, whose musculature is inherited from their origins as draft animals. Over in the United States, at the other extreme, it is all about tenderness and 'marbling', a nice descriptive word for the bands of intra-muscular fat (as opposed to inter-muscular fat), and rather less about the flavour; hence the popularity of the Angus and Hereford cows there. By and large, the more grass in the cow's diet, the less fat there will be and, therefore, the shorter the cooking time needed. Equally, the more marbled the steak, the less of it you will be able to comfortably digest. (The best

example of marbling you will ever see is on the fabled Wagyu*
beef, which we will revisit later on in another context.) Other
countries have their own traditions. All of which feeds an essential truth that I learned early in my researches, to the effect that
there is no such thing as the perfect steak: it all depends on
what you are looking for.†

Farmers who don't have the luxury of their own private
box scheme or hospitality market are most commonly paid by
'deadweight' (the carcass); just as we saw in Chapter 3 that
there is a farm-gate price for milk, so there is a daily deadweight price for beef, averaging around £4.17 a kilo at the time
of writing, rather less if it is a retired milker. So the cow in our
example might earn the farmer 300 × £4.17, or about £1,251.
In an ideal world, everything has its market and everything has
its price, from the £195 a kilo at retail for a piece of Grade 5A
Wagyu fillet to the £1 for a kilo of shin.

This is where we might choose to ignore, for a few minutes,
the siren temptations of the corporate marketing departments
and actually take the trouble to know a little more about the
animal who is about to provide our meal: its provenance, its
welfare, its diet, its additives and, yes, its eventual death. And
we might want to understand the terminology: what is meant

....

* Wagyu cows are any one of four strains of black or red cattle coming out of Japan, and whose standards are fiercely protected by the
authorities. Generally hand-reared and deeply marbled, Wagyu beef is
sought-after and expensive.

† Personally, and maybe only twice a year, I'm going for a small
(170 gram), grass-fed, dry-aged rump steak, cooked medium rare, served
with French fries and a peppercorn sauce, and not an onion ring in sight.

by 'organic', by 'pasture-fed', or by 'traditional', for example. Right now, it is perfectly legal to call your beef or milk 'grass-fed' providing that you can claim to have inched yourself over the halfway line: 51% grass content is fine; the rest can be more or less whatever you want it to be.

It pays to take an interest. Food fraud is rife in our continent and beyond,[4] especially in matters of labelling, the addition of water to add weight, and illegal additives. After all, it was only back in 2013 that we found that what we fondly thought was French beef in our lasagne was more likely, after analysis, to be a retired runner-up from the 3.20 at Chantilly. The Pasture-Fed Livestock Association (PFLA) has been lobbying for years to get more honesty into labelling, and their current CLEAR[5] initiative, supported by many activist organisations, includes a manifesto worthy of your attention. It includes a mandatory method of labelling, enforcement measures, benchmarking, independent assessment, and clear, accessible presentation.

But for now, we are in the delightfully simple position of standing in an organic pasture in Hampshire, looking at a Belted Galloway who has never been in a building in his life, and whose diet has been just about completely gleaned from what he has found in the fields and hedgerows.*

After a good life, what happens in his last journey?

* This cow will have spent time grazing freely on the woods of Blackdown; occasional organic supplements are offered to remind him of humans and prevent him from going completely feral.

Down on the sandy fields of Sussex, I ask Shon Sprackling how he decides which cows are to be taken to slaughter, and when. Shon is the farmer who raised the Galloway whose sirloin I had eaten back at the Horse Guards, and I am standing with him on one of his fields.

'I normally know instinctively', he says. 'I just look for the right conformation of condition and fat that's going to lead to the best beef.' He thinks a bit more, and then adds: 'It's an age thing, too. Ever since BSE, you get more money for a cow that is under 30 months than over, so I have to be driven by that as well. It's a bit ridiculous, as good native breeds like the Angus and Galloway here don't even really mature until after 30 months. It's just an old system, designed to allow us to crawl back into Europe after BSE, but which makes no sense now. At its worst, it means that some of the very best beef out there is going to end up as cheap mince in a curry house.'

Shon keeps his animals outside all year round, on grazing that he has access to, over a twenty-mile radius. He explains the system of traceability that begins before the chosen animal is even born, and that works all the way through into every cut of beef in each butcher's shop, restaurant or private customer who buys from him. He defends the system when I say that it all sounds complicated.

'I don't think it is', he says. 'All I need to do is get the paperwork in order, ditto the organic livestock documents, and make sure that both ear tags are on and readable, which can be an issue when a cow is out all year, and grazing round thorn bushes. In return, I think Britain has the cleanest and least abused system out there. When consumers are really confident, which they justifiably are, then the market can grow. Plus, it has made the theft of livestock a lot more difficult.'

Once he has selected the animals to go for slaughter, he calls up the nearby abattoir that he uses, and arranges transport.

'The first time this animal will step inside a building is also the last', he says. 'It will have spent every minute of its two and a half years outside, grazing on whatever grass it finds.' It is not surprising that farmers like Shon, who walk the walk of grass-fed beef, just as much as they talk its talk, sometimes get disheartened by how much the term 'grass-fed' has been deliberately devalued and confused by people who would like the kudos and extra money it might imply, without incurring the effort. 'Consumers are entitled to believe that what is being sold to them as grass-fed hasn't actually spent seven months of its year eating cereals or biscuit waste in a barn.' Depending on demand, and the time of year, this cow will eventually go in one of three directions: the premium beef section of Guildford's Sainsbury's, the organic market at Shaftesbury in Dorset, or Shon's in-house farm shop, yet another coloured pin in the burgeoning artisan food shop map of modern Britain.

Shon is confident in the treatment that his cow will get at the abattoir, which is why he always sends his animals there. He knows that it will be back a few days later in quarters (the little butchery on the farm doesn't have sufficient ceiling height to take a half cow) and that it must then hang in the cold room until it is ready to be converted into the recognisable cuts, steaks and mince that I have spent half a lifetime looking at in our local butcher's shop.

'Do you want to watch it go through?' he asked, which was easier said than done, as no abattoir in the south-east wanted anyone from outside wandering around the premises if they could help it: the relentless pickets and vilification of staff by the broad church of anti-meat activists had seen to that.

The abattoir visit would have to wait a month or two, and I would instead get straight down into that butchery.

⇌

Lee was making sausages for his father's butcher's shop before he was five years old.

By the time he was ten, he knew his way around the anatomy of most of the classic farm animals, and the names of even the most outdated cuts. And for the next 30 years, sometimes in a boning plant, sometimes in a butchery and sometimes in a supermarket, meat is all he has ever really done.

I have come to spend the day with him at Shon's dry-hanging store and butchery at Rother Valley Organics, to try to understand how the carcass that has returned to the farm from the abattoir completes its final metamorphosis to the cuts of meat that you and I would recognise. After all, this is where my pub steak would have been butchered.

'This has been hanging for 35 days', he explains, underlining the sheer length of the process between the cow being selected for slaughter and finally ending up on a plate in the Horse Guards. With a finger of his chain-link gauntlet, he points out the tell-tale dark 'facings' of skin, before heaving the whole back leg off the hook and laying it down on his work surface.

Lee has two knives: a small, narrow-bladed one for the boning and scraping, to be done with the delicacy and precision of a surgeon, and then a larger one to shape the cuts and steaks when the time comes. Any meat that does not fall into the categories of cuts or steaks goes into the waste bin, or into a box for eventual mincing.

He points out the leg bone, the knuckle at the top of the silverside, the aitch bone and the heel. Once those pieces are clear, he starts to cut away the silverside joint from the outside of the leg, and the topside from the inside, both premium roasting joints, for a while to the disconcerting tune of Alphaville's 'Forever Young' blasting out from the radio. And, as he goes, he talks about the snobbery that persists around the finest cuts, and expresses a common opinion that it is the best chefs who can find ways to release the flavours of the cheapest cuts of all. I watch in awe as his knife makes multiple swift incisions and tears that remove the connecting ligaments and, for an instant, see the true artistry in his work. It is a process that transforms the enormous leg to nothing, and fills the waiting boxes with joints, cuts and meat for mincing. A tiny bit of me wonders what would happen if he injured his hand.

When I ask him what will become of the giant leg bone after he is done with it, he reflects on the gentle irony of a situation that means that it might go for dog bones, at one extreme, or for marrow bones in the very best restaurants, at the other. 'But don't get me started on the legislation behind pet food', he adds. 'There's far less legislation behind baby food than pets these days.'

Butchery is infectious, and each time I go back to that cold room, I find something else to learn, to admire or puzzle over. How the fatty brisket is reduced by four-fifths, and in a thousand cuts, before it becomes the rolled joint with eight pieces of immaculately-spaced string; how the hind quarter is much harder physical work than the forequarter; how the top rump came to be so underrated, the salmon cut such a rare treat, and how the skill in seamwork lies in instinctively knowing where you will find each seam before you even lift the fatty skin. I hear apprenticeship stories, how butchery runs in the blood, and of why to stew a shin but never roast it. For me, to quote Paul Simon out of all context, these were the days of miracle and wonder.

'Now the posh bit!' Lee smiles, and he manhandles the long loin off the hook and onto his workbench.

'I always start with the fillet', he says, pointing out that its tenderness comes from its position as the softest muscle of all supporting the ribcage. He pats one end, the chateaubriand, and calls it, with mild disapproval, the most tender bit of all. Lee is a flavour man from his hat to his white butcher's wellies, and personally prizes that over tenderness. By the time he has finished, there are eight fat fillet steaks in the box. There is a strange beauty to them, among the industrial backdrop of his workplace.

'Now for the rump. More flavour. Slightly more cooking.' It is a more complex job, too, harder on his hands and tools as he forces the sinews away to the tune of the Beach Boys' 'Wouldn't it be Nice', but soon he has 24 rump steaks alongside the fillets. Next is the sirloin, the cut I had all those weeks ago, and we end up with 28 of them. And all the while, I am learning, fresh-minted in the cold air of the butchery, this new language, of chining and tomahawks, of Jacob's ladders and côte-de-boeuf; things that I have only dimly been aware of in French bistros and at American barbecues, but now see face-to-face.

Finally, after he has been working for maybe two hours, he tackles the ribs. He has been asked to create a tied five-bone rib roast, a treat for someone's Christmas dinner and, like the other cuts, its recognisable form starts to emerge from the unfamiliar shapes as hand, gauntlet and knife fly around. I think that he is genuinely proud when he lays the rib roast down in the box. I would have been, too.

'A hundred and twenty quid or so', Lee says, when I ask him what it would sell for. And I could see why. In food, as in everything else, there is good expense, and bad expense.

What is in front of us when we finish is the component parts of about a quarter of a cow; a cow who fed on grass and clover, wild herbs and hedgerows, and who went inside a building for the very first time on the last day of its life. The various cuts will go to the farm shop, to boxes and to pubs like the Horse Guards, the mince into burgers and the waste probably into fertiliser. This is the sum of respect that Emma demanded back there at our dinner table.

Leaving the shed, and blinking into the intermittent winter sunshine, I find myself hoping that I will never take a piece of meat for granted again in my life.

⌇

Next stop, the high street.

That weekend, I ask the manager of the butchers in my local town how come his small display of beef consists only of prime cuts. Sirloin at £30 a kilo, rump steak at £25, and fillet at £50, but there was no cut physiologically recognisable as coming from anywhere else on the body of a cow. Skirt, chuck, shin, blade, brisket, even silverside, all conspicuous by their absence, all mere echoes from a faraway time when dinosaurs and Mrs Beeton roamed the earth. The evidence on the display shelf suggests that we no longer have an appetite for chuck dice or oxtail. (In the allied world of sheep, the same applies to mutton, which is now largely sold to consumers appreciative of their Pakistani and Bangladeshi heritage.)

'I'll try displaying bavette from time to time', he says, rolling his eyes with the air of one who has fought this battle too many times to think he can win it. 'The ones who have been on holiday to France recently might buy it. Other than that, at weekends, it's steaks, prime joints or nothing.' It turns out that his Saturday shoppers are quite happy to learn about 'thrifty' cattle when watching *Countryfile* on a Sunday evening, but would run a mile rather than be thrifty themselves. I tell him it seems strange that he is giving more space to some A5 grade Wagyu (the best), at £195 per kilo, than he is to stewing steak.

When I was a boy, there were two butchers in our little town, one of whom, according to my mother, had a habit of heavily lodging his thumb on the scales each time he weighed her purchases, which meant she eventually shopped with the other one, who was merely rude. Sarcasm was a small price to pay for getting all the meat you had paid for. People these days tend to get misty-eyed about the shopkeepers of yester-year which, on the evidence of my local town, they probably shouldn't. I can still smell the meaty sawdust on the floor, 50 years later, and remember his straw boater and the dark blue butcher's stripe apron straining over a belly that was enormous ahead of its time, as he delivered his insolent one-liners to a captive clientele.

'That will keep the family quiet', he said, eyeing me with venom and without a shred of humour, handing over the parcel of meat to my mother, as if keeping children quiet was what he and his produce had been put on earth for.

Fifty years on, his genial successor is partial proof of the welcome slowing down in the relentless decline in the number of independent butchers in the United Kingdom. Since the dawn of the 21st century, we have lost 60% of them, down to an all-time low of 6,000,[6] in tune with that great marketing fiction that we are 'time poor' these days and therefore need to do all our shopping under one roof, or buy ready meals that have been processed industrially on our behalf. But now there is emerging a committed group of consumers – and by no means all of them from the high-income groups – who are willing to base their shopping on factors other than convenience and price, and for whom the butcher offers an alternative to the pre-packed, shrink-wrapped offers on supermarket counters. In the crowded echo chambers of our food shopping thought processes, sales of beef in butchers is slightly up, whereas in supermarkets it is down.[7] Don't weep for the latter group yet, though, as they still sell you nearly £1.8 billion of beef alone each year,[8] a handy 81% of the total market.

'The most important thing for me is how the animal was raised', says my local butcher, 'and if I have to go a little further for that, I will, including visiting each supplier at least once a year.' Tesco apparently do this as well, which is good news, but when I checked out their supplier, Boswell Farm, I discovered that it was in fact a mere invention of their marketing department, a 'distinct' brand name, and part of a plan to 'simplify' their ranges. In other words, not a farm at all, even though they called it one.[9] The presence of that knowledge in my brain tantalisingly left the question of what the construct 'Boswell Farm' had been designed to achieve, but I never got an answer when I asked them.

'Ultimately', the butcher says, wrapping my silverside in some paper, 'it's simply about respect.'

And yet, in the financial battle between artisan food and industrial food, there can be no possible doubt who is winning.

In their annual accounts for the financial year ending April 2019, Tesco, the UK's largest supermarket with 27% of the market, reported full-year operating profits of around £2.21 billion, or around £32 for each one of us living in the UK, whether we shop there or not. Its chief executive received £4.6 million in remuneration (around £2 million less than he would go on to receive a year later), and the shareholders, of which you are statistically quite likely to be one if you have an occupational pension, received a dividend of 9 pence a share. By any reckoning, this was a great performance.

In contrast, the average business income of farms in the UK

is £51,900[10] (basic payment + earnings), out of which everything else has to be taken, including wages and investment. Go to a lowland grazing farm, and that drops to £12,500. A sizeable percentage of farms that I spent time on while preparing this book were either losing money or just about breaking even. The ones that were owned by the farmer were asset-rich (the real estate) but cash-poor (the income), whereas the tenant farmers didn't even have the asset to fall back on. Just about all of them had had to find other things to do to make the books balance, a way of life that has been the lot of the smallholder since time immemorial.

The only thing for sure, it seemed, was that the percentage of that pound's-worth of food at the retailer that made its way to the farmer was falling fast, at 15% the last time I looked.[11] The field in which my Belted Galloway was finished, for example, inasmuch as these values can be accurately calculated, earns five times the income when it is rented out to Argentine polo teams to rest their ponies out of season. In stark contrast to the popular image of the grumpy, whining farmer, most of the ones I worked with were just desperate to find a formula for producing good food that they could be proud of, but which also paid the bills, and to be paid for producing food rather than just managing land.

This situation has many parents, starting with the inevitable power that something huge, like a supermarket, has when it is dealing with something tiny, like a farm – and, of course, how it chooses to use that power.

'I get £60 a tonne for my potatoes', said one farmer to me, asking not to be quoted by name. 'It's a funny old thing that I couldn't buy a kilo bag at the local supermarket last weekend for less than a quid. Even allowing for the middle man, that looks like a profit margin of somewhere north of 500% to me.'

But it runs much deeper than that. In a country whose population spends exactly half the percentage of their net income* on feeding themselves that they used to 30 years ago, and a fifth of what they spent 70 years ago, cheap food is often the deceptive lantern on the moor that we have learned to follow unthinkingly, never mind the consequences. Cheap food is all too often the illusion of choice, the holy grail behind which all the iPhones, budget flights and cars can hide. Only the USA (6.4%), and Singapore (6.7%) spend less than the UK does, at 8.2%,[12] while France (17.3%)[13] and Germany (14%)[14] seem to have retained the belief that, in the matter of food, you get what you pay for.

In common with much of the western world, we have this curious notion that, once you have put your bank card away in your wallet at the check-out, somehow the transaction has been done and the payment is complete. Nothing could be further from the truth. Michael Pollan, who has forgotten more about food than you and I will ever learn, puts it this way, when explaining what else you must include in the tally: 'Society is not bearing the cost of water pollution, of antibiotic resistance, of food borne illness, of crop subsidies, of subsidised oil and water, of all the costs to the environment and the taxpayer that

....

* 10.6% of our expenditure is allocated to food and non-alcoholic drinks, according to the ONS Family Spending Survey (2019). Slightly less than we spend on 'recreation and culture' (13.2%).

makes cheap food seem cheap. You can buy honestly priced food, or you can buy irresponsibly priced food.'[15] And that doesn't even take into account the costs to our own health, and the future costs to the National Health Service. A powerful report, last updated in 2019, estimates that for every £1 we pay for our food at the till, we pay an extra £0.97 through subsidy taxes, and then to 'clean up, treat and mitigate the environmental and health costs' of what we have just bought.[16]

As I walk the ten miles home from Shon's farm, down the old droving road that used to take cattle eastwards towards Guildford and its market, I reflect that I need to balance the story of my pricey steak with some cheaper, more obviously accessible beef, and to try to follow its own story with the same diligence with which I had followed the Galloway's. I know where I will have to go for it, all £1.99-worth of it. Maybe it will be from a different part of the cow's anatomy (the forequarter or flank), but it will assuredly be beef, and if the cow is more anonymised and homogenised, it is no less sentient, and no less worthy of being honoured, than the Belted Galloway that had made my steak. It was time for a visit to the Golden Arches.

But in the meantime, we had a significant obstacle to jump over back on the farm.

7. VULNERABLE COW

'The fold stands empty in the drownèd field,
And crows are fatted with the murrain flock.'
WILLIAM SHAKESPEARE,
A MIDSUMMER NIGHT'S DREAM

Winter.

Sentinel crows on empty trees. Cock pheasants strutting defiantly alone in the ruts of the silent fields. Rime on the sagging steel of the barbed wire, ice on the lips of the iron-black puddles. Cold nuzzling its fingers into the hardened land. These are the bits you don't hear about on *Farming Today*.

The storm from earlier in the week has passed, and we are moving the ten remaining heifers that are still out on grass back to the barn, to weigh them and to work out which two or three should be sent away for beef.

As November drifts into misty December, the farm jobs change subtly, too. All but three of the bulls and a handful of the cows are in the routine of barn life by now, hierarchies long since established and hay and silage being devoured at the rate of 10 kg per cow per day.

On an A+ practical farm, I remain a D– theoretical farm labourer, full of little mistakes and mishaps, of stiffness and a craving for comfort. But I am there, and I have a functioning pulse, and that makes me just about better than no one at all and, anyway, I know where the digestive biscuits are hidden. It is no accident that Friday, my work day, is also always bedding day, when we parcel out new straw to freshen up the nicely manured layer from last week. Masks on to avert the risk of farmer's lung* from the resulting dust, we spread out the straw as evenly as we can across each of the pens, pushing away as we do so the inquisitive cows who are never above supplementing their traditional diet with a bit of wheat or barley straw. As the season progresses, so the level of the floor rises up and up until, once or twice in the winter, we remove it all and place it on the large heap beyond one of the farm gates, where it will rot down and become welcome fertiliser for the fields come the spring after next. As on other farms, the manure heap grows in size inexorably these days, as regulations (Farming Rules for Water) basically forbid its application during the autumn and winter months, in order to avoid run-off pollution into watercourses.

....

* A nasty allergic disease caused mainly by breathing in the dust of slightly mouldy hay or straw, and in which a chain of hypersensitive reactions ends up causing inflammation and swelling in the lung tissues, and thus breathing problems and illness.

A farm of 27 fields has many miles of fences and at least 60 or 70 gates, all of which need monitoring and repairing as the years roll on. And, once that is attended to, there will be culverts that have collapsed, or giant boughs of oak that have fallen and blocked paths or tracks. Then there are the various pieces of machinery that, however well they have been maintained, find ways of going wrong the precise week we are about to use them. Moreover, the hedges between two sets of fences will generally be substantial, ancient and peopled by the occasional huge oak tree, and always looking to grow into the fields and remove precious access to grass. On occasion, one of the Border Leicester sheep will get its fleece stuck fast in the triffid-like brambles that shoot out from the hedge, and will stay there motionless until a human being comes to release it. So winter is a time for farm housekeeping, or rather even more farm housekeeping than the summer.

Since it is a flat, lowland farm prone to wetness, all but a handful of the cattle are now in for the rest of the winter. Just three stock bulls will see it out in Church Field down by the A3, as will a group of heifers at the other end of the farm. There will be plenty of grass for both, supplemented from time to time by a little hay and some organic feed. Excepting these few cattle, the empty fields will ring only to the call of the strutting cock pheasant, the mew of the ever-present buzzard and the metallic watch-spring rasp of the jay, as she scatters up to 5,000 acorns a season across her territory.

Our farm is orderly, but not neat. There are probably over a thousand large trees in all, so inevitably boughs will sometimes drop off in high winds and, occasionally, whole trees come down. Instinct brings the cattle in to browse every leaf within reach, often before anyone knows the trees are down. If they are not a danger, or in the way, they are left where they are for the increased biodiversity their slow deterioration will bring. After all, a fallen oak, if left undisturbed, can sustain an entire ecosystem for a hundred years or more, including over 280 species of insect alone.[1]

As any conservationist knows, it is obsessive tidiness that is the enemy within.

Tidiness, and disease.

There is always a day when winter finally starts taking itself seriously, when any last residual warmth has been bled out of the farmyard concrete, and when the Ural Mountains represent the last high ground before the icy fingers of the east wind extend across the A3, through our jackets, and into our very bones.

And it comes as little surprise that it arrives on the one day we have scheduled the annual testing of the entire herd for TB, a day when the only certainty is that we will be standing around for hours at either end of the crush,* passing all 122 animals before the vet for the two injections that, three days later, will bring a sigh of relief or a sudden downgrade in the ease of our lives. Robust but for the time being exquisitely vulnerable, each Red Angus parades past.

....

* A robust cage for holding livestock safely on farms while they are examined or treated.

Like most things we do, the testing is a process that has been honed to simple efficiency over the years. John and I round up each pen's cows and drive them into the crush. When they are immobilised in front of him, Keith, the vet, shaves two neat squares in a vertical line down the thick of the neck, takes a micrometer reading of the thickness of a fold of skin on each, and then injects one milligram of mashed and deactivated tuberculin into each square. The top one is for the red needle, which contains harmless bird TB (to avoid endless false positives); the bottom one is for the blue needle, and contains the real thing. With any cow older than two years, we also take the opportunity to test for other latent diseases such as bovine viral diarrhoea and leptospirosis, which is done by Keith's assistant, Rachel, by lifting up the tail and drawing a syringe of blood from the vein running up its middle. In a list of veterinary jobs, I imagine that hovering around the business end of the cow must rank low. Rachel once played cricket for Scotland, so I guess she understands a challenge.

From John's point of view, there can only ever be one desirable answer when Keith comes back three days later, which is to have precisely 122 non-reactors, where the lower fold of skin is the same size as it had been on Monday, or smaller than the higher one. Anything else borders on the unthinkable.

'How often do you have to tell the farmer that they've got a reactor?' I ask Keith.

'Not often round here, thank God', he says. 'Once is enough.'

Up to now, John and Emma have never had a 'reactor', which is just as well, as the stakes are high. If we have one,

129

just one, the individual is slaughtered and nothing can be sold off the farm for breeding until we go 'clear', which means two clear tests three months apart. Which would wave farewell to the spring bull sales, for a start, on whose success much normally depends. In theory, we would be unlucky to have a case, as the nearest one this year is twenty miles down the A3 towards Portsmouth; the real battle is being waged far further west in counties like Gloucestershire, Dorset and Devon. But, being on the edge of an infected area, all our cattle are still inspected for TB annually, as opposed to every four years if we weren't.

A potted history runs like this. Tuberculosis (TB) is a bacterial infection that has been with us since the dawn of time. Human TB first became a serious problem in Victorian times, as people crowded together, often in unsanitary conditions, in greater and greater conurbations. Contaminated milk was known to be a frequent culprit, particularly in the case of children, who often went on to die. (To put it into context, around 2,000 people a year were still dying in the UK from bovine TB in the 1930s.) From the 1920s, when the tuberculin skin test for cattle was developed, through the 1930s, when pasteurisation neutralised its most dangerous effects, and into the 1950s, when compulsory testing was introduced, the problem grew less and less severe. Indeed, outside the West Country, bovine TB had virtually been eradicated from the national herd by the mid-1970s, at which point progress went sharply into reverse. This was partly due to breaks in the testing regime during, for example, foot and mouth disease outbreaks, and partly, since its discovery as a source in 1971, due to the disease being spread by badgers, whose numbers were increasing for other reasons.*

Prevention being better than cure, there is a five-point biosecurity plan in place for farmers to adopt, that includes restricting contact between cattle and badgers, managing cattle feeding and watering, stopping infected cattle joining the herd, preventing spread from neighbouring farms and observing strict discipline with manure. 'Keep your badgers healthy by good husbandry practices', says John when I ask him about it one day, 'and the cows should be OK. And no need at all to cull healthy badgers, as infected ones may well move into the vacuum they leave behind.' It is a view I hear echoed time and again by vets: cull, but only if it is completely unavoidable.

As with any numerous species, viruses and bacterial infections have played a significant role in the history of man and his cattle. It was once much worse than any of this.

$$\Longrightarrow$$

During the early 1960s, scientists working in the Serengeti National Park in Tanzania started noticing an exponential but inexplicable growth in the number of giraffes.

....

* A quarter of a century after the 1997 Krebs report identified badgers as a significant source of infection and recommended a controlled cull in 30 hotspots, the issue of badgers, cattle and TB remains a toxic one, often exemplifying the feeling of many farmers that the urban majority are unwilling to engage with their daily problems in an evidence-based, rather than an emotional way. The best that can be said is that some progress has been made, although not in the form of the vaccine that the report's authors thought might solve the problem by 2007.

It took them around ten years to work out a long sequence that, in reverse order, finished with the giraffes being attracted by taller trees to browse on without competition, which themselves had been enabled by fewer forest fires, due to the grass being much shorter than normal at the end of the dry season, which had happened because there were four times the usual number of wildebeest to graze it, which had thrived because they were not being infected by rinderpest* from the buffalo which, in turn, were not catching it off domestic cattle, which didn't carry it because they had recently been vaccinated. This was in fact a 'trophic cascade'† which became part of what is now known as the Serengeti Rules,[2] and marked an important staging post in the eventual eradication of the worst disease ever to affect cattle.

If the Bible is partly historical, then it is likely that the plagues of cattle mentioned in Exodus were rinderpest epidemics. From the moment that humans learned to crowd and fight together, until it was finally declared extinct by the World Organization of Animal Health in 2010, rinderpest wreaked its periodic devastation of herds the world over. Passing quickly from cow to cow through direct contact and sharing grazing or water, and presenting as discharges and violent diarrhoea, rinderpest was an infectious viral disease that had up to a 100% mortality rate, normally within a week. Like smallpox, which travelled around the globe on military campaigns, shipping

---

* From the German for 'cattle disease'.

† A strong chain reaction brought about by the introduction or removal of a predator in an ecosystem.

lanes and slave routes, so rinderpest moved down the old droving roads that brought faraway cows to market. One of the first
historically recorded epidemics in England came in 1348–49,
when the human population was still on its knees from the
effects of the Black Death. If you wanted a Shakespearean turn
of phrase, then the word 'murrain'* would have covered it, and
many other disorders to boot.

If we have learned anything about cattle and disease, it
is that the latter so often appears, and then goes out of control, as a direct result of people trying to make a little more
money by breaking rules and cutting corners. In 1865, a cattle trader called John Burchell, for example, 'whose speciality
was buying inexpensive eastern European cows, shipping them
across the Baltic, and selling them to English dairies',[3] brought
a consignment over from Estonia to Hull, a port that he well
knew already had lousy standards of policing the rules. Two
vets signed the cows off, and they went by train to Smithfield
market in London, from where they duly went away with their
new owners to all parts of the kingdom, implanting rinderpest
wherever they fetched up, and causing a national catastrophe
that was part of an even wider continental one in which up to a
quarter of a billion cattle perished. If anything good can be said
to have come from the whole grim episode, it was that it was so
bad that even a complacent government couldn't ignore it any
more. Slowly and sporadically, quarantine came onto the menu
of dealing with livestock conditions as well as human ones.

....

* A dated term that covers all livestock diseases.

On the face of it, rinderpest, whose closest viral cousin is measles, makes foot and mouth disease look like a sideshow. The middle of the 18th century saw an outbreak in England that lasted over ten years, decimating entire herds, almost entire breeds, across the whole country. Biosecurity was an infant idea in 1745, and farmers often turned their eyes away and ignored the evidence of infection within their herds rather than slaughter their cattle for the paltry compensation that the government offered. It was particularly severe in the West Country, effectively killing off the Gloucester cow as a mainstream breed; there is a tipping point in most things in nature, and rinderpest proved adept at testing it over and over again. Back it came over regular intervals around the old droving roads, even in the face of tireless work on a vaccine in Holland, making its last major British appearance in 1877. Even as late as the 1890s, a big outbreak in eastern and southern Africa killed somewhere around 85% of all the cows, and sporadic outbreaks continued for another 100 years after that.

Vaccines became increasingly effective during the 20th century, but even so, an epidemic ripped through Sudan during the 1980s, killing millions of animals as it went, the problem in Africa exacerbated by the fact that buffaloes and antelopes were vulnerable to it, and could not be stopped from spreading it. The last known outbreak on earth was recorded in Mauritania in 2003, as rinderpest became only the second disease in history, after smallpox, to have been eradicated by vaccination.

No one can entirely prove it, but it seems highly likely that mass outbreaks of disease in animal species, just as in our own, only started when man started to corral animals into crowded static enclosures, rather than have them running freely over the plains and through the forests. It is not for nothing that the adoption of agrarian life has been called by anthropologists the 'worst mistake man ever made'.[4] Indeed, there is a compelling theory that the book of Genesis in the Bible, with its story of the Fall from grace, is no more than an expression of the collective memory of the hardships of this new stationary life, which, as we saw in Chapter 2, introduced drudgery, property ownership and misogyny into our human experience for the first time.[5] The theory also suggests that organised religion, often in the form of an inbuilt fear of animal 'watchers' (the notion that you were never safe from being observed), was the way that sedentary man was persuaded towards good behaviour, in a way that he hadn't needed to be while in his small hunter-gatherer groupings. Once you start to look at the Old Testament and the Torah as a series of public health announcements, it is hard to stop. Lessons in safe sex, if you like, a few millennia before safe sex was invented. 'In the sweat of thy face shalt thou eat bread', and that was before we even got on to the plagues of cattle.

⚌

Three thousand miles over the Atlantic, a peculiarly American equivalent of rinderpest was bringing havoc to the growing cattle culture of the country in the latter half of the 19th century.

At its most basic level, Texas cattle fever was simply a disease caused by ticks dropping onto the grass off passing Texas Longhorns, in whom the ticks were endemic but without bad effect, before reattaching themselves to the local non-Texan cattle, who would generally get infected and die within days, and do so in their thousands. In the 60 years or so up until the 1930s, when it was brought under control by the twin hammer of science and the power of the state, the fever killed millions of cattle and shone a spotlight into the many uneasy opposites in American farming of the time. Cows of Spanish descent in the southern states, for example, versus those from Britain, in the north; drovers versus farmers and ranchers; south versus north; science versus nature; ranging versus barbed wire.*

The main problem was that the Texas Longhorn was a lot more valuable anywhere other than in Texas, up north in the Chicago meat markets, for example, and that they therefore had to be driven up there by cowboys. Given that there was an extremely high chance their cattle would catch the fever, and therefore die, from a passing column of Texas Longhorns, farmers from Missouri and other transit states simply took the law into their own hands. Herds were driven back by armed bands to where they had come from, cows were deliberately stampeded and drovers targeted and killed under what became known as the 'Winchester quarantine'. Even when they came by train, many towns refused to let them pass through, let alone be unloaded. Eventually, no fewer than eight states outlawed the movement of cattle that came from below the 45th parallel between March and December.

....

* Invented, to a less than universal welcome, around 1873 as a more flexible and resilient substitute for the thorny *bois d'arc* hedging that had been generally used until then.

The greatest contribution of Texas cattle fever to civilisation was that its intractable awfulness finally led to the notion
that only science could solve this kind of problem. Away from
all the fighting and machismo, the bar-room brawls and the
stockyards, three young scientists of the USDA's Bureau of
Animal Industry discovered in 1888 the protozoa that caused
the disease, in 1890 that it was transmitted by ticks and, in
1905, that it could only be by cooperative state effort that it
would finally be brought to heel.

By 1917, cattle fever had effectively been controlled, and
southern cows were free, once again, to go north.

And on it goes.

On February 19th, 2001, in a small family-owned abattoir
in rural Essex, someone noticed a vaguely familiar disorder
among two batches of pigs, one from Buckinghamshire and
one from the Isle of Wight. By the time, seven months later,
that the final case of the 2001 foot and mouth disease (FMD)
outbreak was confirmed at Whygill Head farm in Cumbria,
over six million cows, sheep and pigs had been killed on over
10,000 farms,[6] £8 billion had been hurled at the problem and
whole swathes of countryside, particularly in the Lake District,
had been closed to the public for months. Herds and flocks
that had taken generations to bring together were incinerated
in the blink of an eye. 'Cattle ... shot in the fields by a police
sniper, killed one at a time with the crack of a rifle, until the
fields around the village looked like something out of a war
movie.'[7] It even managed to delay that year's general election

by a month, while the authorities fought to get control of the situation.

If anyone thinks that the Covid-19 restrictions were extreme in 2020, then they ought to have been a livestock farmer back in 2001: 'On every ringing hill, there were sky-blackening pyres of animals being burned, the barbecue stench filling the air. The village school was closed due to the "smog" from the roasting animal flesh. Troops in Land Rovers, rifles sticking out of the front window, going up and down the lane, the soldiers having been conscripted for the slaughter of the animals. We were under siege from our own side', wrote a farmer from west Herefordshire.[8] If you want to drain colour from the face of a farmer of a certain age even now, just say the words 'contiguous cull' to them. The cost to farmers unable to export their livestock for endless months, and of the slaughter of entire pedigree herds that had taken decades to build up, is incalculable. 90,000 animals a day were being exterminated by the time the authorities got fully into their enthusiastic stride, mainly fit and well ones that were at no more risk of being infected than you are of being a concert pianist, which I assume is a small one. The contingency plan didn't really exist, and the ministry was instead reduced to sending out diagrams of how to build fires with railway sleepers, and how to stack dead cows on them.

In Tony Blair's Cool Britannia, you listened to urbane computer modellers at Imperial College,* rather than, say, to the

----

* The same ones who predicted, four years later, that bird flu would kill 'up to 150 million people'. In the six years it ran, it actually killed 282. (www.statmodeling.stat.columbia.edu) Other idiocies are also available.

practical Dutch, who calmly brought their own FMD outbreak under control by a mixed programme that included vaccination. Britain's high-energy Prime Minister, who once said that 'sometimes it is better to lose and do the right thing than to win and do the wrong thing', showed in a few short weeks that it was also quite possible to lose and do the wrong thing as well. If the problem had been dealt with by a freeze on all movement from Day 1, instead of the Chief Veterinary Officer having to fly abroad to explain what needed to be done in person to the Prime Minister, it might just have remained a manageable problem. As it was, dysfunctional government, added to a Whitehall culture of non-cooperation with other departments, as the Anderson report later pointed out, made for '31 days during which a serious veterinary problem became a disaster'.[9] At a stroke, farming had become a sub-branch of the disinfectant industry and, by the time they had finished, one in seven of the UK's livestock had been incinerated.

Granted, it was always going to be serious. FMD does not have the same grim mortality rates as rinderpest, far from it, but it is a nasty condition and difficult to control: 'Contrary to the views of some', said the Anderson report, 'it is not simply an equivalent of the common cold. Infected animals may suffer acute stress and pain. On recovery, their long-term health and condition may be affected, with serious economic impacts.' And cows are particularly susceptible to the airborne virus, which can often drift innocently in their direction from, say, a crowded piggery upwind.

Once again, human fingerprints were all over the body. The final report stated that the outbreak had started on a small farm in Northumberland where the farmer had not only fed his pigs with 'untreated waste', but had also concealed the first outbreak from the authorities. Because many local slaughterhouses had shut down over the years, livestock was having to make longer and longer journeys which, much like the spreading of Covid-19 to all parts in early 2020 by returning half-term skiers, meant that it was fundamentally too late for regional controls once the problem was identified. The situation was then compounded by driving the slaughtered cattle (some of which were inevitably infected) huge distances across the countryside to approved incinerators, and by a metropolitan government that was persuaded more loudly by its PR advisers to say that the problem was under control, than by its scientific advisers as to what should actually be done. And all along, the British public were treated to news footage of cows in rigor mortis being trucked in humiliation to their safe disposal. A vaccination programme, which was feasible, at least in the earliest stages of the outbreak, was ruled out by the government on the ironic basis that it would complicate the future export of meat, and deter tourism.

I asked John how it had been on the farm while it was all going on.

'We were lucky', he said. 'The real damage was going on in the north and west, and the worst that we had to do was shut the footpaths, stop exports and hope upon hope that it didn't come our way.' He thought about it for a bit longer and then added: 'The scarier one for us was about five years later, when it started off in the waste pipes of the government laboratories at Pirbright, just up the road from us. That made us properly worried.'

Even so, we were starting to learn the lessons. The 2007 Surrey outbreak, despite the 'strong probability'[10] of its tragi-comic beginnings actually taking place in the very establishment that was supposed to be working on a vaccine for the health of farm animals, stayed as exactly that: the 2007 Surrey outbreak. Thirty-seven days after it started, it was declared to be over.

As an afterthought, you could argue with some coherence that the whole cull had virtually nothing to do with health, and everything to do with trade. It was the arbitrary insistence of the body governing world livestock trade[11] that you could not have foot and mouth disease in the system if you wanted to export, and that vaccination wasn't an option because future tests couldn't differentiate between an animal that had the disease, and one that had just been vaccinated. All over Africa, for example, foot and mouth disease is just part of the daily round. All through history, in fact.

Fundamentally, certainly when left to its own devices, *Bos taurus* is pretty robust.

Like the simplest kind of internal combustion engine, it actually takes quite a lot to make a cow go wrong. After all, vegetation indirectly looks on the cow as a means of convert-ing sunshine into disturbance and manure, just as we look on it as a source of protein. Indeed, after four months on the farm, the most common complaint that I came across, and therefore the cause for the most frequent intervention, revolved around the hooves, the points of which can be disposed to grow in the wrong direction, and into which low-grade infections can develop from our wet ground. But overall, our stock is very healthy, and I never fail to notice that John or Emma checks each and every one of our animals each and every day. Cows select the diet best suited to them, if it is available, even allegedly to the extent of seeking out willow (the source for aspirin) when they are injured or are feeling off colour.[12]

The reason why humans can't eat grass is that we have no device to process the cellulose; our stomachs have just the one chamber, which acts as a giant blender, mixing our food with acid and bile so that it breaks down what we have eaten into nutrients that are then dispersed around the body to do more or less useful things. A cow doesn't, as is often suggested, have four stomachs, but one stomach with four chambers. In the first of these chambers, called the rumen (the origin of the term 'ruminant'), is a giant holding tank containing bacteria that break down cellulose; in the second, the reticulum, the food is regurgitated back up to the mouth to give the grass a second going over, otherwise known as chewing the cud. This process allows the cow to binge eat, according to availability, and then process at leisure, say, in the safety of the deeper forest. Most of the nutrients are then absorbed into the body from the third chamber, the omasum, other than the least digestible food which makes its way down to the fourth, the abomasum, which works much like our own.

As a prey species, cows famously have 330-degree vision, binocular immediately in front, monocular around the sides, and only non-existent immediately behind the head; technically, they have reasonable eyesight but poor depth perception.

They have excellent hearing,* again probably evolving from the days when they were carefully avoiding large carnivores, and an acute sense of smell. While their digestive system means that they tend to spend a large amount of their day eating (possibly seven hours), they spend rather less of it sleeping, and even then in many little bursts rather than in one go. In the league table of animal sleeping arrangements, topped by the giant armadillo which snoozes for at least 80% of its day, and propped up by the giraffe at 7%, the cow manages about 16%.† It does occasionally occur to me to wonder what our own cows did with the 60% when they weren't eating or sleeping.

Always somewhere in the back of my mind was the vexed question of antibiotic use. Although by no means the worst target species (that honour goes to the ultra-intensively farmed pigs and poultry), cows have generally been somewhere near the front line of the over-use of antibiotics over the last 50 years, both prophylactically (indirectly to promote growth) and therapeutically (mainly to get rid of ailments that intensive farming brings). On the east side of the Atlantic, regulators have belatedly, but effectively, woken up to the time-bomb of antibiotic resistance (ABR), which happens when bacteria undergo genetic changes that protect them from antibiotics, whereas on the west

....

* 16 Hz to 40,000 Hz, in comparison to humans at 20 Hz to 20,000 Hz, which is why keeping the noise down for cattle is often thought to be an important component of keeping their stress levels down. And why cowboys probably didn't shout 'yee-hah' as often as they do in the films.
† Washington Educational Faculty. If you must know, the three-toed sloth sleeps only 60% of its time.

side, they haven't. Around 80% of all antibiotics administered in the US are used on farm animals,[13] compared to a figure of around 33% in the UK,[14] where they have been banned as a growth promoter in feed since 2006, and where their general use is, happily, dropping fast.* As trade deals are reached, and a vibrant market in meat exports continues around the world, we probably need to be asking ourselves how happy we are to buy meat that has used 5.4 times the amount of antibiotics per kilo than our own.[15] Or that includes growth-promoting hormones that would be banned over here.

This book is about cows, and not worldwide health threats, but it is worth repeating the World Bank's assessment that 'by 2050, drug-resistant infections could cause economic damage on par with the 2008 financial crisis', and the World Health Organization's view that ABR is 'one of the biggest threats to global health, food security and development today'. As ye sow, so shall ye reap, and so long as we continue to demand that our livestock grow at twice their natural rate, in a quarter of their natural space, ABR will be keeping scientists awake and nervous, as it probably should the rest of us.

As has been alluded to earlier, the quite remarkable thing is the extent to which the cow has changed shape and size at the behest of humans, and the speed at which it has done so. Ten thousand years ago, as an aurochs, it probably averaged 1.8 metres of height at the shoulders, and weighed a ton and a half. Nowadays, you can take your pick from anywhere

....

* Down by 27% between 2014 and 2016. (House of Commons report, September 2018)

between the little Irish Dexter (just over a metre high and weighing in at 400 kg) and the Chianina from Italy, which reflects almost exactly the dimensions of its distant ancestor. Over the last two or three hundred years, the size and weight have increased and decreased almost as a result of fashion, but in certain parts of the world, such as the USA, size continues to head remorselessly upwards: those Smith & Wollensky's rib-eyes have got to come from somewhere, and there need to be plenty of them. Any butcher will continue to delight in a bonanza of prime cuts from a huge slaughtered cow, just as any stockman may wince at the birth problems that succeeding generations will have to undergo.

'I think these ones have got as small as they need to, or should do, for now', said John one morning as we parcelled out the hay and silage for them. 'I think I probably need to go in the other direction for a bit.'

It seemed like Robert Bakewell speaking to me across the centuries.

There is more.

At 9.00am on May 21st, 1995, a young man called Steve Churchill died in an Edinburgh hospital, a few weeks after first complaining of symptoms including hallucinations and a lack of balance. Twenty-five years or so earlier, a dairy cow on a Sussex farm ate her first supplement of meat and bone meal in her evening feed, supplement that included remnants from the spinal column of a sheep that had died of a disease called scrapie. The two events are cruelly related.

For some medical reason, probably a 'freak genetic dysfunction as a consequence of recycling animal protein in ruminant feed', this diet triggered within the cow a neurodegenerative disease that, five years later, presented as Britain's first confirmed case of bovine spongiform encephalopathy (BSE). At this stage, you might ask yourself why it wasn't identified for another six months after that, and not confirmed for another two and a half years. By the time it was, Britain had entered another of its dire animal health crises, at the end of which 4.4 million cows had been killed (40 times the amount that had been infected) and Britain's thriving export trade in beef had been halted for a decade.* One infected farm became two, two became five, and five became many, many hundreds. The symptoms in cattle – aggression, depression, hypersensitivity, tremors, abnormal posture and lack of coordination – were depressing enough to watch on television, but catastrophically more so for the farmer concerned.

Worse was to come. In 1990, and despite all scientific assurances to the contrary, the disease was found to have jumped species, first presenting in a Siamese cat called Max, and then vaulting to thirteen other species. Other animals followed, even a tiger in Newquay Zoo. Torn between the need for openness (which would admittedly have had immediate devastating consequences in the farming industry) and keeping a lid on it in the approved Soviet style, the government continued for a long

....

* I remember furtively meeting someone in a dark car park, during the worst of the crisis, to buy my illegal four-rib (beef on the bone was banned). I might have been less cavalier if I had known what was to come.

time to do the latter. Then in late 1994, four years after the then Secretary of State for the Environment had gone on national television at a country show to persuade his little daughter to eat a burger, to underline to us that he thought the beef 'completely safe',* the first humans started to develop the variant Creutzfeldt-Jakob disease (CJD) version. There could be no doubting where it had come from, or that all 178 of them who contracted it went on to die from it; after all, a diagnosis was also an inevitable death sentence. Most of the victims, a fact that helped the scientists to isolate the cause quickly, were teenagers, including Steve Churchill: CJD was not unknown in old people, but very rarely in the young, and never, ever as the variant. It could only have come from a cow. In retrospect, it seems a minor miracle that the number of casualties was as small as it eventually was.

If it was possible to make the government that presided over the subsequent 2001 FMD crisis look almost competent, then the way the government of the day handled BSE managed it. If it was feasible to shatter confidence in British food by embarking on measures that were supposed to sustain it, then, yes, they managed that as well. Even the compensation scheme of only 50% offered to farmers for slaughtering affected cattle

....

* Required watching on YouTube, if you wish to see a slightly cocky British minister feeding his young daughter a burger that is demonstrably unpleasant, and far too hot for her. Mirrored, in June 2005, by US Agriculture Secretary Mike Johanns telling everyone, 'There is no risk whatsoever. I'm going to enjoy a good steak', a week before announcing confirmation of the infected cow that he had been implicitly denying.

encouraged rule-breaking and deception. Beyond that, it was an episode that shone an uncomfortable beam of light into the cynical way that the get-rich-quick elements of the industry went about their business, and the wider effect that these methods brought in their slipstream. The government gave a tragic but convincing demonstration of the Dunning–Kruger effect, a cognitive bias within which we are routinely bad at the things that we automatically think we are good at – like, for instance, running the nation's rural affairs just because we have a wealthy landowner or two in the Cabinet. For the sake of balance, I should point out that the US government, when faced with the issue of BSE when it had drifted south from Canada, were just as dilatory, evasive and inactive as Britain. Governments seem to find it much easier to take action against other countries' sick cows than their own. (Most British farmers that I spoke to were of the opinion that each time the French found a case of BSE, they would just quietly dispose of the animal under the heading of 'bovine flu' or some other such imaginative term.)

If there was ever a good time to be a cow in Britain, then the 1990s and 2000s was manifestly not it. BSE, as one writer on agriculture lyrically put it, 'was the harvest of betrayal, the betrayal of a gentle, long-suffering creature that had been the servant and companion of mankind down the ages. Whatever the true nature of the mysterious prion at the heart of the sickness, it would surely not have afflicted the hardy, unimproved cattle of the Tudor grazing marshes, or the herb rich summer pastures of the high mountains.'[16] Precisely.

Apart from the seemingly obvious inadvisability of eating mechanically recovered spinal cord meat, and of keeping notifiable things quiet for eight months too long, the key take-away (no pun intended) seems to be the oldest one: the more you play around with nature, the more she will eventually play around with you.

You would be forgiven for thinking otherwise, but we have cultural evolution* on our side, apparently, and cows don't.

⸺

They talk about driving rain, but never driving drizzle. They are wrong.

Heading back to the farm on a damp Thursday morning for the results of the TB testing we have done three days earlier, I begin to realise how deep I am in all this. I have lain awake half the night before, and feel the looming results as keenly as if it was a medical test on myself.

As so often in my short farming career, most of the action takes place beside the cattle crush, this time driving the cows back through in the rain, to get the two patches checked for reactors. My job is to hold the vet's increasingly sodden file, noting down the readings as he checks them off.

'1021', Keith calls out, 'fine. 1038, fine. 1006, fine.' My old friend 1025 pushes his way into the crush, giving me the same insolent look we had exchanged a few weeks ago when he kicked me. '1025, fine.'

....

* Cultural evolution is the concept that, of all species, only humans evolve knowledge, ideas and discoveries cumulatively, which is one reason why we have progressed as far and fast as we have. It is a concept that has generally evolved, it seems, to elude career politicians.

Each 'fine' is a step closer to a clean bill of health for the coming year. Sometimes he sees one that has reacted, but so long as the first (avian) jab has reacted more than the second (bovine) one, we are OK. In one of the gaps while John is rounding up the next group, I ask Keith if he thinks that we have learned the lessons of the last 30 or 40 years.

'On balance, yes', he says, after a pause for thought. 'Back then, the whole animal health game was badly funded, and anything but driven by the science. The joke ran that people only became government vets because they couldn't make it as "real" ones. Besides, animals moved all over the place without any proper paperwork, meaning that when something did happen, there was no telling how far, and to where, it had spread. The 2001 foot and mouth was the real wake-up call.'

'Look at that folder', he says, after I ask him what has really changed. 'Each livestock animal has its own unique twelve-figure code, which gives it history and traceability throughout its life, and long, long after. You buy a steak in Sainsbury's nowadays, and they can trace it all the way back to the backside of the cow it came from. Same in a pub. Same anywhere.'

'What would happen, say, if they got an outbreak of foot and mouth over there?' I point at a neighbouring farm, not wanting to tempt fate by using ours as an example.

'I guess that there would be an immediate national freeze on livestock movements. After which they would work their way out from the source of the outbreak in concentric circles until they had no cases. And then slaughter what they had to, and work as quick as they could to get things back to normal.'

I ask why they don't just vaccinate them all, and he explains that to do so would risk not being able to tell vaccinated cows from diseased ones, a problem that may or may not have been sorted out by 2025. Some time later, when I ask Simon Doherty, senior vet and animal health lecturer from Queen's University, Belfast, what one thing he would change so as to prevent rampant cattle disease in the future, his half-flippant answer shouldn't surprise me as much as it does.

'Ban Ifor Williams trailers', he says, before adding: 'Don't get me wrong, they are excellent. But it is the constant and relentless movement of livestock up and down the country in trailers like those that persuades me that we're just waiting on the next one.' Then, with a smile, he adds that he had been told as an undergraduate in the 1980s that he would never see another foot and mouth epidemic in his lifetime. 'You can't blame me for being a sceptic', he says.

Developmental farming specialist Peter Bazeley backs this view up later on, by pointing out to me that the vast increase in recent times of masses of animals living alongside masses of humans, as in the so-called Chinese 'wet markets', will almost inevitably lead to a procession of H5N1-type infections and viruses, any one of which could be extremely serious. It puts a slight but annoying qualification on the otherwise attractive idea of including livestock in the network of peri-urban farms that are springing up around many of the world's cities – itself, alongside farmers' markets, a vibrant solution to much of the de-democratisation of food. The little Friesian cow against the backdrop of that tower block – such a great photo-opportunity for the local politician – just may also be harbouring tomorrow's zoonotic disease.[17]

On we work through the morning, from bullocks to heifers, to cows and, finally, 121 beasts later, to Tiger, the four year-old bull that I had first met out in the fields all those months ago. Tiger is so calm, so gentle, that we don't even need to move him to the crush: John just feeds him a handful of hay through the rails of his stall, and Keith leans in to check the measurements on his vast, powerful neck.

'1072', he says, checking the number off the ear tag. 'Fine. All done for another year.'

If I am tempted to think that this clear round is mere routine, just another predictable outcome of a box-ticking exercise, I am mistaken. A few days later the *Farmers Guardian* carries an article about a Pembrokeshire dairy farmer who has lost his entire herd after a bovine TB outbreak, the same day as Keith cleared ours. Everything that he has spent five years building up, a hundred prime Wagyu crosses, killed in the space of a couple of hours on his farm. 'I will never forget leading cows to a man with a gun, and seeing unborn cows die', he said. Well, you wouldn't, would you? After all, 30–40,000 British cattle are still slaughtered each year on the grounds of TB.[18]

The next crisis might just be around the corner, as in farming it always is, but we should take encouragement from the green shoots of growth in farmers' markets, artisan food, interest in provenance and improvements in traceability, all building blocks in the construction of a less fragile system.

Down in Hampshire, we are lucky. We can breathe again.

8. THE TRAGEDY OF
THE COMMONS

....

'*When cattle ranchers clear rain forests to raise beef to sell to fast-food chains that make hamburgers to sell to Americans, who have the highest rate of heart disease in the world (and spend the most money per GNP on health care), we can say easily that business is no longer developing the world. We have become its predator.*'
PAUL HAWKEN

'*If men were angels, no government would be necessary*'
JAMES MADISON,
FOURTH PRESIDENT OF THE USA

....

If the setting was bleak and joyless, I have to say that my £1.99 burger was anything but. It was delicious.

The beef patty, with its attendant ketchup, onions, dill pickle and mustard, sat within its bun on a carpet of slightly apologetic shredded lettuce in its little cardboard box. It was cheap, and exactly what I had wanted, something that had been familiar to my taste buds for over a quarter of a century. The sauce, which managed to be both tart and sweet at the same time, reminded me of some sad teenage memory, and of stolen unromantic evenings hard by the local cinema. All around me in the rainy and ill-lit car park of the drive-through McDonald's on the edge of Petersfield, people sat in their metal and glass bubbles, thoughtfully ingesting their Happy Meals, their wraps and their Spicy Veggie Ones, absorbing calories for the day ahead just like their cars absorbed petrol or diesel for the journeys to come. This was less about food as an event, and more about food as a routine fuelling process.

I didn't have time to savour the aftertaste, as I had work to do. In the back of the Land Rover were concealed two stillborn calves that the law dictated we had to present to the local hunt kennels who, for a fee, would dispose of them. That was one of my jobs for the day, apart from anything to allow me to understand that farming isn't just about new life.

Any livestock farmer will tell you that death is embedded in farm life, and the irony of the calving season, full of new life and optimism as it is, is that death is never that far away. It is the same for farrowing and lambing. But we have had a good season so far, with 40 healthy calves to date, and ten more expected over the coming days. Aside from the twins in the back of the vehicle, all has gone well. Other than the occasional hormonal mother who resents any intrusion, all is calm.

'I like to think that our deliberately keeping them on the small side has made for easier calving overall', John had explained earlier that morning. 'We actually have to intervene very little.' Generally, he checks up on cows that are approaching calving three or four times each day, and the signs of an imminent arrival are pretty unambiguous. 'I'll do one last round at about eleven in the evening and then, if they all look OK, I'll leave them to it.' Most days at this time of year, he will come back to a barn that contains one more animal in the morning than it did the previous night.

Coming, as we do, from a species that is dependent on its parents for around 20% of its long life, it is something of a miracle to watch for the first time a new calf, not yet 30 minutes old, pick itself up and stagger around for a while, before attaching itself to its mother's udders for a feed and then wandering off to check out the surroundings. When John says 'on the small side', he means around 40–45 kilos, and he knows instinctively which cow will probably need intervention and which won't. Once born, we put iodine on the navel, weigh them, and then eventually put the ear tag in that will be their identification for the rest of their lives. If the calf is having a problem feeding, because she or the mother is exhausted, for example, she will receive a supplementary feed of colostrum,* which is an essential element of her growing immune system. We then segregate them from the other cows in a small pen, where they can gather strength, bond and avoid the clumsy nosiness of other mothers. Other than that, the calves will just get on with life, becoming quickly more inquisitive and socialising readily with the other new-borns in the shed. In a few weeks' time, we will

....

* Colostrum is the first milk that a baby mammal receives from its mother.

turn them joyfully out into the fields for the first time, each in its own carefully selected group, and they will grow on the fat of the land, and to the rhythm of the lengthening days, at the rate of about one kilo a day.

As a breeding farm and working business, we have a hierarchy of desirable outcomes for each of the new-borns, ranging from the dead twins in the back of the Land Rover behind me, at one extreme, to the production of a valuable and saleable breeding bull or heifer, at the other. In between, there are a whole range of possible lives in store for them, some of which will end with an early trip, say at eighteen months, to the abattoir, some of which will breed generation after generation of new stock for us. The livestock is the working capital of the farm, and how well or badly this process goes will directly influence the income stream for years to come.

For a few weeks, the whole place throbs with the pulse of new life, and the dark days of deep midwinter have started to become a frosty memory.

But let's return to that burger for a moment. I think we moved on from it too quickly.

The cows that provided the meat are obviously no less deserving of my respect than the Galloway that produced my sirloin in the Horse Guards Inn all those months ago and yet, within the homogenised conveyor-belt anonymity of the 2.36 billion or so burgers that McDonald's sell each year worldwide, it is respect that just seems harder to deliver. The distance, both actual and philosophical, between me and the cows that supplied that meat, just seems too great – as if, through an industrial process of alchemy, it has simply become a commodity, like potash or potatoes. More immediately relevant, it was hard for me to understand how my £1.99 had adequately compensated for all the component costs within the process: the farmer, the feed, the transport, the abattoir, the bun, the lettuce, the sauce; and its share of the capital cost of the building, the rates, taxes, staffing and a hundred and one other things. Even the CEO's modest remuneration package of $18 million* needs a little bit of my cash to help it along. I couldn't fault the burger for taste, and I am well aware that McDonald's have worked hard on welfare and quality within their supply chain but, even allowing for the company's fabled economies of scale, and for the fact that some things on the menu may be sold as loss leaders, there was something strange about the low price.

Ask not for whom that burger fries; it fries for you. Well, statistically it is certainly likely to. Since that day in 1937 when Richard and Maurice McDonald first opened a drive-through restaurant in Pasadena, California, trying to cash in on the new craze for the automobile life, the McDonald's fast food habit has spread out of the United States like an unstoppable, savoury tide, with 36,000 restaurants in 118 countries at the time of writing.[1] And, as with McDonald's in Pasadena, so for Burger King (Florida), Wendy's (Ohio) and a hundred others that probably failed, or got bought up, or stayed under the radar. Described by Eric Schlosser as both 'a commodity and

---

* 2019 figure, just 1,939 times that of one of his median full-time colleagues. (www.businessinsider.com)

a metaphor' for how we live now,[2] the key to fast food has always been convenience, repeatability and, above all, uniformity. You produce something as cheaply as you can, consistent with it being delicious and legal, and then market the hell out of it, often to children who may come to recognise a logo before they know their own name. In fact, in 1993, District Eleven in Colorado Springs was the first school authority to raise revenue by inviting fast food businesses to advertise in their hallways and on the sides of their school buses, a trend that was quickly followed by others until even a child whose parents managed to keep them away from the advertising at home, was powerless to ignore it once they went to school. It clearly worked: a couple of dozen years before, there had been just twenty fast food outlets in the entire city; ten years after, there were 21 branches of McDonald's alone.[3] A brilliantly effective franchise scheme simply enabled the company to grow quickly, and without risk, while recruiting an army of reliant entrepreneurs to push it all along, and get rich themselves. *

One of the standard criticisms directed at people who argue against fast food culture is that they are food snobs, trying to belittle the habit that has enabled billions of people to buy cheap, satisfying and fun food. That may or may not be the case, although it cannot possibly disguise the underlying effects that this diet has had on people's weight and health, and even on social eating habits. However, this is a book about the

---

* Thomas Friedman's 'Golden Arches Theory', which asserted that no two countries that hosted a McDonald's would ever go to war, looked pretty good until Armenia and Azerbaijan started battering each other over Nagorno-Karabakh.

history of man and cow, and there can be even less doubt that, in only a half of 1% of the time the two species have worked together, fast food has changed everything. From land management through to what we feed and medicate our livestock with, the cow is now often little more than an industrial resource for a meat-obsessed world, its route to market controlled by alarmingly few boards of directors. Alongside the chicken, which largely went from something you carved at a lunch table to something whose bits you ingested from a cardboard box behind a steering wheel in not much more than a single year,* the cow is all too often just a commodity, and it matters.

Life is good at McDonald's. As much a real estate business these days as a restaurant chain, in 2021 they managed corporate earnings of $7.5 billion on sales of $23.2 billion,† which looks like a healthy 32.3% margin to me. It means that a good proportion of my money was headed straight to the grateful shareholders, and suggests that they and their franchisees aren't exactly struggling to achieve that £1.99 price. Looking a bit deeper, I became anxious to understand why it was going to take McDonald's so long to stop deforesting the planet,† but I met with a determined lack of reply to my questions.‡

....

* 1983, when the Chicken McNugget was introduced.

† McDonald's Purpose and Impact Statement: '[We] remain committed to eliminating deforestation from our global supply chains by 2030.'

‡ Not answering my questions on deforestation (seven of them in all) became a bit of a habit with McDonald's. You can draw your own conclusions as to what this silence on important issues signifies, but it is hard to avoid the idea that sheer size and power means the big burger companies feel no need to defend their processes.

I mean, if clearing rainforests is a bad thing, then why would a good citizen wait until 2030 to stop causing it? Why not take the temporary supply chain hit for the good of the planet, and stop immediately? Other than that, the big burger outlets are doing no more than riding bareback on the system. We can all go to these joints as often as our busy lives will allow us to, but we can never pretend to ourselves that our burger habit hasn't changed life for cows for ever. With 50 billion burgers eaten in the United States alone each year, it is probably not food snobbery to suggest that we have an issue here, and that issue is a relentless increase in the number of cattle we need to feed the habit.

To illustrate the point, one company, JBS Five Rivers from Greeley, Colorado, has a one-time capacity of 930,000 cattle; that is one tenth of the *total number* of cows in Britain, on just a handful of sites, and roughly the same as the number of people in Southampton and Portsmouth combined. With numerous other feedlots each having over 100,000 head in single locations themselves, it makes blaming climate change on Daisy having a quick belch on a regenerative meadow in Oregon seem a bit strange. Eat and enjoy your burger by all means, but it's probably best not to kid yourself that the cost of the habit stops at your own digestive system, and wallet. Instead, as you slide the trash from your meal into the bin, you are in fact linking straight back to an unremarkable event on a small piece of common ground in Oxfordshire 200 years ago, as we shall shortly see.

But back to that burger in Petersfield and its staggeringly low price. One answer of many is that its low price is largely artificial. McDonald's, along with just about every other food establishment in the UK, have been enabled to pay the farmer as little as they have because the consumer's financial relationship with the beef in that burger is in reality multi-faceted: we pay just about as much again as taxpayers to subsidise it as McDonald's did in the first place to buy it. In whatever form, direct subsidies to the farmer (such as the old farm payment scheme) are accompanied by indirect ones, like the removal of 'normal' taxation such as inheritance tax and local rates, and added to by the even more indirect costs of cleaning up at our expense the environmental damage that so many farms still produce.[5] One calculation is that farming, as an industry, is worth £9 billion to the UK economy each year, but that the benefit of that £9 billion is almost entirely wiped out by the mostly hidden costs of propping it up. Basically, we are paying our farmers to enable them to sell as cheaply as the often inferior imports that would otherwise replace them, and which may well not have the welfare, hygiene and sustainability standards that we insist on here. But then again, until now, the subsidy system has rewarded people more or less in direct proportion to their starting wealth, so we shouldn't be too surprised at any effects of its other madnesses.

The publication in July 2021 of the compelling National Food Strategy, Part 2 ('The Plan') set out a possible road map out of the muddle. Right now, with the twin convulsions of Brexit and the Covid pandemic, would seem the appropriate time to start a food system that at least begins to serve the planet, alleviate poverty and improve human health. After all, as Mary Quicke had pointed out to me all those months ago on her dairy farm, this is in all probability our modern 'Corn Laws moment'. The 2021 update, the aim of which is to make us well, not sick, create resilience in food systems, restore nature and tackle climate change, and meet the standards we expect on health, environment and welfare, makes a series of recommendations. Of these, the key ones are probably a sugar and salt tax, an 'eat and learn' initiative in schools, guaranteed support for farmers until 2029, and £1 billion for a better food system. But the recommendation that won't make the headlines, even though it should, is the need for a Global Farming Metric that can provide a common framework for measuring farm sustainability.

The report's author also argues for a 30% reduction in meat consumption, rather less than the figure we arrive at in Chapter 9, but it disappointingly fails to make the true distinction between a pasture-fed, low-input conservation cow in England, and one raised on food that is not natural to it, in a feedlot or cleared forest on another continent. The enthusiastic launch by McDonald's in November 2020 of the Double Big Mac, with its signature *four* burgers in one bun and 77% of the recommended daily intake of saturated fats, suggests that the owners of the business may not quite see the meat and fat problem in the same way as the report's author.

One of the things that the earlier version of the report points out is that we grow about 64% of our own food in the UK, and import the rest. So far, so easy. So long as we insist on similar standards in our imported food, those sound like pretty well balanced figures. But the problem is that we already don't: we allow Danish bacon in, for example, where the pigs have been kept for the first few weeks of pregnancy in sow stalls that have been illegal here since 1999, and we still enable the sale of foie gras, despite a production process that we have outlawed; we import oilseed rape that has been coated in neonicotinoids that have been illegal here since 2017. And that is before we even think about striking a trade deal with, for example, the USA, with the beckoning finger of growth hormones and other delights.

The truth is that I should probably have been paying around £4 for my burger that day in Petersfield, even if, actually especially if, that means that it is a treat I enjoy half the number of times that I do currently, and if McDonald's have to downscale their operation a bit to cope with the new reality. As it happens, I actually *was* paying around £4, but only half of it at the till; the other half would be in the form of my annual tax bill. Same with you. When it comes to paying for your food in Britain, you are in the world of mirage and illusion. And not just in Britain.

The industrialisation of food production and supply chains has brought many benefits, not least of which was the supermarkets' ability seamlessly to keep food on our tables when the country suddenly found itself in lockdown in March 2020. It has also been able to reduce the price of some foods, though not all, to a level that people living below the poverty line can cope with, and has brought us much increased food safety and a variety of diet and convenience that our grandparents could only have dreamed about.

But, as we start to blink into the full glare of what developments climate change will probably be sending our way over the next 50 years, regardless of the actions we take now, we might also think that honest pricing will force us into that most sustainable of all dictums, the one that gently suggests that less is more.

The deeper I get into this, the more it seems time that our relationship with the cow gets a fundamental re-evaluation.

⇌

Over 80% of beef sales in Britain go through supermarkets.

So the Saturday after my £1.99 burger, I find myself standing by the giant meat cabinet in the equally giant local Tesco superstore, wondering what's new, where it came from and whether I can be tempted to buy some.

The meat in that cabinet shares whatever it can of the attention span of a consumer who has over 40,000 products to think about under that one roof, which fact in itself may be a contributor to the overall problem. I mean, try counting the things you have in your fridge, cupboards and bathroom, even in your life, and ask yourself if you really needed to choose them from 40,000. Personally, I struggle to choose one from three in normal life. Too much choice, in my experience, is sometimes more stressful than too little, and it generally leads to higher waste levels, not to mention a greater demand on the planet's resources. Wendell Berry described the effects of this phenomenon nicely back in 1980: 'The idea was that when faced with abundance, one should consume abundantly, an idea that has survived to become the basis of our economy.'[6] Precisely. You could be forgiven for thinking that some of the big corporations rely on it.

I was clocked by the in-store security cameras long before I had finished counting and inspecting the 52 different offerings of beef and beef derivatives in that cabinet ('Security to Aisle 4, please', said the PA system a tad too cheerfully for my liking). And that's not counting all the prepared meals like lasagnes that lurked in other parts of the store. The great thing about aggregating and harvesting millions of pieces of data, something that the till records and Tesco Club Card provide for them, is that they can gain in one snapshot a very clear summary of what the average British consumer requires, beef-eaters included. And what they require nowadays, based on what I saw, is, in order: mince, roasting joints, diced Irish lean beef and various shrink-wrapped steaks. Consolation for the lack of detailed visible provenance ('slaughtered in the UK'; 'slaughtered in Great Britain'; 'from trusted farms'; and our old friend 'Boswell Farm') came in the pricing, which appeared to be about 20% below the artisan butcher in our village, and in the undoubted freshness that is underwritten by a highly sophisticated supply chain. If you were a busy shopper, you couldn't fault the choice, price and probably the quality of what was in that cabinet. With the possible exception of the shrink-wrapping, this was a good substitute for any one of the mid-price butchers that supermarkets have rather forcefully replaced over the last 30 years or so. But there remain significant issues.

Supermarkets react to, and direct, public opinion. On the one hand, they try to convince us that it is we ourselves who have demanded vegetables that conform to an exact size and shape (because it happens to make their supply chain operation easier), but on the other, they eventually have to go along with the things we feel strongly about, like climate change, over-packaging and animal welfare. This is when their power, so often a curse if you happen to be one of their suppliers, can quickly become a force for public good: a company with annual sales above £50 billion has earned the right to make things happen if they want to, and to happen quickly. But it's a trick that only works if each consumer understands their own power and acts on it – which, in a country where people routinely go home to be silently furious with their dog about things that have publicly annoyed them, is a disadvantage.

A good recent example of this, in August 2020, was when Greenpeace challenged Tesco's social media claims that the supermarket was actively working against deforestation and, to that end, didn't buy meat from Brazil. Sort of right. They didn't actually buy meat from Brazil, according to Greenpeace, but they bought meat that had been fed on soya about whose provenance they had absolutely no idea. By devolving that tricky bit of the supply chain to a system of credits, they could claim to be supportive of the Greenpeace campaign, while actually buying meat from two UK suppliers who happened to be subsidiaries of a huge company that is repeatedly linked to deforestation in the Amazon.[7] Tesco didn't reply to my various requests to see how things had developed since this all blew up, but they are on record as subsequently asking the government to order food companies to ensure that all food sold in the UK is deforestation-free.[8] It may still be a muddle, but you get the feeling that it is a muddle going in the right direction.

Supermarkets are still generally just about a force for good in the way we live now, some much more than others, and I am tempted to believe that most of the problems that arise with them do so because of the sheer volumes racing through their complex supply chains, and not some conspiracy or other. Where they make mistakes, or worse, it is usually because we – the consumers – tacitly give them our permission by not making a sufficient fuss about it.

All this matters, because, if and when calf number 1025 makes the short walk into the food chain, wherever he ends up, we owe it to him to ensure that it is as humane, respectful and undamaging as it possibly can be.

—

One spring morning in 1832, a political economist from Oxford University found himself staring at a bunch of cattle on a piece of local common ground, and idly wondering why the animals were 'so puny and so stunted', and why the common was 'itself so bare-worn, and cropped so differently from the adjoining enclosures'. He had a point. It was, by all accounts, half-wrecked.

He was called William Forster Lloyd, and from his associated researches eventually emerged his celebrated theory of the Tragedy of the Commons. Because the indirect ramifications of what he set out nearly 200 years ago will appear over and over in our story, it is worth looking at them in a bit of detail. What Forster Lloyd asserted in his paper was that, given a collective asset (e.g. the common itself), our instinct is always to over-exploit it for our private benefit (meaning the owners of the increasing numbers of cattle who overgrazed it). Because the herdsman owned the animals, the profit came purely to him; equally, because the pasture was a commonly held benefit, its gradual deterioration was shared by everyone. And because 'the *privatised* gain would exceed his share of the *commonised* loss, a self-seeking herdsman would always add another animal to his herd',[9] until the common was ruined and they all had to go and find new land. It's a trick that mankind has been pretty good at, especially since the industrial revolution.

You can pick any example of this that you fancy, from the deforestation of Easter Island in the pursuit of logs to help build and move the statues, to the relentless industrial extraction of more fish than our oceans can sustain, and the phenomenon will keep on proving itself. Perhaps a good modern illustration comes in the frequent sight of 2,000 wilderness-searching tourists converging simultaneously on a summer's day on a pretty Cornish beach to 'be alone' with nature. In a way, it has mutated to be the Tragedy of Progress in that, as humans, we have turned out to be much better at inventing things than we are at developing ways to live with them once we have done so. In the matter of beef, it is the notion that meat (the 'common') can be an ever-increasing part of the diet of an ever-increasing number of people worldwide (the 92% of the 7.7 billion who are meat-eaters) when it simply can't.

The tragedy of the commons is the new reality of the way our modern society overfeeds itself. We blame it on the farmers and fishers, but we shouldn't: we are mostly liberated people with the freedom to make our own choices. At the moment, the bill for the choices we make is picked up by empty hedgerows and silent skies.

'In the corpulent West', wrote A.A. Gill, 'food has ceased to be a big political problem, or even a minor one. The problem isn't too little, it's too much. This is by far and away the biggest social change in two thousand years of politics: finally, government has achieved what it was set up to do – feed everyone.'[10] Contrary to what many people say and think, half the world being overfed doesn't directly lead to the other half going hungry. What it does instead is lead to Mickey-Mouse-logic supply chains (European cows being fed with soya that travels 7,000 miles from fields that were once rainforests, for example) that simultaneously disrupt common sense and local food sources, and then to self-inflicted health problems that divert resources that could have been offered to the genuinely needy in poorer countries.

While you might occasionally be forgiven for thinking otherwise, we are all sentient beings with capacious brains. I'm not making a value judgement that says the £24 steak is somehow a better thing to buy than the £1.99 burger. Far from it: both more than met my expectations of them, and both were more than enjoyable. But every one of us has the responsibility to try to understand more about the impact of the food decisions we make, because not to do so is to invite others, who may not have our, and the planet's, immediate welfare at the top of their agenda, to make them for us. Then we go and complete the circle of madness by wasting 31%* of the food we produce, chucking 9.5 million tons of it each year into landfill in the UK alone. 'Cheap oil', says Betty Fussell with

---

* 31% is an average figure between the US and the UK. (UN environment report)

impressive brevity in her book *Raising Steaks*, 'created cheap fertiliser which created cheap corn which created cheap beef.' She might have added that it all came together to produce a cheap food habit.

If you accept and follow the logic, the upshot is simple: we need fewer cows. And, if we are to achieve that, people like me need to eat that steak, that curry, that burger, as an occasional privilege and not as a routine right.

You as well, if you're a meat-eater, and still reading.

And it is time to exercise our right to politely question the tactics of the mass fast food chains like McDonald's, Subway, Wendy's and Burger King, not necessarily for the quality or the welfare standards they adhere to, but because their business models appear to rely on the growth that comes from persuading us to eat more beef, and more often, than the planet can possibly sustain. In other words, stopping them damaging our 'commons'.

And as they're not doing anything illegal, it's down to us to change our behaviour.

～

One morning a few weeks later, John shows me his grubby blue book for the first time in a month or so.

'All done', he says with an enigmatic smile. 'Fifty-one calves from 44 cows. Twenty-two of them heifers and 29 bulls.'

I ask him if he thinks it has been a good calving season, if he is happy.

'Yes – we just lost those two twins you took to the kennels, so all the others survived.' He shows me the book, which sets out in neat statistical form the mother of each calf, the father, the birth date, the weight and the all-important tag number. In the right-hand column, he has noted down comments on the condition of the calf and the behaviour of the mother, all of which will later become vital leads as to what is planned for them down the line. I am amazed at the difference between the weight of the smallest surviving twin and the largest single calf, which is more than double. As a reflection of John's determination to stop the size of the individuals spiralling upwards, any bull calf with a birth-weight of more than 50 kg is castrated. 'All OK' is the expression we want in the right-hand column, because it means that there are no problems at all with the birth or the new arrival, and 'All OK' is what has been written 41 times. His biggest complaint is that there are too many sets of twins, which tends to become a habit and can weaken the cow, or produce freemartins.*

Most of them are fathered by our resident three bulls, Tiger, Saturn and Dancer, but, for eight of them, John has brought in semen from a bull called Paringa Iron Ore, a vast and handsome eleven year-old from the Riverlands of South Australia, and another from Canada called Rum.

'Why do you do that?' I ask, subliminally feeling that Tiger might have been short-changed.

'It just removes the risk of my selling a calf to an existing customer that ends up being too closely related to another one in his herd. Also, it freshens things up a bit, and adds some

---

* Freemartin: genetically female, but with male characteristics, and therefore infertile.

hybrid vigour.' He smiles. John always smiles when he is talking about hybrid vigour, rather like the Queen when talking about horse racing. 'And, with a small heifer that is just learning her trade, it is sometimes safer for her not to have the undivided attention of a large, enthusiastic bull.'

By now, spring is chasing down winter in earnest and, as if to prove the point, in the great oaks to the east of the farm-house, jackdaws are flying to and fro in the slanting sun with wood for their nests. The soundtrack of the farm seems to have found its own echo in the burgeoning birdlife at its peripheries, the green woodpeckers yaffling low across the adjacent pastures urgently alerting us to the awakening earth below, and the many promises it holds. From the margins of the fields, mole-hills progress away from the hedges, more each day, like little platoons of earthy children playing grandmother's footsteps in a garden. Gradually, as the northern part of our planet tilts inexorably once again towards the sun, the farm is emerging into a new season, and each dawn brings with it brighter greens and a gathering sense of approaching bounty.

'We'll be letting them out in a week or so', says John, look-ing back in the direction of the cattle barns. 'I think you'll enjoy that.'

9. SCAPEGOAT COW:
A BOAT TRIP THROUGH
MY BRAIN

April

....

*'The energy required to refute bullshit is many
times the energy required to produce it.'*
ANTHONY WARNER, THE ANGRY CHEF

....

For a moment, they just stand and blink at the sunlight, like Beethoven's prisoners in *Fidelio*.

But only for a moment. Before the first swallow of the summer has the chance to flit down into the depths of the farmyard to join them, they are off.

The long winter confinement is over and, barn by barn, we are letting the cattle out to the waiting fields. John normally has to do this later than other local farms, as his low-lying land stays wet for longer. Ironically, this spring there is a cold drought, and he has an agonising equation that balances, on the one hand, that he will run out of hay and silage by Sunday week and, on the other, that the fields are still growing feebly in the dry cold of the Atlantic high-pressure system, and that therefore it is still too early; there is a sense that we will pay later. In these days of satellites and nano-technology, it is a reminder that farming still stubbornly relies on what comes out of the ground, how much of it, and how fast.

The first barn is a tale of two cities, of cows who remember with delight the freedoms of a previous summer and who can't get out quick enough, and of calves who have never left the building before, and don't particularly want to now. Motherhood goes out of the window in the stampede, as John and I have to use an unhung gate to push the reluctant calves into the yard, and onwards from there up to where they initially congregate by a shady mound of nettles and winter blackthorn. From there, we walk them down the short track to the gate into what will be their first pasture of the year.

Once they are through that gate, what follows seems to be an expression of pure joy. The cows lead the charge into the sunny field, bucking and running their way around the perimeter like children released into the grounds of a free funfair, all summoned by those deep-grained mob-grazing memories. The calves follow because there is nothing better to do and, maybe, because they sense that it is fun, as well. For a minute or two, the grass is something to run over and not just to eat, to explore and not just to stand upon, as if the feeling of it under the hooves is a life force of itself. After them, we take some of the heifers to a distant field, and then a small group of year-old bulls to one nearer the farm. After a few days, the 'bull-ing groups' will be completed by the arrival of Tiger, Saturn and Dancer, each to their respective collection of heifers and calves.

By now, it is lunchtime, and I choose to watch the bulls, calm now, and newly settled. My old friend, 1025, comes towards the fence, much as he had all those months ago, that evening when I first leaned over the gate with John. Briefly, he eyes me up as he passes, and briefly as well, I give him a weak smile.

It is weak because I know something that he doesn't. I know that he wouldn't be in that field with that group if the plan was for him to be one of our breeding bulls, or someone else's for that matter. But he hasn't yet fulfilled the promise of his early months, and he is now officially one of our beef cattle, and that changes everything.

It is time for me to think about the cost of my beef habit.

⇌

On November 29th, 2006, a 380-page report was published by the United Nations' Food and Agriculture Organization (FAO), complete with the dystopian image on the front cover of the sinister long shadow of a cow cast over a desert, entitled, funnily enough, *Livestock's Long Shadow*. That, too, changed everything.

I think you just sighed there, dreading, perhaps, the coming argument. Indeed, if you don't eat meat, or you do and really don't think there's a case to answer, you can move straight on to the next chapter, which is about stories. Otherwise, make yourself a strong coffee, and plough on.

The report's central finding, certainly the one that got all the publicity, was that the livestock sector accounted for 18% of global greenhouse gas emissions, far more than had been imagined before. Almost immediately, and from both sides of the argument, people started to discredit it – including the FAO itself, which reduced the figure down to 14.5% seven years later. However, the emissions accusation was joined by other, perhaps less arguable ones, based on land degradation, deforestation, water usage and pollution, and biodiversity. The debate has raged ever since, with the meat lobby on the one hand claiming that the true emissions figure is far, far lower, and that this lie was halfway round the world before their truth had got its boots on, and many climate campaigners, who continued to doubt that it had gone far enough. It didn't matter, though, whatever the truth. We live in a world of headlines, and the genie was well and truly out of the bottle. From that point on, cows would be under suspicion, to the extent that no story could credibly be told of man's relationship with cows in this modern age without at least pausing to examine it.

Even so, when Christiana Figueres, a former senior member of the United Nations Framework Convention on Climate Change, announced in a 2018 conference speech that meat-eating should be abolished, you could say that she was trying to push a very old rock up a very long hill. After all, we've been eating the stuff for around 2.6 million years, and cooking it for about half a million of those. Meat-eaters, she added, should be treated like smokers and made to eat outside restaurants, because meat is 'bad for the planet and for our health'. 'How did we get to this point', mused one academic, 'where food sources that humans have relied on for millions of years are now considered backward and objectionable?'[1]

As a meat-eater who also claims to be a conservationist, I cannot morally – or practically, for that matter – ignore the fact that as much as 96% of all mammalian biomass is now composed of humans and their domesticated animals.[2] Meaning that everything from elephants and rhinos to voles and mice has to fit into the other 4%. Nor that around 70% of all birds on earth are chickens. We can debate the details all we like, but with our own species (which only represents 0.01% of all living things) having managed to cause the loss of 83% of all the world's other wild animals, and half its plants,[3] and then more or less replace them with domesticated livestock, we cannot possibly say that there isn't a case to answer, or that choosing to eat meat doesn't carry costs.

Equally, there is no credible way that a meat-eater like me can begin a defence of their habit by claiming that their diet is efficient. It simply isn't. A huge amount of research has been done as to just how inefficient it is,* but a crude averaging out suggests that, for every kilo of beef I eat, it takes ten kilos of feed to provide it.† A grass-fed cow has a much better ratio than a feedlot-finished one, obviously, but the fact remains that most

....

* Painstakingly laid out in Simon Fairlie's excellent *Meat: A Benign Extravagance*, Permanent Publications, 2010.

† The figure for pork is 5:1; for chicken 2.5:1 and for farmed fish around 2:1.

of the energy put into any animal I eat has leached out into the environment long before it arrives on my plate. The sweet spot is only achieved when the cow is predominantly eating stuff that we can't, like grass or lucerne.

Water use is more complicated. There is an oft-repeated figure of it taking 100,000 litres of water to produce one kilo of beef,[4] which makes for a good, shocking headline from time to time. The logic, if we can call it that, is that you count every drop that falls from the sky (which is a lot in a rainy country like the UK) onto a field that grows the hay that feeds the cow. It doesn't count that the rain was coming down already, or that the overwhelming volume of it ran off and did something else useful afterwards, like provide water for us to drink, or to clean sewage, or provide a medium for fish to swim in. A grass-fed cow in an already wet country uses remarkably little extra water, aside from the 180 litres or so that will be used by the abattoir to clean up after it has gone through. The problem occurs when you rear your cattle in deserts, as in the Australian outback, or in feedlots in a parched US state. 'The amount of water consumed by a beef cow', as Simon Fairlie writes drily, 'appears to be a function of your political position.'[5]

Rather to my surprise, a year into researching and writing this book, I still eat meat on a regular basis, but I eat less of it, less often, and very differently.

Maybe like you, I have too much going on in my life to absorb more than a grossly reductive version of the many arguments on both sides, so here is how I have arrived at where I am, regarding nutrition, ethics, emissions and biodiversity loss. At no stage do I claim to be right, and, with all its unscientific imperfections, this is just a short private boat trip through the canals of my layman's brain.

⇌

First, health.

We have started in the unconscious part of my brain, the cerebrum, and this is what is going on within the forests of neurons that I hope are still functioning there.

Ever since the early 1960s, when Ancel Keys' celebrated work in the USA first pointed to the dangers to health in multiple ways of a diet that contained too much fat meat, carnivores and omnivores have been on the back foot, philosophically at least. The original theory became mainstream within the space of a generation, and along with it came the idea that we would all probably be healthier if we dropped meat altogether. Omitting from his results the fifteen countries where the evidence inconveniently didn't support his theory, and just keeping in the seven that did, Keys enthusiastically promoted the idea that the saturated fats from a high-meat diet lead inexorably to cardiac problems, cancer, diabetes and obesity. With the tacit support of a US administration that was keen to sell more cereals, his hypothesis neatly overturned two million years of evolutionary logic, and quickly but unaccountably became received wisdom. The mistake, as it so often is, was to confuse correlation with causation, and anecdote with evidence: the real issue was that the people presenting with, and dying of, these problems, were people who already had high levels of unhealthy foods in their diet, like fries, starchy bread and fizzy drinks, and a high probability of a sedentary lifestyle. Keys' trick was to link just the meat element with the high fat with the future illnesses.*

When I ask nutritional therapist Monique Stone to explain what she thinks the real problem is, she is unequivocal. 'We evolved alongside and ate large herbivores, who put nutrition back into the soil, and we thrived on the diet. The useful argument these days should not be between a meat-based diet and a vegetarian one, but between processed food and unprocessed food.' Both main diets are fine, she argues, so long as they comprise as little processed food as possible. 'Unprocessed foods are what our physiologies have evolved to thrive on, with a cascade of downstream effects that links with our digestion, produces enzymes and builds muscle. How is it possible', she continues, 'that food our species has been eating for two million years is suddenly bad, indeed suddenly worse than a meal consisting of largely synthetic ingredients produced in a factory?' I see her point. It will still take a giant leap of faith to convince me that a factory-processed cell-based alternative burger is either better for me or is, in any sense, meat. Vegetarians manage without meat and, if I ever get to that point, so will I. For the time being, I feel that the hundred trillion microbes cheerfully multiplying in my gut will find it easier to keep me safe and well if I send them down stuff that they are evolutionarily adapted to, which includes meat.

....

* The initial Seven Countries Study, as it is known, ran from 1958 to 1964, and included cohorts of males between 40 and 59 years old, in the USA, Finland, the Netherlands, Italy, Greece, Japan and what was then Yugoslavia.

The recommended diet that Monique goes on to describe seems to chime with the one I have tried to follow for the last decade, from Michael Pollan's seven-word summary of his own 2009 book, *Food Rules*: 'Eat food. Not too much. Mostly plants.'[6] And then I add three of my own: 'Plenty of variety.'

If we are going to eat beef, then we need to do it in moderation, and well. For me, this includes trying to avoid buying varieties that might be more of a health time-bomb than others, such as when it is smoked,* or, like Wagyu, when it has a serious amount of marbling (aka fat) in it. Gillian Butler's 2021 paper for Future Foods[7] was unequivocal in its conclusion that truly pasture-fed beef would give you considerably more good Omega-3 fatty acid concentrations than standard non-organic, cereal-fed beef, and considerably less problematic Omega-6. Her point is that, to influence human nutrition, you first have to influence the cow's; and the higher the percentage of grass forage in its diet, the more Omega-3 you will get in yours, especially in dairy. Other than that, the answer to most dietary choices is that too much of anything is quite likely to be bad for you, the hint being in the word 'omnivore'.

Obviously, there is much more nutritional research opposed to meat-eating out there, and most of it probably a lot better than Keys', but, in my case, it absolutely fails to overturn two million years of evidence to the contrary. There are some arguments between which it is simply not possible to straddle

....

* Don't panic. Eating five rashers of bacon a day, every day, raises your risk of getting colorectal cancer from 5% to 6%, or 6% to 7%, depending on whose research you accept. My parents both got that cancer, so I desist.

yourself, and, for me at least, blaming good animal fats for the damage that bad sugars are doing is one of them. So I am an omnivore, albeit one who is vegetarian around five days a week. While I don't think the vegan diet is right for me, or that it sounds much fun, I can sympathise with the issues that its adherents often face. When young nutritionist Aarti Kavita tells me that she has spent her eighteen months as a vegan politely but consistently being asked by her friends to justify her choice, I recognise the problem, and we both agree that, within a decade or so, meat-eaters will probably be in the same boat. I just like the idea expressed by Anthony Warner, that 'no food should be feared, no choices deemed "wrong"; we should be free to embrace the huge variety that the world of food has to offer us, not restricted in our choice based on the moral values and pretensions of others.'[8]

My grandmother frequently told me to do 'everything in moderation'. She died in a one-vehicle car crash, so it was all a bit academic as to whether she was right, but I like to think she might have been. Apart from her driving, which was awful.

=

Which brings us neatly on to morality and ethics, so our journey pauses for a while in the prefrontal cortex, where I think that sort of stuff gets mulled over.

Historically, my species eats beef, drinks milk and wears leather shoes because we always have, and because we have come to accept and elegantly sidestep any moral contradictions that doing so might involve. If animals have rights that humans can't override, including the right not to be owned, not to be killed and not to be eaten, then my eating beef is obviously selfish, in that it causes the death of the cow, impacts heavily on the environment and possibly adversely affects the global poor. And my drinking milk alters the natural life cycle of the cow and keeps her under constant pressure. I am causing damage and, possibly, suffering when I don't even have to. As I am when I father children, drive my car, buy a new shirt, fly off on holiday, own a dog, sit on a leather sofa, watch television, eat chips or turn on the central heating, because modern life is complex, and there are no easy solutions. At least no easy solutions that I have yet found.

The morality of a behaviour is dictated by society and, like it or not, over 90% of that global society still eats meat from time to time. I also know that there have been huge welfare advances for livestock in the last 50 years or so, not least in Temple Grandin's ground-breaking work on reducing the stress of the last journey through an abattoir. Finally, having watched gulls eviscerate living shearwater chicks, stoats tear the throats out of rabbits, and sick roe deer starve to death in the nearby wood, I believe that the life of a prey animal can very often be better in captivity than out in the wild. That doesn't mean it always is, just that it can be. And therefore should be, which is the bit that a meat-eater must not duck.

From a monastery some 40 miles west of Warsaw, one of the foremost scholars of animal ethics and Hindu studies tells me gently over a long conversation why he feels I may be wrong. Kenneth Valpey, an Oxford academic and a practitioner of Vaishnava Hindu devotional yoga himself, is a long-term subscriber to the principles of environmentalism and complete non-violence, and follows a tradition that goes back two and a half millennia. Through the devout and genuine prism of his beliefs, he could no more eat the meat of a cow than I could shoot a bird off the bird table outside my kitchen window. He says that the cow's gift to the world is simply the milk that nourishes its people, and the manure that helps to fertilise its land, and explicitly not its flesh. I remind him that Mahatma Gandhi himself once ordered a calf of his to be shot, as it was in terrible pain, as an attempt at an argument that these things are multi-faceted,[9] but it cuts no ice. While he may regret the extreme politicisation of the cow in modern Indian politics, he tells me instead of some of the legends from which are carved out the more general Hindu beliefs: of the Brahmin's special cow, Nandini, and of the martial king Vishvamitra's attempt to trick it from his possession; of how this fails, and of how the peaceful Brahmin power is the true power. They are beautiful stories, which I am happy to hear.

Legends don't prove anything, but their lessons can steer our thoughts usefully, so I ask him instead how it is for devout Hindus living, say, in a fast food-obsessed culture like Britain's, with a McDonald's or Burger King on every street corner, and he smiles and just says: 'No question. It is hard.' He ends by reminding me of Leo Tolstoy's famous quotation: 'As long as there are slaughterhouses, there will always be battlefields', and says that it has been a pleasure to talk with me about such an important subject. And that is it; he has talked *with* me, and not *at* me. But his quiet wisdom simply takes me to a line that I find I still cannot, and do not want to, cross. It's just how it is.

As a point of observation, three beef farmers, a dairyman and a vet that I met during my travels had all given up eating meat themselves somewhere along the line. 'One day in the abattoir as an undergraduate was all it needed', said the 70 year-old vet. A few months later, I was to see what she meant. 'I know these animals too well', said one of the beef farmers. 'I'd just rather not do it.' It is a highly complex moral issue, with no pleasing right answer.

But there is help and guidance available for us. Back in 1979, a set of 'five freedoms' were formally proposed by the UK Farm Animal Welfare Council. These are: freedom from hunger and thirst, freedom from discomfort, freedom from pain, injury and disease, freedom to express (most) normal behaviour, and freedom from fear and distress. These, particularly the last two, usefully enable us to benchmark the background story of the meat we are eating if we want to, if we are prepared to find the time. In my experience, retailers and restaurants who are proud of the welfare standards of the animals they serve, shout about them, and those who aren't, keep strangely silent on the matter. As we will see later, this concept of our welfare obligation is enshrined in an 'ancient contract' that tries to persuade us that it is not all a giant choice between ethics and economics.

So having accepted any ethical contradictions that infest my omnivorous diet, the pressure is then on me to do it as 'well' as I can. That means doing the research, whenever I buy beef, that satisfies me that the animal has had a good life which ended when it was led gently to a death about which it knew nothing until it happened. Basically, meaning that it hadn't come through a joyless feedlot eating soy from a cleared rainforest and belching out CO_2 as it travelled hundreds of miles to my plate. In this digital world of readily accessible information, there is no excuse for eating meat with low welfare standards. In other words, finding a butcher or supermarket I can trust, paying a little bit more and eating it a little bit less often. And yes, it is more expensive and yes, you can find out all of those things, every time, if you just make the effort.

And no, I probably couldn't knowingly tuck in to calf 1025, or his brothers and sisters. There are limits to everything, and you are now in a rather private chamber of my brain, so it is time to move on.

The second hurdle is cleared, but maybe by slightly less distance than the first. We should be grateful that our brains work most of this stuff out without disturbing us.

⇌

With the issue of greenhouse gases and climate change, it all becomes a little more complicated. Well, for me it does. This is science, and you have now arrived in my frontal lobe. Welcome. Unlike you, I only started learning this stuff in my fifties and sixties.

The science is mind-bendingly complex, and it is neither clever nor useful for laymen like me to pretend that they fully understand it. My starting point is based on Pascal's wager, a handy philosophical position from the 17th century which asserts that, even if the existence of God is unprovable and unlikely, the benefits of believing in him vastly outweigh the risks of not believing in him, if he does exist. So even if I find the group-think around the subject occasionally unsettling, the support of over 90% of the world's scientists is good enough for me, and I buy it.

So then I have to split the problem into two parts: the emissions that cattle naturally cause (mainly by belching), and the emissions that cattle indirectly cause by the way we farm and trade them. All too often, these factors are conflated by both sides into one misleading emissions claim that supports a current argument. According to the FAO report, the emissions split about evenly; it also disarms at a stroke that nice omnivore argument about all those millions of bison a couple of centuries ago being OK, so what's the problem now? (Hint: the bison didn't cause the expenditure of tons of fossil fuels, tons of nitrogen fertiliser, abstraction of river systems and vast swathes of forest clearance to keep them going.)

This now gets technical for a minute or two. With regard to the first part, I have accepted that the FAO scientists know more than me, and are right when they say that 86 million tons of methane leak into the atmosphere directly from livestock each year, plus another 18 million from their manure. On the one hand, methane (CH_4) is 28 times worse than carbon dioxide (CO_2) at warming the earth over a 100-year period (and livestock produce around 40% of our annual emissions of it);*

* 'Methane Explained', *National Geographic* article by Alejandra Borunda, January 23rd, 2019. The other 60% comes from bogs, wetlands, energy production, sewage farms and volcanoes.

on the other, it is currently 200 times less concentrated in the atmosphere than CO_2, and has an atmospheric lifetime of about twelve years, against CO_2's 100 years.[10] Add the 7% of that other group of warming gases, nitrous oxide (N_2O),[11] much of which comes from agricultural activities, and I cannot reasonably duck the accusation that my eating beef is helping to warm my world. I can't even point at John's slow-reared and pasture-fed cows in my defence, as a number of reports conclude that intensive cattle rearing is actually better for the climate than its organic equivalent, as it all happens quicker. Indeed, the main recommendation of the FAO report is not that we do away with livestock, but that we shove them all into efficient factory farms. This is annoyingly complex, but then most things are: the real problem is that we conduct most of our arguments in jet black or snow white, and always at full volume.

I'm not sure that things are quite as simple, or as bad, as *Livestock's Long Shadow* suggests, if you add a few other factors into the mix. First, that science is already starting to come up with mitigation strategies for the emission problems of cattle: for example, researchers found that a high dose of seaweed added to their diet reduced their methane output by 20%, while red seaweed (if they can ever find a way to grow it commercially) reduced it by no less than 68%.[12] The addition of probiotics or organic acids into the microbial community of their guts is also being explored in academia, and you get the sense that the start of the solution is not too far over the horizon. Furthermore, the idea of 'livestock on leftovers' – animal production on resources that are never in direct competition with human food production – will benefit both the climate and biodiversity simultaneously.*

Secondly, we can all effectively reduce the carbon footprint of our beef significantly by simply refusing anything that has, or whose food has, travelled between continents to get to us. When McDonald's, for example, tell us that it will take them until 2030 to stop indirectly causing deforestation, I suspect that we can join the dots for ourselves as to their corporate priorities, and then decide if we are happy with it. Personally, the thought of another decade of needlessly evicted sloths and parrots deprived me of my fast food burger habit overnight. Also, bear in mind that no less than a third of the FAO's original figure of 18% of global emissions being due to livestock farming came from deforestation,[13] which presumably most meat-eaters would want to avoid anyway.

The third 'hang on just a moment' moment is already with us, and has been for ever. Grazing lands naturally sequester carbon, and the more they are grazed in a way that mimics nature (meaning intensively and for brief periods, while avoiding overgrazing), the more they sequester carbon. Some activists disparage this argument, but it is a fact. Just ask yourself if a company of the sophistication and intent of Microsoft would pay an Australian ranching business half a million dollars'-worth of carbon credits to sequester 40,000 tons of carbon on

....

* The Scandinavian research that came up with this ('Future Nordic Diets', Karlsson et al., paper for Nordic Council of Ministers, 2017) also suggested an 'efficiency diet' that included one serving of meat a week, two or three of fish, three of eggs, 66% of current milk consumption and loads of fruit and vegetables.

their behalf, to help them become carbon neutral,[14] if they felt the science was bogus. The cycle of the old-fashioned mixed farm, where carbon sequestration balances the livestock emissions that are required to make it work, is a model to which many younger-generation farmers are now returning. The truth is that the land needs the cow, just as the cow needs the land, but it also needs farmers and policy-makers who recognise this.

This is where the need for open-mindedness comes in. A leading food campaigner explains to me the complexity that ensures that for every housekeeping (e.g. wastage reduction) and technological gain, there is also the remorseless and compensating increase in meat consumption, which ends up neutralising the good.[15] So, at the risk of repeating myself, there is no question in my mind that our future on the planet partly relies on us eating less meat, better-raised meat, and less often. It is simply not credible for the average omnivore to pretend that they couldn't eat more sustainably. Besides, the area of land needed to grow all our vegetables is dwarfed by a factor of 50 by the land needed to graze our livestock.

Each of our life choices has an impact. 'Nearly every one of us, nearly every day of his life', wrote Wendell Berry back in 1970, 'is contributing directly to the ruin of this planet.'[16] The cow was here, and we were eating it, millennia before the car, the heating boiler and the aeroplane. None of us has the answers, but we all have enough available science to stop passing the responsibility endlessly upwards and away from ourselves. When a lady once asked me, with the wings of her disapproval beating energetically in the air above, if I truly understood the emissions cost of my 'beef habit', which I did, I found myself retrospectively wishing that I had asked her the same question about her Land Rover. The one that, statistically, she will use for only 4% of its expensive life,[17] with its diesel engine and Greenpeace stickers.

The way we conduct agriculture in our demanding capitalist world has helped to reduce poverty and yet simultaneously trash our own environment. We don't need to do it this way, but it is not of itself sufficient reason for me to give up on meat – other than beef from cleared Brazilian forests, for example, which research suggests produces 700 kg of CO_2 emissions per kilogram of beef,[18] or twenty times the standard rate for an organic cow in the UK.[19] What I would say is that, for any instance that I found of a multinational bending the rules by finishing a cow sustainably[20] but not caring too much about how much forest got cleared for it to be born and raised, I could point to 50 or more ordinary beef farmers doing their level best to grow their beef responsibly. Food policy-makers have to make that distinction just as I have, and not pretend that it doesn't exist. And whether we like it or not, this leads to all sorts of complications on the desirability of that sacred cow of post-war economics – unrestricted free trade.

Again, it is down to us, the consumers, to do the research, diligently going beyond the feel-good platitudes of airy corporate annual reports and the wistful belief that getting someone to plant a few trees somewhere somehow absolves us of our fossil fuel habit. One of the biggest risks right now is the sometimes comical corporate 'greenwashing' involved in the headlong race to claim carbon neutrality. It took Greenpeace to point out, for example, that only 3% of BP's investments, at the time of their 'Beyond Petroleum' rebranding exercise, were going into clean energy; and by then, 'the many petalled sunflower was drenched in four million barrels of oil spilt in the Deepwater Horizon disaster'.[21]

The third hurdle is cleared for now, but this is a long race, and I suspect its height will go up a little each time I come past, unless we get our act together on meeting our emissions reduction goals.

If anything makes me give up beef, it will be our failure to halt and reverse the effect that modern livestock farming has had on our world's habitats and biodiversity. Welcome to the limbic system that controls my emotions.

As we found in Chapter 2, only a dozen or so of the roughly one and a half million identified animals on earth have been successfully and profitably domesticated, that fraction of our planet's species who now, with us, make up 96% of our biomass. Much of the rest of the animal kingdom is in fast decline, passive participants in what has become known as the Anthropocene (because man is causing it) sixth extinction. Not all, but much of this decline has been caused by the way we farm. From the destruction of 50% of our tropical rainforests for raising cattle or growing crops to feed them, to the loss of a similar amount of our wetlands, drained for farming as well as combating malaria and building cities, we have systematically degraded our five main ecosystems. The price of this is 16,000 known species in decline and endangered, with 10% of that number critically so.[22] We have become a pirate species.

Let's just take, as one example, Brazilian rainforest clearance, roughly three-quarters of which is down to increased cattle ranching,[23] and see what biodiversity pressures might emerge from an agribusiness cutting out some more new farmland to serve the growing foreign market for beef. Leopards and apes will lose the space they need to roam, wintering hummingbirds and warblers will arrive back to find their habitat destroyed, and toads and other amphibians will lose the damp areas they need to survive; sloths will have no trees to hang off, and the beetles who live on the sloths will lose their home, too. On average, 137 species of life form are driven to extinction each day in the world's tropical rainforests, so it's reasonable to work out that 70% of that is down to cattle ranching activities.[24] That's not a misprint, by the way, that's each day. We shouldn't be that surprised about this, in the context of our long history: axe-heads and weapons have been discovered in pits together with long-extinct animals dating back as far as 100,000 years, in Suffolk, Devon and many places in between. It turns out that man's appetite has been helping cause extinctions since long before agrarian life started. More recently, only 1,100 years ago, the Norse invaders of Iceland managed to destroy 40% of the island's vegetation by overgrazing and deforestation. Habitat destruction runs deep through our DNA.

This is a great pity because, as we will see in Chapter 13, the cow can be a wonderful biodiversity engineer if left to its own devices and farmed in a way that goes with the grain of nature. The cow clears the vegetation that prevents other plants rising, and so adds to biodiversity. Livestock-induced biodiversity loss is an idiotic man-made solution to a man-made problem, wished upon us all by people who should know better, and creating many human casualties as collateral damage. And the problem is not just where the cow grazes, but what it eats when its numbers outgrow the available natural foraging. Somehow, we have got ourselves into the position where a third of the world's crops are simply grown and used to feed livestock that can already live off something – grass – that covers about 20% of the planet's dry land. Right around the world, but particularly in South Asia and South America, ecosystems are being trashed to grow inappropriate food for animals that should be simply leaning forward and eating the grass that they are standing on. And, as the developed world gets increasingly interested in solving this problem locally, it also has to be very careful not simply to relocate it to the tropics, just because its governments can afford to subsidise good practice at home.

Sadly, there is no question that my meat habit, and yours if you have one, is causing extinctions. The tragedy is that it really doesn't need to. Indeed, the opposite should be true. In fact, the direction of travel in clearance in the Amazon was actually being reversed until Jair Bolsonaro came to power in 2018 as the 38th President of Brazil, and with him, a darkening disregard for biodiversity, not to mention the human rights of indigenous populations.*

....

* Encouragingly, the pressure on the 'deforesters' is intensifying. On May 5th, 2021, an open letter to the Brazilian legislature from 40 or so of Europe's biggest food organisations, including all the main UK

There is a figure out there somewhere for the number of cattle that the world can safely sustain, without the need to steal other habitats, and it should eventually dictate the number of times we can eat beef each month. Actually, a fiendishly complicated paper[25] has already worked out that, in 2050, you would have 22% fewer cattle on earth than otherwise, if they were all fed only on what they could graze, plus the fodder from crop residues that humans can't eat, like brewer's grains, and not on cereals grown especially for them. This would allow for 26% less land needed for livestock cereals, which, in turn, would release the land for 'human crop' production, perhaps starting with horticulture, in which we have managed to descend into the position where the UK is only 23% self-sufficient in fruit and vegetables (the figure is 75% for red meat), or for some form of re-naturing. The figures for pigs (a 91% reduction in numbers) and chickens (85%) are eye-wateringly higher, and bring the general requirement to about 50% less livestock on earth. This is borne out by the consensus among the 30 or so experts I discussed this with, that 'we need about half the cows we've got now'.* Interestingly, when I put this figure to one regenerative farmer near Berwick, his reaction, an outlier that was punctuated with the occasional colourful expletive, was that far from needing half, we needed treble. I love colourful expletives, so I listened on.

....

supermarkets, threatened to pull out of sourcing food in the country altogether if the issue isn't dealt with.

* Incidentally, it's a number widely supported by academic research, including the EAT–Lancet Commission report on 'Food, Planet, Health'.

'How so?' I asked him.

'Because you will need a huge national herd to be deployed to the arable areas that have been trashed by monoculture and chemicals.' He waved an arm down at the once super-fertile Tweed Valley. 'That process will take twenty years. Once you've done that, then you can have your 50%.' He then talked cheerfully of one day trying to buy 5,000 cattle and kick-starting the process locally, a sort of army of mobile ecosystem engineers.

You can agree with his point or not, but it is hard to argue that the removal of livestock from the modern arable farm, and its indirect replacement with chemicals, has not come at a hell of a price, and that it is not just deforestation trashing our biodiversity. Take an insect net, or a local bird book, or a botanist, for that matter, into a 50-acre field of sugar beet and see how that all goes for you.

On a blisteringly hot day on a Hampshire café pavement, Philip Lymbery, the CEO of Compassion in World Farming (CWF) and a vegan himself, made the same point to me from a different perspective, when I asked him if the future of the cow on earth involved being eaten by people like me. 'Absolutely', he said, slightly to my surprise, 'and for at least 50 years. The sheer effort of repairing the damage we have done to the world's topsoil needs cattle now more than ever.' As a vegan, he longs for a day when we do not need to eat meat; but as an honest commentator, he also recognises the cow's central role in improving the organic matter of our soils.

So then maybe we all just end up eating beef about a third as often as we do now, overcompensating so as to allow for the new people who will justifiably want to try it as well. The twice-weekly burger becomes fortnightly, the steak monthly, and the beautiful Sunday roast quarterly. The key is to change all agricultural priorities, and not just meat, from 'producing high quantities of food to producing healthy food'.[26] Later on, we will look at how this might be achieved without further disadvantaging people in food poverty.

I have stumbled into the last hurdle, but it has just about righted itself for now, ready for the next circuit.

—

You have reached the end of your private tour around my brain, and have probably come to no particular conclusion, which is exactly as it should be. I am more than aware that someone else could have processed the exact same information and come to an entirely different set of conclusions. I also know that I have only selectively skimmed the surface of this complex issue – but then, you have to start somewhere. One of the extra problems that we have to contend with nowadays is that, whatever point our opinions start from, the wonks in Silicon Valley will try to ensure that they are doomed to circulate in an online echo chamber of similar thoughts that both harden them and isolate them from any reasonable contrary argument. Throw in a few needy influencers, and it all risks becoming circular.

Ultimately, the question of what I eat is never quite as simple as the purists would like me to believe. For a start, it is generally a household matter, and not my choice alone. It is the subconscious averaging out of many inputs, including season, manners, budget, knowledge, balance, ethics, health, tradition, time available and, not least, the practicalities of what the other people in the home would like to eat, or who is coming to supper. If we were religious, it might include that; if we are feeling adventurous, which we increasingly are, then that will be a factor. If there is a food story in the news (think back to the French horses in Birds Eye's beef lasagne in 2013), we may well be swayed by that. But perhaps the main architecture of our weekly meal plan, such as it is, simply comes from habit and budget: we just come back to our tried and tested favourites because it's easier and cheaper. The genius of our brains is that they tend to sort all this out for us without us having to think too much about it, via short-cuts within the cognitive process known as heuristics. It is a good reason why we should view with intense suspicion the prophets of certainty.

Our own home is not a world of wellness tools, oura rings, lifestyle choices and ancient West African berry smoothies. Like most people, we just try to get good, reasonably balanced food on the table a couple of times a day, and then eat it together if we possibly can, sometimes with a nice bottle of wine lubricating the process. Finding greater pleasure in what we eat together, and sometimes even cook together, has become one of the big changes of our years of on-and-off lockdowns.

So, for the time being, I eat beef, but under specific conditions, while acknowledging the marginal costs of what I am doing, because the arguments haven't turned over for me 2.6 million years of my species' evolution. If those costs, the 'tragedy of the commons' that we first met in Chapter 6, continue to steepen, eventually I may have no honest option other than to become a vegetarian. But definitely not now. And definitely not by choice.

Right now, the urgent problem that we need to be tackling is not one of dietary choices so much as our relentless removal of nature and natural processes from the business of livestock farming. From all farming, in fact.

⇒

My sandwich is finished, and 1025 has wandered back to rejoin the main group.

'Turning out' day, with its dappled sun shining through the oaks above me, and the ever-present metallic pings of their resident jackdaws, is a powerful reminder of the inexorable trundling on of the seasons on the farm. For all its latter consolations, winter for the livestock farmer is something to be survived, a time of relentless work needing to be done, and of equally relentless expenditure. The turning out of the cattle signifies so much more than the swapping of one site for another: from this point on, the cows will generally keep themselves alive, fit and well, without human intervention.

As I stride back to the yard to see what is next on the list, I find myself more conscious than ever of the minuscule nature of my walk-on part in the long story of this farm. Bulls, labourers, hedges, even outbuildings, come and go over the centuries and sometimes all that is left are the stories.

Many, many stories.

10. THE CATTLE OF
A THOUSAND HILLS

April/May

....

*'Knowledge is a sacred cow, and my problem will be
how we can milk her while keeping clear of her horns.'*
ALBERT SZENT-GYÖRGYI,
HUNGARIAN BIOCHEMIST

....

Late spring, and fields of dandelions are the gift of the cold
drought from the north.

On a track festooned on either side by the last of the white
blackthorn blossom like a bridal train, tiny leaves are appearing
on every branch, except the ash. My grandfather had an old
saying, part of which was: 'ash before oak, in for a soak', but
now a vicious fungal disease has consigned it to irrelevance, a
stinging reminder of the price we pay for our careless worldwide connectivity. Trade moves, plants move, people move and

with them move the invasive species and viruses that are its price. Somewhere, an invisible blackcap calls out his territory, as clean and insistent as a new resolution.

Walking cows with John is one of the great pleasures of the job, and hardly counts as work to someone who loves walking anyway and just needs to be outside as much as possible in the short days of early spring. Down the paths it is easy, just a question of leaving the gates at either end in the right state at the right time, and letting the cows choose their own speed. Crossing a field from one side to a gate over at the other, where they have new grass to interest them, and a choice of many different directions to peel off in, is an altogether more nuanced operation, guiding but not pushing, obliquely shepherding them in the direction of the other gate, almost as if wanting them to go that way is the very last thing on our minds. Herding cows through gates in the middle of a run of fencing is well-nigh impossible, so we have 'Hampshire gates' in most of the corners, which are effectively no more than a small section of fencing that can be unhooked, opened, and then put back together again once the cows have gone through.

'Did I ever tell you about Princess?' asks John as we walk along. I am idly watching a cock robin feeding tiny grubs to his mate on a branch of hawthorn, and so have to redirect my attention.

John has a habit of suddenly coming up with some random fact, or a long-forgotten story, each one a tiny piece in the giant jigsaw puzzle that makes up the history of the farm, another drop in the reservoir of his deep experience as a cattle farmer.

'About 25 years ago, when we very first thought of running a Red Angus herd alongside the Devons, we went up to the Royal Show at Stoneleigh to see them being shown, and learn a bit more about them. That's what these agricultural shows are all about. We saw a heifer that had got second prize in the class, fell in love with her, and put a bid in on the spot. Very unlike us. She was as near perfection as we had ever seen in the breed.'

That's the thing about starting a new herd: it's not just a question of buying a few suitable cows. It is an exercise in research, travel, contact-making, risk and, above all, investment. It's walking away from depths of knowledge, resources and friends that have been built up over a lifetime. It's like a greengrocer suddenly becoming a fishmonger, with many of those old procedures and contacts now meaningless.

'Anyway, we agreed a price, £2,000, which was more than we had ever paid for anything at the time. But it kind of made sense on the basis of us wanting to establish a wonderful new bloodline. Even then, I think we thought that we had got a great deal. A few weeks later, I drove up to the farm near Harrogate to collect her. Lovely lady who owned the place, but a stockman who made me feel uncomfortable from the second I got there. When we got her home, we got a straw of semen from the best choice of bull we could find, and then waited to see what came out.'

I tell him that it seems to me that much of farming is like that, just waiting to see what eventually comes out.

'Well, what came out nine months later was a minuscule and ugly little calf, who stayed minuscule, and an increasingly bad-tempered mother who turned out to be completely dry, and utterly disinterested. So not only had our inspired genetic planning gone for a ball of chalk in the size of the calf, but the expensive mother wasn't even going to look after it. By that point, my children had changed her name from "Princess" to "Old Bag", and Old Bag she stayed until, in due course, we took both the mother and calf off for burgers, and got about 500 quid for the pair of them.'

'Which only goes to show', he adds, pulling a gate to behind him and roping it up, 'it only goes to show that you don't need to be a novice to get duped. I'd been farming for over twenty years at the time; I was even judging at shows. But I'd been judging South Devons, not Anguses, and I had been flattered and deceived by the cosmetic work they had done on Princess before the show, and by the look in her eye when we studied her.'

We walk on in contented silence, John probably recalling the pain of the incident, me rejoicing in the fact that so much of farming is still about storytelling.

＝

And those stories have been running for at least ten millennia.

From Genesis 12 to *Animal Farm*, the cow has had a permanent role in our human story. In *Animal Farm*, it is the cows who bring about the revolution by breaking into the grain store and chasing the men away when they turn up, but it's the pigs who swiftly end up running the show. And it's a safe bet that you wouldn't have wanted to be a cow in the Bible.

Starting with only two of you after the great flood, and always painfully aware that you could be the next

God-appeasing sacrifice on the altar if you were sufficiently perfect, you would have quickly become inured to your place as a pawn in man's fractious relationship with his deity. From Pharaoh's dream of the seven fat cows being eaten by the seven lean ones to the pestilence wished upon the cattle in the field, whatever happened to you was unlikely to be anything other than bad news. And when the people started worshipping you, as the Israelites did the golden calf, they were put right in no uncertain terms by God through his messengers. Fundamentally, in the Middle East where cattle and their ancestors were endemic, cows appeared on the menu from Day 1, whereas pigs, which weren't, didn't. And still don't.

But the cow as a focus of storytelling goes back a whole lot further than Genesis.

People on this planet have been looking up into the night sky for thousands of years and seeing, 490 light years away, a group of nineteen principal stars that, when they tried very hard, their imaginations could and did configure as a bull. You, also, can find it on any clear winter's night by following the line of Orion's belt upwards about five times its own length: it is called Taurus. The light that radiates from it will tell you, rather more elegantly than I can, that mankind has found supernatural significance in cattle since long before he domesticated them. In culture after culture and dynasty after dynasty, from the Babylonian astrologers to the story of the Minotaur and beyond, the cow took its central place in the narrative of the people.

In no culture in the ancient world did the cow and bull play such a crucial part as in early Hinduism, where the scriptures are plump with stories of cows and kings, bulls and Brahmins, and of their part in the search for dharma, the four truths. Long before early Britons were tucking into deceased cattle, the Vedic texts had persuaded followers to forswear beef for ever.

Wherever you look in the ancient world, the ancestor of the cows on our farm had significance. In Egypt, Apis was always one in a long line of perfect bulls, revered as the embodiment of the god Ptah. These bulls were housed in a temple for the duration of their lives and then encased in a giant sarcophagus when they finally died. And opposite them was Hathor, 'the gentle cow of heaven', whose milk was fed to the infant pharaohs so as to make them divine. Bulls came to be seen as the embodiment of kings on earth, which goes some way to explaining why so many of them were buried, as it were, with full military honours. Intriguingly, the Swazi people in southern Africa still sacrifice a black bull at the winter solstice as a stand-in for their king.[1]

Far, far to the north, among the foggy icefields and fjords of Norse legend, the first human, Aurgelmir, was brought into being by a cow called Auðumbla, after she had first nourished herself on salty and rime-covered stones, and licked them into the shape that now acts as our bodies.

As seen in the famous Landseer painting of 1867, 'The Wild Cattle of Chillingham',* our mythologies eventually created the

* As a study of character, and painted by a man who was often racked with mental illness, this is a worthy equal of the more famous 'Monarch of the Glen'.

two archetypes to which we still cling, that of the rampaging bull as the embodiment of power, together with the latent violence and strength with which to impose it, and the gentle cow as the nurturing, nourishing bringer of life. It has inexorably led to the extremes of a public bullfight in a *plaza de toros*, on the one hand, and the gentle 'Cow Who Jumped over the Moon' in the children's story, on the other. More so than in the narrative of any other animal that we have domesticated, we still cannot help but differentiate wildly between the male and the female.

In the pleasing British tradition of eventually consigning all myths into pub names, none is better known than the Dun Cow, who is a savage beast if you happen to live in Warwickshire, a generous but disappointed giver of free milk in Lancashire, or the inspiration behind the foundation of the city of Durham.

Three thousand miles east, it was rather a different story, and its long-term effects still influence the highest level of Indian politics to this day.

—

Even before the Minotaur was creating havoc in Knossos, early settlers were arriving in the Indus valley as pastoralists, for whom cattle were of immense significance. It was fine to kill them for sacrifice, was how their thinking originally ran, but not fine at all to kill them for food. As their own gods quietly took shape within an organised religion, so too did their animal others – Nandi the bull, who carries Shiva, for example, and Kamadhenu the wish-granting cow – and cattle came to symbolise a life of non-violent generosity. Ironically, it is thought that the influences for shunning beef came eastwards with the

Semitic people and *Bos taurus*, rather than westwards with *Bos indicus*, an eastern descendant of the aurochs that had split away over half a million years before. It is rather more likely that the Aryan settlers in northern India started running out of draft power to pull their ploughs, and simply put a mandatory stop to the habit of eating the animals that provided it. There is a misconception that Hindus regard the cow as a god, and something to be worshipped, when in fact they simply see it as a symbol of life itself, to be protected and venerated. Killing and mistreating animals is generally believed to generate bad karma for both the individual concerned and for society, because 'the essential element of Hinduism is not in fact, belief, but social organisation'.[2]

The status of the cow has punctuated Indian politics since before the founding of the modern state. So much so, that there is a direct line of descent between the establishment of the Cow Protection Movement in Punjab during the British raj and the assertiveness of domestic politics today. The Indian Mutiny of 1857 was partly caused by the notion that the grease on the cartridges with which the British equipped their native soldiers, and from which the soldiers would have to bite the caps off, was variously pork fat, which was unacceptable to the Muslims, or beef fat, which was anathema to the Hindus. A century later, the cow was a totemic presence in the anti-Muslim riots that preceded full independence, itself an event where the cow was unwittingly centre-stage, too.

Even now, as the world's largest democracy rapidly modernises and reaches out into the rest of humanity, domestic politics have a habit of getting snagged on the metaphorical horns of that all too un-metaphorical cow. In 2017, for example, it took a decision by the Supreme Court to prevent a full nationwide ban on the slaughter of cattle that the government wished to impose. As it is, six Indian states and territories have imposed it anyway. A few years later, the government was forced to postpone the new 'Cow Science Exam', in which students were to be tested on how indigenous cows produce gold in their milk, and on the extraordinary powers of their dung and urine. Officials of the ruling BJP party continue to assert that cow dung protects the earth from radiation and that the 'cow is the only creature on earth that inhales and exhales oxygen'[3]. Wherever Indian politics go from here, it is likely that the obliging cow will be trotting not that far behind.

It is curiously against this uncompromising background that beef has become the fastest-growing food in Asia. Devout Hindus regret bitterly that vegetarianism in India is now at an all-time low.

⇌

In stark contrast to the mother-cow as the focus of service and love, perhaps nowhere do storytelling and violence collide with more startling effect than in the *plaza de toros*.

Bullfighting has been going on since Roman times; indeed, it is likely that the arena at Mérida in Spain was hosting bullfights 2,000 years ago, and it still is now. Aficionados – well, Ernest Hemingway anyway – insisted that the spectacle started to go decadent after May 16th, 1920 when the great matador Joselito lay dying on the sand of Talavera, killed at the age of 25 by his 1,547th and last bull, and his arch-rival Belmonte went into the first of many retirements, from which he never quite recovered.* Certainly, the opening decades of the 20th century are known now as the spectacle's golden era. And yet it continues today in eight countries, mainly those where Spanish is spoken, but particularly in Spain, a seeming anachronism that defies the softening sweep of history. For all the pomp and circumstance involved, bullfighting boils down to little more than the rather violent telling and re-telling of familiar stories.

The story it weaves is one of valour, as of, for example, Manuel García Maera, who once killed a bull even though he had incurred two dislocated wrists during that very *corrida*, and who died at 28 of TB not in, but 'under his bed fighting, dying as hard as any man can die'.[4]

It is about beauty, about the slowness and closeness of the pass, the balletic insolence of the puny matador against the mighty bull, and the contrasts of burning sunlight and dark shadow in which the action takes place. *Sol y sombra*, as Jan Morris once wrote, 'a mirror both of Spain's delight, and of her lingering poverty'.[5]

It is about danger, and particularly the knowledge that just about every fighter will at some stage be gored painfully and dangerously. Accumulated records suggest that 534 matadors have been killed in the last 300 years, one of the more recent being Víctor Barrio Hernanz in Teruel, live on TV in 2016, at the age of 29. In 2013 alone (figures for other years are

---

* Like Hemingway, Belmonte finally shot himself. This was after his doctor insisted that his accumulated injuries meant that he could no longer smoke, drink, ride horses or make love. Apparently, he did all four activities in the immediate lead-up to his suicide.

unreliable), 31 matadors and sixteen mounted picadors were wounded by the horn of a bull, in a total of 661 fights. The risk of death is the key to the *corrida*'s honour code, and 'the potential bartering of life for life is central to its logic'.[6]

It is a story of culture more than art, though it invokes nonetheless the art of Velázquez, Goya, El Greco and Picasso, but an art in which the artist is in constant danger of death. It is about passion, honour and, above all, about the moment of truth, another name for the kill. It is even about humour and archetypes, where the disapproval of the crowd can be expressed in the mass throwing at the matador of the only thing keeping them comfortable – their cushions – or the occasional bottle of *manzanilla*.

Above all, it is a story of the bull itself. The breeding of a fighting bull is the polar opposite of how John breeds and raises one of the Red Anguses back on the farm. Where we breed gentleness, they breed fury. Of them all, the fabled Miura bulls from Seville are generally seen as the most ferocious, and therefore the best; they have nobility, and are calm in normal times, but completely mad when roused. Everything that can possibly be done, genetically and behaviourally, is done, so as to end up with a short-tempered, elite fighting machine. Substantially smaller than a standard beef bull, and with low, slanting horns that are neither too long nor too short, they are tested for bravery when they are two, and what defines them in the ring is their courage, their simplicity and their complete lack of experience. Of all the qualities bred into them, there is a focused relentlessness that can see them chasing the same person in a fast-moving crowd for over a kilometre, and a subtlety that means the only sign of an imminent charge can be the slight raising of the crest of the neck muscle. For the bull, the first fight is designed to be the last, so no one ever knows how he will react, if he will run straight, or if he will see through the deceptions of the cape or, later on, the *muleta*. All they know is that the longer he lives in that ring, the more he will learn and the more dangerous he will be.

It was a Miura bull that killed the great Manolete in front of 10,500 people at Linares in 1947, goring him deep in his right thigh before succumbing from the sword wound that had been inflicted on it; they carried Manolete out of the arena, still bitterly complaining that he wanted to continue. From then on, the discreet pressure from matadors on the breeders to produce more docile bulls, and ones that may well have had their horns subtly shortened, grew more intense.

52% of the Spanish people would like to see bullfighting banned,[7] as would, I might guess, a rather larger percentage of people from outside the country. No account of bullfighting could reasonably ignore the tormented animal, skewered in the back by *banderillas*, sleek with its own blood, making its last desperate stand for the entertainment of the watching crowd. Nor can it pass by the fate of the picadors' horses, blindfolded so that they cannot articulate the natural terror they should feel, and sometimes fatally injured in the opening passages of the show.* The sight of any animal's newly dead body, let alone one whose generosity has supported man for ten

* 200 die this way each year, according to www.theanimalrescue site.com

millennia, being towed by mules across the sand in front of a large crowd who have come for the pleasure of seeing it killed, should be enough to give even the most robust constitution pause for reflection.

Personally, I don't like it, and I don't care much if this makes me culturally naive, or plain soft. Bullfighting seems unarguably and unnecessarily cruel, and my pledge as a meat-eater is to remove as much cruelty as I can from the process; and it is also because the fabled *agresividad* (aggression) of the bull is, in truth, the reaction of a terrified herd animal deprived of company, where, very often, 'isolation means death'.* Also, it is widely believed that the fighting spirit of a bull actually comes from the mother, which kind of spoils the whole, masculine point. If we are looking deep down for a reason why something so apparently out of place continues to this day, then perhaps George Monbiot has a point when he says that 'the absence of monsters forces us to sublimate and transliterate, to invent quests and challenges, to seek an escape from ecological boredom'.[8] In other words, it's an entertainment service for our missing inner caveman, and probably needs to come to an end.

Deep down, maybe it all reminds us that, in nature, violence is never far away.†

---

* *On Bullfighting*, A.L. Kennedy, Penguin, 1999. A rather more measured account of bullfighting than Hemingway's, in my view.

† For the record, I was enabled by Covid's various lockdowns to avoid making the choice as to whether to subsidise an activity I disliked by attending a *corrida* or, on the other hand, writing about bullfighting when I had never witnessed it.

And then there are all those superstitions.

For most of the modern era, and until surprisingly recently, it has normally been all about religion. The manner in which the cow arrived in storytelling and superstition generally, but not always, carries the faint odour of priests influencing the behaviour of their people, as we saw back in the Old Testament. Like a reprise of those old Bible stories, animals continued to take their place as unwitting agents of a ruling class that wanted its common people to feel watched. In an age before formalised power structures and laws, keeping the populace uneasy was probably as good a way as any of keeping control.

Once you embark on it, the list of superstitions goes on for ever, getting increasingly mad as it does. Let's ignore the easy ones like cows lying down meaning rain (which it doesn't), it being bad luck to make an offer for a cow that is not for sale, or having to tell cattle about deaths in the family. Or the ones that are borderline common sense, such as not singing in a milk shed, and it being bad luck to strike a cow by hand rather than with a stick. Most of them are much more bizarre. If you had found yourself at a funeral in Germany in the Middle Ages, for example, you were likely to find a cow among the mourners, as they alone understood the route to heaven. Further to the west, in Ireland, you might find a cow that had recently given birth with a candle tied to its tail for a week or two, to deter the fairies from stealing any butter. Obviously. Just like burning a calf alive protects the whole herd from witchcraft, tarring a cow behind the ears stops pesky witches stealing the milk, and feeding mistletoe to the first calf of the year brings good luck, rather than a seriously upset stomach.

Then there's that biggest of all urban myths, the one about cow tipping: the notion that what drunken rural lads get up to after a night on the tiles is to leap into a neighbouring field and upend a sleeping cow. Leaving aside the fact that cows don't sleep on their feet (unlike horses, they don't have the ability to lock their legs), and that they would probably run a mile before you reached them, scientists have also calculated that you would need a force of between 1,360 and 2,910 Newtons to achieve it, well beyond a couple of boozed-up students. Pausing briefly to celebrate living in a world where academics are actually paid to work that kind of stuff out,* even YouTube, 'the largest clearing house of human stupidity the world has ever known',⁹ cannot come up with even one un-faked example of it.

One of the few bright spots in medieval times, a rare light-hearted interval in a life that was generally given over to hunger, subsistence, illness and uncertainty, lay in the delights of a Bestiary. Bestiaries were beautifully illustrated compendia of animals both real and imagined, and seem to have existed for entertainment rather than any particular moral improvement. One 'animal' that made an occasional appearance was a reprise of Pliny the Elder's explosive cow, this one called the bonnacon, a mythical bull-like beast who, finding itself disadvantaged by horns that curved inwards and were therefore useless for self-defence, farted out a potent stream of dung that burned anything in its path that it didn't like. If you approached a bonnacon, it was wise to do so in full armour, so they said,

....

* Oh, yes they are. University of British Columbia study, 2005, conducted by Dr Margo Lillie and Tracy Boechler.

and presumably having arranged some robust laundry facilities before you left home.

In light of all the above, it is verging on the miraculous that a minor country doctor had the idea, on May 14th, 1796, to take fluid from a dairymaid's infected hand and scratch it onto the skin of an eight year-old boy called James Phipps.

It was a simple act of inquisitive research that changed humanity for ever, and it is where our story goes next.

11. A TIME OF GIFTS

May

....

*'You have not lived today until you have done
something for someone who can never repay you.'*
JOHN BUNYAN

....

At the end of April, we start dispersing the bulls.

That, after all, is what the farm is in business for, to produce fine pedigree Red Angus bulls that go to distant parts of the kingdom and beyond, normally to bring a combination of hybrid vigour and small desired changes to other herds. John has sold ten of them to nine different farms in the last couple of weeks, and he celebrates by inviting me to spend the morning with him at the crush, sprucing up the ones who are heading off soon. Prowler, who is moving to a herd of South Devons near Alton after the weekend, seems to have spent a happy week rolling in shit, which has now matted on to his backside and legs in a cleaning challenge of industrial proportions.

'When you sell a car, you take it down to the car wash, and then valet it, don't you?' asks John, when I complain. 'Same with a bull. It's part of the after-sales service. Even though the deal has been done, first impressions are important.' I tell him that most of my cars had died before I had got round to selling them, so the valeting bit never really happened, but he remains adamant.

So, for half an hour or so, I crouch down by the bull's back legs, wetting, softening and then twisting off large lumps of shit by hand, before rough-combing back some sense of order. In his fourteen months of life, he has grown from a skittish 40-kilo calf to a muscular and assertive half-ton bull, radiating well-being and, up close and personal, it is hard not to be impressed. From time to time, Prowler swings the tip of his tail into my face with an accuracy that belies his status as a clumsy quadruped. Through it all, I marvel at his forgiving patience with me and with the process. On occasion, he goes down on his knees and makes a half-hearted attempt to crawl underneath the front of the crush, but basically, he just lets me get on with it. This is the dividend of John's careful genetics, and of a year of introducing as much human contact as possible into the bull's young life. That gentleness is one of the things the farm is best known for, as we have seen.

At business school, they talk about 'unique selling propositions', and selling these young bulls is, indeed, the still point around which the working life of the farm revolves. This is not just in terms of the income, which is obviously important, but of John and Emma's reputation in the Angus world and beyond, which stretches out into the future as a reliable income stream. When Prowler leaves the yard in a couple of days' time, it will be the end point of a long and painstaking production process, and he will be buffed up like a new Bentley leaving the forecourt. The money paid for him is a capital investment by someone else's business, like a factory buying a new piece of plant, and it has been the ongoing currency of farming since Neolithic times. If all goes well, he will repay that value many times over for his new owner through the progeny he sires on his new farm, and ultimately, when his breeding work is done, his flesh will make its way into the food chain, and other parts of his body into all those different products we first met in Chichester in the prologue.

The contents of that Ifor Williams trailer, when it finally bumps its way down the track and on down the A3 and beyond, is a microcosmic reminder of the unconscious generosity and usefulness of cattle that has been with us since before the Dark Ages, and of their gifts.

Two gifts from them, for the time being, and one from us.

━

At 3.50am on September 11th, 1978, a 40 year-old medical photographer breathed her last in the Catherine-de-Barnes Isolation Hospital in Solihull, England.

Exactly a month earlier, she had complained of feeling unwell. Within days, she had developed unsightly red spots on her back, limbs and face, but her mother, who had nursed her daughter through smallpox as a child, was sceptical, and reckoned she merely had chickenpox. Nine days later, and too weak to stand unaided, she was admitted to the local hospital where, only a few days before the World Health Organization was to declare the disease eradicated, she eventually died.

The autopsy confirmed that Janet Parker had died of smallpox, having inadvertently been exposed to it in the anatomy department of Birmingham Medical School about five weeks before. Five days earlier, a distraught 49 year-old professor* who blamed himself for the lack of biosecurity that had led to her death, had killed himself in his garden shed. He left a note which said: 'I am sorry to have misplaced the trust that so many of my friends and colleagues have placed in me and my work.'

As it turned out, she was the last person on earth to die of a disease that had harried mankind since the dawn of modern time.

It is hard to overestimate the awfulness that smallpox had brought in its wake over the preceding centuries. Killing around 30% of all those who caught it, smallpox was an acute and highly contagious virus, characterised by a high fever and distinctive skin rash that, when the scabs dropped off, led to hideous scarring that often stayed for life and, as often as not, blindness. As with other viruses we have recently come to know, it came in a number of distinct strains, one of which (the haemorrhagic type) you really didn't want to get: it killed 96% of its hosts; if it was going to kill you, it would do so within about sixteen days of catching it, normally from severe toxaemia.[1]

---

* Professor Henry Bedson, who headed the school's smallpox laboratory.

Like every other disease that has developed with man, it spread easily around the world, sometimes on the boots of crusaders, sometimes in the blankets of roadside innkeepers and sometimes on the lips of sailors. By the 18th century, it was killing half a million people a year in a Europe that had five times fewer people in it than it does now.*

The relationship between smallpox and cowpox had been long known, and inoculation of some sort had been taking place for centuries, with varying degrees of success. But it took Edward Jenner, a doctor who himself had been inoculated as a small boy, to understand the efficacy of deliberately injecting material from the milder disease of cowpox, in his case from a dairymaid called Sarah who had contracted it from a 'docile Gloucester called Blossom',[2] into the arm of that eight year-old boy, thereby giving immunity to the worse disease. The boy duly became slightly ill for a day or two, recovered fully, and so became the first person in the world to be part of a scientific vaccination programme. We may raise an eyebrow at the kind of parent who would allow this kind of high-risk intervention in a healthy child, but then science's great leaps forward have often been enabled by equally great leaps into the dark. After all, we didn't get the electric light by making constant little improvements to the candle.

From that point on, the medical profession has found much else to covet in a cow. The scientific approach known as 'One Health', whereby human and veterinary medicine are

----

* Worldometers.info (a site that includes a live feed that allows you to see if your continent's population is rising or falling at the moment).

brought together to find links and opportunities between the two, has ebbed and flowed over the years; some scientists, such as Rudolf Virchow, Sir William Osler and Calvin Schwabe have enthusiastically supported it while many others have simply found animal medicine unworthy of their consideration. Right now, in the wake of the zoonotic Covid-19 virus that may well have started its life with a sick bat in a cave near Wuhan, it is back in fashion again.

Unlike bats, cows are remarkably similar to humans in many ways, allowing scientists from the Beatson Institute, Glasgow to work out that a molecule used in a vaccine to protect cattle from papilloma virus can also be used to protect thousands of teenage girls from developing cervical cancer. At the same time, the 2015 Nobel Prize for medicine went to two scientists who worked out that a veterinary drug called Ivermectin, used to treat worms and parasites in livestock, could also be highly effective at protecting humans from the devastating tropical disease of river blindness.[3] And into the future, it is quite possible that a long observation of how cattle fight East Coast fever will come up with a vaccination for malaria, which still kills over 409,000 people each year.[4] In Uganda, for example, a country where access to modern human drugs is routinely harder than it is for veterinary ones, there is a long tradition of people successfully taking courses of antibiotics that were originally meant for cattle, so much so that it is regarded as an informal extra layer of the country's health system.[5]

But if we step out of the laboratory and into the doctor's surgery, the cow's involvement in our welfare increases still further, and there are well in excess of 100 drugs to which they have contributed: from the bovine insulin that was used to keep diabetic patients healthy before biosynthetic insulin came along, to treatments for safe childbirth, upset stomachs, and the prevention of anaemia and blood clots. The stickiness on that sticking plaster in your kitchen cupboard comes from boiled bones and hide, and you don't even want to know where the material for your stitches probably came from, when you last had to visit the Accident and Emergency department.*

On a sunny summer's morning in 1988, a rather unusual cargo was being loaded on to a chartered Boeing 707 at Gatwick airport, bound for Entebbe in Uganda.

Thirty-two in-calf dairy cows were making their long way from multiple farms in the south of England to villages in Uganda, as part of what was to become an ongoing initiative to create smallholder dairy farming in the country.

One of these, an English Friesian heifer called Gracie, used to graze high above the Taw Valley in mid-Devon and, 32 years later, I find myself staring into the same fields with her former owner, David Bragg. These days, the field contains someone else's Simmental-Belgian Blue crosses, as David has long since retired as a farmer himself, but the fences and folds in the hills hold firm to their old shapes and contours. Above us, the sky is unfeasibly blue between the towering thunderclouds. To our

....

* Purified collagen.

right, the death rattle of a magpie passes down the hedgerow in search of unfledged songbirds.

Leaning over a gate, David tells me of the early days, of how, every now and again, it turns out that two wrongs actually *can* make a right. Of how, on the one hand, the grim six-year civil war in the Ugandan bush that had followed the overthrow of Idi Amin had ravaged the country and caused, depending on whose account you accept, somewhere near half a million deaths and a complete loss of livestock. And how, on the other, the insanity of the then EEC's milk quota system was causing farmers in Britain to slaughter perfectly good dairy cattle that they could no longer afford to keep. He talks of the strange connections and coincidences that make things happen in life, and of how the meeting up of a group of British farmers with the Bishop of Mukono, who just happened to be a livestock expert himself, married up the two problems into an imaginative solution, and led directly to that first consignment of cattle wandering up the ramp into a cargo hold at Gatwick, and to the establishment of the charity Send a Cow.

'A few years later', he says, in answer to my question about what happened to Gracie, 'I went out to Uganda to see for myself. It was a trip that changed my life.' Gracie was there in her village, right enough, but the other things he saw on the trip would lead him to sell his farm and spend the next thirteen years travelling around Africa as an employee of the charity, helping to coordinate its efforts on the ground.

'Anyway', he says, 'in 1996, BSE stopped us in our tracks sending cattle out there, and the whole direction of the charity changed from being provider of livestock to agent of education.'

Three decades later, Send a Cow operates in six African countries,* each in a way that strives to be appropriate to its climate, culture and traditions. In that time, it has provided numberless cows, along with the tools and education that have helped to turn smallholders into more effective and confident farmers, and has taken its place as one of the tens of thousands of initiatives that are helping to reduce overall world poverty. The original idea of sending a British cow to a tropical village has long since metamorphosed into supplying locally crossbred versions using AI, where the parasite- and drought-resistance of the regional breeds has been crossed with the improved dairy quality and capacity of breeds like the Jersey to produce a logical local solution. Besides, in a world that is trying in its clumsy way to move away from fossil fuels, shoving a cow onto an aeroplane would no longer be a good look.

'Also, a 10,000-litre-a-year Holstein would be next to useless in the tropics', says animal health expert and Send a Cow trustee, Simon Doherty, 'and it's a lot more efficient to send a flask of semen straws than a cow on a plane.'

He then explains that the actual cow isn't the only thing to have changed.

'It's all designed to be a hand up, not a hand out. We are trying to help to create sustainable organic smallholdings within communities where often the women are the farmers as the men are away in the towns and cities trying to get work, and that can only be done holistically.' As an illustration of the lengths that they go to adapt to the local

....

* Burundi, Ethiopia, Kenya, Rwanda, Uganda and Zambia.

circumstances, Doherty explains that, where HIV/Aids has produced orphaned child farmers, they might well be given goats or sheep, which are generally easier to deal with than cattle. There has also been, as you might expect, a recognition of the role of wildlife in agriculture, where the two try to exist alongside each other.

There is no empowerment like that of taking your own family out of poverty, and initiatives like Send a Cow's, working with other organisations such as Tusk and the Brooke Horse and Donkey charity, use livestock as the axle around which the rest of the enterprise can rotate and, eventually, succeed.

'It helps these communities to become more resilient', says Doherty. 'At a time when climate change is exaggerating the effects of the dry and wet seasons, the cow's role in providing compost, manure and the organic improvement of soil structures is a vital one.' He then describes the cumulative effect of the process, where local farmers are impressed and copy the model themselves, and where the national governments end up providing the AI technicians themselves, and therefore feel more in the loop of control. 'It can sometimes mean less cows, not more; three productive cows are better for the community, and for the world, than ten just owned for the status value.'

The charity's approach also embraces the concept of One Health, an 'approach that recognises that the health of people is closely connected with the health of animals and our shared environment',[6] with ever-expanding populations of humans and livestock living in closer and closer proximity, and thus providing opportunities for zoonotic diseases to spread from one to the other. The charity works together with doctors, vets, farmers, environmentalists and epidemiologists to research, educate and set up prevention strategies for diseases like rabies, anthrax and Ebola. This can be as simple as a visit to a village by a health professional, or as sophisticated as the development of a new vaccine against, say, the Rift Valley fever virus. Doherty is at great pains to point out that, to have its best impact, Send a Cow cannot ever work in isolation.

These days, anything involving a cow has its critics and it may well be that there will be a name change at some stage, as much as anything in recognition of the way the charity has evolved.* In a way, this would be a shame, as the sustainable service cattle provide to organic smallholders all over Africa is extremely important, and as far away from the fast-food-driven, high-intensity feedlot farming we have become used to in the developed world, as Kentucky is from Kigali. Besides, eating beef is very, very far down the priority list for most of their smallholders, maybe something for a wedding feast or occasional festival. Quite apart from anything, without the means to refrigerate it, a regular supply of meat is always going to be a problem. There is something deeply hypocritical in the western world that has exclusively created the emissions that have warmed the globe, lecturing Africans on what they may or may not farm and eat, so as to reduce them. It's a new form of moral colonialism that probably has Africans blinking in astonishment. As one commentator observed with wry elegance: 'Those of us who live in countries where social security

....

* Indeed, in April 2022, the charity finally changed its name to Ripple Effect.

payments cover the unemployed's supermarket bills may need reminding that, while meat is the rich man's luxury, in many parts of the world it is the poor man's necessity.'[7]

Back above the Taw Valley, David Bragg talks with passion about what it all amounts to. 'Ultimately, it's about the cow as the driver of fertility, where the cow farmer becomes a grass farmer becomes a soil farmer. We don't tell people what to do so much as enable livestock to do something for them that it has been quietly doing since time immemorial.'

'It's about the cow', he repeats, 'as a vital enabler, both for the soil and for the people who farm it.'

This is another gift that we want from the cow.

⇌

'So what do cows want from us?'

It is a rainy afternoon in Hungerford, Berkshire, and I have come to see animal behaviour specialist Lindsay Whistance, who has made a life's work out of trying to answer that question. It is also one that I have been asking people on and off for more than a year.

'I mean, for all that they give us. What do they want in return? And do we give it?'

She thinks for a bit, and then says: 'A good life, worth living.' And then, after a pause: 'Do we give it? Sadly not. At least, not enough.' I dimly remember another welfare specialist telling me: 'You tell me how much you are prepared to spend on it, and I'll tell you how much welfare you can have.' Whether we like it or not, this trickles directly down from the amount that we are prepared to spend on our food.

'If we put animals into an unnatural situation, as we have with cows, then we are obligated to do certain things for them, including protecting them from predators, and being their attentive carer, keeper and harvester. It's known as the "ancient contract".'

'Harvester?' I interrupt.

'Yes. We will eventually harvest them. And the problem is that meat has been downgraded in its importance over the years, which has led to a lack of respect for the animal that has lost its life. That matters. As a nation, we don't know animals any more; we have lost the ability to connect the cow in the field with the milk on the supermarket shelf, or the burger in the fast-food joint. And it therefore doesn't even strike us as strange that we have knocked the stuffing out of the ten-tons-of-milk-a-year Holstein dairy machine, or anonymised the provider of those burgers. And we are not counting the cost of the real damage of the illnesses we inflict on them by the way we make them live, as, by and large, we are eating them so young that the problems haven't really developed. So much of what we know about them is based on our observation of them in unnatural behaviour settings.'

She talks about bull-fighting as an example, and how she thinks that there could be virtually no worse way of depriving an animal of its natural needs: through isolation, taunting, violence, death and, above all, tutoring a prey animal to be as violent as it can. She is not criticising livestock farming so much as pointing out that we have forgotten the other side of the bargain.

I ask her if a cow can be happy. 'I don't really like that term in this context', she says, 'as we only know it as a human emotion. However, I absolutely believe that a cow can be content, or not.' She tells me that, by comparing human and animal brain scans, scientists have seen that the same bits light up at the same kind of stimuli. 'So, yes', she says, 'there is no question that they undergo positive and negative emotions, like we do.'

'What's the answer, then?'

'Allowing them to live as close to their natural state as is practical in the farming context', she replies, the same as so many others have before. This literal *re-naturing* of farming and, by extension, its animals has been a powerful recurring theme in my recent conversations.

'And how do you start?'

'With the children', she says, without hesitation.

It is market day in Ashford, and we're bundling round the M20 with a ton of bull in the trailer, and all John can talk about is the prospect of his all-day 'Full Monty' breakfast.

'The café is the best reason to go there', he says, beaming.

Time was when every town of any size had its own livestock market, often in the town square, but these days the two closest, in Salisbury and Ashford, are both nearly two hours away, the latter tucked away on an industrial estate by the motorway. These markets are still the engine room of the livestock trade, where animals are sped through the ring in double-quick time, bought by butchers, traders and other farmers. Van Gogh's 'Sunflowers' it manifestly isn't, but it is a quick and efficient way of realising value in the business, and a rare opportunity for farmers to gather and exchange gossip. Given the underlying loneliness of the profession, and the previous year of social distancing, this is no meaningless fringe benefit.

Today we are taking Dancer, whose wonky feet mean that he is fated to suffer health problems all his life, and who may well pass those problems on to his descendants if he is allowed to breed any more. It may be that someone buys him to bulk him out further on some rich pasture, but it is more likely that it will be a meat trader, and that this is the first step on his last journey. He joins about a hundred other cows in the yard behind the auction ring, many of them superannuated dairy Holstein-Friesians for the cull, gaunt and strangely shapeless after a ten-year life that might well have produced 100 tons of milk for the human race. Dancer looks relaxed, proud even.

'These will be for burgers', says John of the angular Holsteins as we walk around before the auction starts. He explains how, in contrast to his private bull sales, this is a world of little gambles, big volumes and small margins, where bets are taken on the future price of beef and the capacity of each cow to fatten up a little bit on more bountiful pastures. Someone buying a half-ton 'store' cow for, say, £1,000 is simply banking on selling it, slightly bigger, for maybe £1,150 a few months down the line. John hasn't bought a cow for years now, so this is all about Dancer – and, of course, browsing out of mere professional interest.

The ring is small, and all the business is done by kilo rather than cow, at breakneck speed between the auctioneer and no more than a dozen short-haired, checked-shirted, middle-aged men on wooden benches immediately around the ring, and he knows them all. There is an unspoken uniform for a day off the farm, and they are all wearing it. To my knowledge, no one from the stands behind places so much as a single bid all morning.

'She's a belter', the auctioneer says, of a particularly lovely Limousin heifer, with a wide top and a generous bottom. She gets maybe two turns of the tiny ring before disappearing out to the yard. '£2.55 to Thompson', he says after some lively bidding. It is the highest price we see all day, which, multiplied by her weight, will earn her owner around £1,400, less commission. At that price, 'Thompson' will likely be finishing and not butchering her.

'He just needs a little more time', the auctioneer says of a petite Black Angus steer, and starts the bidding at £2. I watch the nods and twitches and nose rubs down below, and keep my own hands firmly in my pockets. He is heading for a pasture, and gets £2.30.

A three-quarter-ton Holstein-Friesian comes in, ten years old and tottering slightly. 'Nothing prime about her', chuckles someone nearby, and she goes for £1.10. The chances are pretty high these days that your burger this evening was your metaphorical milk provider a fortnight ago. We see Jerseys, British Blues, Hereford crosses and many variations of Angus until, finally, Lot 233 comes in, all 1,035 kg of Dancer, and he looks magnificent. Maybe it is that I fed him hay all last winter, that I took salt licks out to him in his paddock, mucked him out and separated him from his group only a few days ago, but I find it a little hard to watch him trotting out of the ring and towards that uncertain future beyond the network of gates and hurdles that lead back to the trailer park. He gets a good price, but I realise that I am still a poor excuse for a real farmer.

John gets over the loss quickly, pockets the voucher and heads enthusiastically down to the greasy spoon café for his all-day breakfast. I buy a burger, and wish I hadn't. I look around instead, and find myself thinking that, if the farming lobby wanted to illustrate the health benefits of an outdoor life, and a diet of grass-fed beef, the occupants of the other tables in the café would be entirely the wrong demographic. Generally pale and overweight, they look like prisoners in some dungeon that just happens to have a full tea trolley parked in it.

Lost in thought, I find myself looking down at John's boots, wishing I owned them.

12. THE JOURNEY OF
A BELT TOLD BACKWARDS

June

....

*'Without craftsmanship, inspiration is a
mere reed shaken by the wind.'*
JOHANNES BRAHMS

....

Finally, the sun comes out, and I still find myself looking at
John's boots.

He is not inside them yet, but I am standing on his doorstep
waiting for him to come out of the house with some paperwork, and they fascinate me. They look like the kind of boots
that I would like to own. If my life has taught me anything, it
is that you can generally tell a man by his footwear.

Those boots came 10,000 miles to be here, from a work-
shop in Adelaide, South Australia. They have a well-worn
elegance about them, like the lined face of an old film star, and

the leather, the stitching, the shape and the welting speak of a long tradition, and explain the high price.

Those boots could tell many stories, and have seen many floors, from the corrugated concrete of cattle yards to the battered and beer-stained carpet of the neighbouring bar. They have walked a hundred farms, kicked reluctant gates rustily open and manoeuvred bales of hay along; stood in the way of ill-tempered livestock, and supported the weight of a tiny rejected lamb on its way to the kitchen. Other than when the weather is as bad as it was last month, I have never seen John out of them, unless they are on the front doorstep.

They are a continuation of one cow's life, and suddenly I find myself wanting something leather of my own to show for my journey, something I can perhaps trace back to the very field it started in.

My own boots are fine but my belt is on its last legs. It gives me an idea.

⟹

Three blocks back from the sea in West Hove, up an outside staircase festooned in buttercup and herb-robert, is the first-floor studio of Wolfram Lohr, one of Britain's 8,400 leatherworkers.*

It is a room of joys, a light and airy room of spider plants and tiny avocado trees hanging from the beams, of the pervading smell of a childhood shoe shop and of a hundred

---

* Capel Manor College prospectus, October 2020. The industry is worth £195 million annually, and the average person 'has at least four leather items on them at any one time'.

different-coloured leathers in small rolls in an open cupboard. It is a room of industry, but also of sensitivity, of theories but of hard-nosed practicalities too. There are handbags in the rafters and belts and marbles in the dark drawers, screws in cigar boxes and swatches of material in wooden wine crates, and always the endless cry of the evening herring gulls jarring through the dusty roof lights. Even the uncleared rye bread and Boursin lunch on a work surface speak of a free artisan spirit.

'You are mad, of course, which I quite like', says Lohr, in reference to my request to buy a new belt from him, but only on the strict condition that I could watch him make it. Born in Karlsruhe and trained as a shoemaker, he was brought to Britain by 'the normal reasons' (a woman) and settled down in Brighton to make a go of it. He lifts up my jumper to measure for the size.

'A man who likes his steak, I think', he muses aloud, like a dentist assessing for cavities, 'and probably goes up and down through the belt holes as the year progresses.' 'If only', I think in silent reply.

He goes to his store and puts two rolled butts of thick oak-bark leather onto the worktop, one brown and one black, asking me to choose. 'It takes them sixteen months to make this. There's only one tannery that does it in the UK, and it's in Devon. The staircase is 450 years old and worn bare. You must go and see them.' He speaks in staccato bursts, and there is an energy and restlessness about him that is all-embracing, an ability for the mind and mouth to be doing something completely separate from his hands on the leather. I choose the brown.

He talks of his hippy days and his environmental campaigning, while he asks me to choose a buckle from a huge selection in an old document drawer. 'This is slow fashion', he says, when I ask him how he squares his leatherwork with the cow's role in the changing climate. 'Buy less, choose well. If they are well made, a man might have just three belts in his adult life, one at a time, each one of which he will wear every day. Maybe 5,000 times. Often they just send me an old buckle, and simply ask me to replace the leather. And remember, it is a by-product of the cow.' We discuss the work of the Sustainable Leather Forum, and its drive for ethical sourcing, welfare assurance and minimising of the carbon footprint.

He lays the brown leather out on his workbench and takes a wooden strap cutter to it, separating my belt from the rest of the hide with a careless precision. I am tragically impractical, and therefore find all craftsmanship mesmerising.

'It's tough on the hands, this work', he says, 'especially when you are dealing with really thick hides like this.' As if in confirmation, I can see the knuckles on the back of his hand whitening as he drags the cutter through the thick hide. He notices me looking at a vertical scar on the bottom of his left wrist. 'Bike crash', he says. 'Titanium plates and three months off. Not good for a sole trader. Worse still when, three days after I go back to work, a pandemic starts.' But he is adaptable ('a craftsman never stops learning') and he loves the fact that his craft is still appreciated in Britain, at least more so than it is in Germany.

I watch my belt take shape. He uses a two-sided template for the buckle end and the end with the seven holes in it, and then thins the buckle end down with an edge beveller so that it can be folded over without creating a lump. 'Each craftsman finds their own way', he says. And then, when he sees me staring vacantly up at the seagulls through the roof lights, he adds with laughter: 'Go on. Write that down. It's good.'

We agree that, rather than go to the pub afterwards as we have arranged, we should drink beer in the studio, and I go to the shop on the corner and buy a four-pack of not-quite-cold Carlsberg tins.

And on it goes. He puts the holes into the buckle zone, ready for the stitching. 'I am a thinking contemporary minimalist, I think.' He compresses the end of the belt into a small return with a beautiful tool, its handle rubbed into a mahogany sheen by decades of use. 'The precision tool company went bust. The new one sent me *this*,' he says, showing me a flimsy new tool up on the workbench. He spits out that last word with contempt, the only time he gets anywhere near anger in the three hours I am with him. 'It's a fucking joke.'

I find myself getting increasingly excited about that belt. He punches out the seven holes and then files off the edges, before treating them with gum tragacanth, and then with beeswax. 'I have a broom fetish', he says, and lovingly shows me a 1969 pure bristle antique he picked up for £15 in London, which I have to admit is gorgeous. Then he goes to the other side of the studio and brings back a hand brush he has made from an old Slazenger squash racquet handle so that he can clean the back areas of the huge workbenches. He applies the buckle and asks me to choose a cotton colour for the stitching that will secure it. We agree on dark red.

Having stitched it, he takes it to a small press where he embosses his brand name by the buckle, a tiny process that delights me no less than any other. 'All these old machines', he says over the noise of spinning, 'are in tune. If not, I know it immediately. A good craftsman is in tune with his tools.' He quite likes that sentiment, and suggests that I write it down too, which I do.

Finally, the belt is ready, and I tell him that it is one of the first made-to-measure items of clothing that I have ever bought, and that it makes me as happy as my first car.

'Excellent', he says, and we toast each other in warm beer and agree that it honours the cow that it came from.

'Go and see the tannery', he insists. 'You'll learn much more about your cow there.'

So, a few weeks later, I take my new belt for a trip to the West Country, back to where it had started, at J. & F.J. Baker, tanners in Colyton, East Devon.

There have been tanners here since Roman times, as there once were in all towns, but this one has been in the hands of the Parr family only since 1862, which I suppose makes them relative newcomers in this most traditional of crafts. Time lies heavily on this place, where the stone staircases are indeed deeply indented by the movement of centuries of boots, where the machinery probably predates your great-grandparents and where the leather itself goes through a fourteen-month process before it goes out into the world. It is the last remaining tannery in Britain that only uses traditional oak bark and stream water in the process which, in turn, allows the grain of the leather to remain in its natural weaves. Even the oak bark dries off for two years before being saturated. For an instant, the thought of fast food becomes incomprehensible.

The word 'tannery' comes from tannin, a naturally occurring compound found in many trees but most notably associated with vines and oaks. Over the centuries, they have been used to 'prevent the disintegration of the collagen fibres of the leather',[1] or in other words, to stop your shoes rotting on your feet. It's a treatment that goes back around 4,000 years, to somewhere in Scotland, and it is listed 'critical' on the HCA[2] red list of endangered crafts. Each time I think about this, about there actually being a formal list of endangered crafts, I rub my new 'Bronze Age' belt appreciatively, and mock the others in my cupboard, with their synthetic heritage.

There is alteration everywhere you look as, stage by stage, the cow's skin slowly becomes leather. The arrival of a pallet-full of salted hides, and their soaking, de-hairing and thinning; the suspended immersion in pits of bark dilution, once for three months, and then again for another nine. This is a process that Stone Age man would have probably arrived at by trial and error, finding out that it worked in the puddles near oak trees rather better than it did in the ones near ash. This is the moment of alchemy. Then there is the drying, the cutting of the sole bends, that hardest and most long-lasting part of the shoe, the water bath to fix the dye to the hide, and the splitting of stock by future function. There is the rubbing of dubbin, and then the cutting.

'There's enough there for another pair of size seven and a halfs', says Andrew Parr, eyeing up a piece of cut leather sheet.

Not sevens or eights, you will note, but somewhere precisely in between.

The physical stages become, for me, an impressionist sketch of dark holes in the ground, of low ceilings, of hanging hides and of the occasional squelch as, somewhere in the darkness, a lone bubble rises noisily to the air, as in a mangrove swamp. If the leather from your shoes came from this tannery, and it probably didn't, it would have spent the first year of its life utterly submerged. Andrew shows me everything – and, as so often in old crafts, everything connects to everything else, or at least it used to.

'Until relatively recently', he says by way of example, 'the hair stripped off the hide would have gone to the local plasterer as a binding agent.' Even the stearic acid from the animal comes back as a component for a process somewhere down the line.

Childishly, I ask him about his trade secrets.

'You're looking at them', he says. 'Of course, there are things that we generally keep to ourselves, like our sources for hides, the exact mix of tannin, and the formula for the dubbin that we apply for the different colours; but the real secret is in our patience. There's just no one else who is prepared to take so long about creating this standard of leather.'

Mesmerised, I watch one of his craftsmen applying brown dubbin to a full hide, to that private formula, to soften, waterproof and gently dye the surface of the leather. What appears at first glance to be no more than a mere wiping of a loaded soft brush over a piece of material, so simple that even I could probably do it, in fact takes about twenty years to perfect. Slightly too thick or too thin, or left fractionally too long, and there will be rings of dark and light across the surface, and it will no longer be a luxury. I ask about apprenticeships, and the polisher smiles.

'Just learned it as I went along', he says. 'On the job.' It turns out that their last apprentice had actually been dead for over 50 years. He was called Reg.

'So who's your market?' I ask, rather proud that, whoever else he mentions, it includes me. 'I mean, it can't be cheap.' Having said that, my belt remains one of the best £100 I have ever spent.

'Three categories, really', he replies. 'Shoes. Especially in Japan, where they really appreciate good footwear, but also to bespoke makers in, say, Northampton. Then there's saddlery, and the whole equestrian market. And finally luxury goods brands. And all of them need different thicknesses and treatments, depending on what they will be spending the next twenty years being used for.' He shows me a handbag from a brand that even I recognise. Some time back in the whenever, a small order would have arrived at J. & F.J. Baker's offices from a craftsman called Wolfram in a bright studio in Hove. And a butt of new leather would have been selected from the store room, maybe a few, and then dispatched to him and stored in a cabinet until one day a writer pointed at it and said: 'That one.'

I find myself surprisingly moved by the eternal tide of human connections made permanent from the one cow that provided the leather for my belt: the farmer, cowhand, haymaker, driver, vet, slaughterman, tanner, craftsman, warehouseman, shopkeeper and end customer who are all small stakeholders in what came from it, bound together in some infinitesimal way by that one animal.

And I am struck at every turn by the 'just-in-case' nature of this work in our just-in-time world. Excellence can sometimes sit uncomfortably in a society of short cuts and quick bucks, but right here things are done simply because that is the right way to do them, and always has been. They could surely take less time, use cheaper synthetic materials and so ship more leather out at the end of each week, but that would be to overlook the essential point. All over the world, craftsmen like Wolfram have come to rely on that indefinable edge, as it is part of what makes them excellent, too.

Near the end of the visit, we reach a pallet with a small pile of brown hides, with the sheen of a pair of military boots.

'That's where your belt came from', says Andrew.

It is time to go yet another stage back.

⸺

'We mostly see what we have learned to expect to see', is how artist Betty Edwards puts it in her book about colours,[3] and the sentiment certainly applies to me.

I have learned to expect the cow in a horizontal plane, with a head out in front and a leg at each corner, or at least lying down. So when I first see a dead and headless cow in the abattoir, suspended by its back legs from a hook five metres above, it is the fact of its being in the vertical plane, and how that somehow exaggerates its size, that gets me first. My brain can cope with everything involved in the process apart from its sheer perceived size in a strange elevation.

It is a day later, and my belt and I have arrived at a small abattoir in the West Country. I am not a writer today, but a farmhand. I have no notebook, and no phone, and the abattoir will remain anonymous. These days, abattoirs, particularly small ones, would fundamentally prefer to do their work without visitors, and you can't exactly blame them, especially when those visitors carry small cameras and expectant notebooks. We have been slaughtering our livestock for more than ten millennia, but it is really only in the last fraction of 1% of that time that it has become this strange, divisive issue. It has taken me a year of effort to get myself inside an abattoir.

A combination of economics, regulation and long-term protests has seen a rapid decline in the number of small, local facilities that tend to serve a small, local market, with 33 closing in the decade after 2007 alone. Great if you are a supermarket or a protester 'bearing witness', as it is termed; less so if you are a cow travelling eight times further than you should, or a farmer for whom the transport mathematics just becomes untenable, and who is forced to sell up to someone bigger, for whom the 'unit cost' can be shared around on a bigger scale. It is not surprising that the 2021 UK Food Strategy Report singled out the desirability of protecting the few small slaughterhouses that are left.

In a world that claims to be trying to become more localised and sustainable, this is a strange situation, but with straightforward reasons: infrastructure costs, including CCTV, head restraints and stunning boxes, have soared; bureaucracy, much of which is multi-agency, has bloomed, with the burden (the cost per animal) falling disproportionately on the smaller businesses; the regulations were drafted with the larger facilities in mind; and waste disposal costs have rocketed, as rule changes have killed competition between by-product collectors.[4] Even the hides, which used to fetch about £45 each twenty years ago, now only get £1, and then only if they are in perfect condition.

That abattoirs are so much better than they once were has much to do with an American scientist called Temple Grandin. Named *Time* magazine's 31st most influential person on the planet in 2010, Dr Grandin is credited these days with almost single-handedly revolutionising the way we slaughter our livestock. Using the intense visual sense which she credits to her own autism, she has seen the final journey through the eyes of the pigs, sheep and cattle who pass through each abattoir, and designed them accordingly. With their sweeping curves and lack of outside distractions, it is reckoned that 70% of all the slaughterhouses in her native USA are now made to her design.

It is Grandin's intense study of how a cow actually thinks that has opened our eyes to a field of study previously either dismissed as mad, or just subsumed into a sentimental pastiche of sweet children's stories from which we never grew up. In the real world, cows have a broad range of emotions, such as rage, fear, anxiety, sadness, curiosity, playfulness and the capacity to nurture. They have long- and short-term memory, and a complex sense of hierarchy within groups and subgroups. There is evidence that some cows have one or more 'anger genes', a genetic overlap with humans that predisposes them to do violent stuff that their more pacific colleagues wouldn't consider.[5] In some ways, they are the same as humans, only without cognition and language; they share with autistic people a tendency towards sensory overload, in the cow's case from the fact that they are seeing, hearing and smelling things with rather more intensity than we do. Little by little, from a start point where she was routinely mocked as being not just mad but, worse still, a female in a man's world, Grandin brought her knowledge to bear. She revealed how you should never chase escaped cattle (as their journeys are generally circular, they will eventually return to where they started), how it takes a cow 20–30 minutes to calm down again after being stressed, and how they will benefit from things being kept very, very simple.

Thus, she continually refined the design of the abattoirs to fit in with the reality of what she understood about the emotions of the different animals. For example, cows prefer to go in single file when they walk and make naturally circular journeys, as we saw above; they seek calm and companionship and they are innately suspicious of things like the shadow thrown by, say, a chimney (could be a hole in the ground), or a length of flapping material hanging off a building (could be a predator). So Grandin built around these needs, with solid sides to the walkways, non-slip flooring and calming lighting, until she had a model that has been replicated all around the world.

Back in the West Country, we are taking to slaughter a two year-old, and much appreciated, bullock from a small herd of conservation Longhorns. He has turned 'a bit cranky' and the owners therefore feel a responsibility to remove him from their land and from the public footpaths that cross it. He has been grazing the moorland edges and it has taken most of the morning to round him up. By the time he arrives at the yard, he has calmed down, like a knee that suddenly loses its pain at the first sight of a doctor. He is well-behaved and handsome in his hide of brown and white, his head held high. We are a solemn little party, ending the life of a beast we would rather see alive, but at least we are doing it in a slaughterhouse that the owners know and trust, and with skilled staff who actually care about what they are doing. By the time he is ready, I have watched a dozen or more sheep move through the process inside the building. I'm not an old hand, but I get it. The duty vet stands in his white wellies with his clipboard, looking as if he would rather be somewhere else.

It happens quickly. Almost before he realises that he is in the stunning box, the sharp report of the bolt gun kills the bullock. For a second, there is silence, but then the busyness of the workplace seeps back in like a spring tide into a rock-pool, and there is noise again. He falls to the ground, and then down a level to the abattoir floor once the side wall is lifted open. Chains, oddly dainty in the circumstances, are applied to his back feet, and then he is hauled up to be worked on. The strength of the nervous kicks of the legs puzzles me and I have been warned that, unlike with sheep where it is the throat that is slit to let the blood out, this will be a cut straight to the aorta.

'Big cow. Lots of blood. You might want to look away.'

Eighteen months has come down to this. If I am happy to go on eating beef, and if I am happy to suggest that others might do so as well, then the only honest thing I can do is watch the whole thing through, not selecting the bits that I am comfortable with and covering my eyes for the rest. My brain comprehends it, even if my insides are noisily rebelling against the message. Deep down, the soldier in me would rather not make a big thing of it, at least not publicly.

'Lot of it, isn't there?' says the same voice, not unsympathetically.

The head is sawn off and slides momentarily across the wet floor towards me with the residual momentum of the last cut. It discomforts me that there seems to be so little resistance within that thick neck to the six-inch butcher's knife, and I find myself hoping that mine would be a tougher prospect in other circumstances. Oddly enough, it makes me feel rather vulnerable. Then the team gets to work. And take away the death, that is all this is: a skilled group of people doing what they do. Cutting away the hooves and they were talking about the fishing season; peeling away the hide, and it was someone's much delayed hip operation; sawing the carcass in half, and we were on to what so-and-so down the road has done with his garden, and how stupid it looks. And all the time, music blaring in the background, a lady in Cleethorpes is getting 24 points on *PopMaster* to the soundtrack of an industrial saw, and the smell of offal.

It seems that every time I get involved in butchery of some sort, Radio 2 has got there first.

By the time the bullock is swung away to the cool room, he has already undergone the metamorphosis from sentient grazer of the moorland margins to provider of beef and all the nameless by-products we met that afternoon in Chichester at the very start of our story. Did I enjoy it? No, not really. Could I have done it myself? Probably not. Was it respectful? Yes. Not precious, but respectful. Was the welfare of the animal uppermost so long as it was alive? Yes, I believe that it was. To pretend that it worked out well for the Longhorn would be ridiculous, of course, but it looked to be as good as it possibly could be. This, after all, is the reality of the meat-eater's world. Without the process of death, there can be no meat. And without complexity, there can be no honesty. During my travels, more than a few people on both sides of the argument suggested that the price for a life of meat-eating should be a couple of hours in a slaughterhouse at the gateway to adulthood. I get that now. If nothing else, we would understand the magnitude of what we are doing when we next order a steak.

As for the hide, they can't tell me where it will be sent, but we all agree that my belt is a very beautiful one.

An afterthought.

A few weeks later, along with a group of Cotswold farmers, I am standing inside Britain's first mobile abattoir. (You probably think I am going on about small abattoirs too much, but it is hard to exaggerate the de-democratising effect that their closure has on our food systems, and on the animals that have to travel further and further to get to them.)

Fitting on the back of a truck, it is no more than an ultra-high-tech shipping container, and yet also a possible genius solution to the not-so-gradual closing down of our network of small slaughterhouses. A ramp leads up to the stun box, which is extended out through the side wall when needed, and from there the carcass proceeds through the various stages until it reaches the chiller room at the back, where it will hang until its temperature has descended to seven degrees Celsius. For larger animals such as cows, part of the roof extends upwards to give the necessary height for vertical hanging. A large Hereford bull went through the week it arrived, and the team are buzzing at the quality of the ultra-low-stress meat that followed. We stand in a circle in the farmyard after our walk-through and agree that it is brilliant. Agreeing that things are brilliant is not what farmers are famous for, so we breathe deep of the air and appreciate the moment.

'Now we need to try to put together clusters of small farmers', explains Jane Parker, who has driven the experiment, and on whose farm it is now sitting. 'And then move it around the locality to support them. We think it will do about fifteen cows in a day, or maybe 25 sheep, so it is perfect for the small-scale farmers who are most affected by the lack of abattoirs.' It is a magnificently simple scheme, and self-evidently what the industry needs.

But first it has to achieve licensing from the Food Standards Agency (FSA) and jump the various hurdles that Defra will throw in its way.

'The individuals are fine', says Jane, 'and even the ministers are supportive.' But with competing divisions and bad communication, the bottomless 'blob' of the civil service constantly finds reasons for delay and objection. The problem, as always, is the regulatory landscape.

The project has been 40% funded by Defra, so it is an exquisitely ironic thought that it is Defra rules which are, for the time being, stopping it happening. A particularly daft one, if you like daft regulations, is the requirement to cover the holding area with something rainproof so that a cow, which has probably been in a rainy field for 50% of its life, doesn't get a bit damp before it gets killed. It is not totally surprising to learn that 59% of all small abattoirs in Britain expect to close their businesses within the next five years if nothing is done.[6] The day I was in the Cotswolds, news came through that another one, this time in Wales, would close its doors within a week.

'It will happen', says Jane, when I ask her if it will fully see the light of day, 'but the authorities will make us fight every inch of the way.'

In fairness, she could have been describing half a century of British agriculture.

⁓

On Monday, we take Prowler to his new home, looking clean, glossy and seemingly confident.

He is calm as we lead him through the crush, and calm as he walks up the straw-covered ramp into the trailer, as if he is looking dispassionately at a new adventure rather than facing the biggest upheaval of his young life. On the seat between John and me is a white A4 envelope containing the bureaucracy of a modern cow's existence: his cattle passport, pedigree, organic standards certificate, declaration of health, his recent TB clearance certificate and, of course, an invoice. For his first eight months, he was allowed to be a child, racing around the pastures with other calves, or nuzzling up to his mother; since then, he has been one of the lads in a section of the main barn, letting his senses educate him into the world around him. From today, he has a man's job to do.

He has been chosen, among other attributes, for his small size, so that he can influence the South Devons that he will sire in that same direction. Beyond that, and the added marbling in those future cuts of beef, he will bring the unknown mysteries of hybrid vigour to his adopted herd.

We reverse into his new yard and exchange livestock gossip for a minute or two with the farm manager who is taking him on. Prowler's future home is organic, too, with all the animals born, reared, hung and butchered on the farm, and with nearly half the produce being sold through the little farm shop at the entrance. It is another enticing glimpse into a non-industrial world of less being more. The six documents are swapped for a cheque, which goes wordlessly back into the white envelope on the dashboard.

Driving back through the Hampshire lanes in a heavy rain shower, past lavender fields and then the beech hangers above Selborne, within whose shadowy contours Gilbert White hunted down his natural histories, I point out a field of lush grass that seems way more advanced than our lowland pastures a few miles to the south.

'Nitrates', says John. 'Can't use it when you're organic. You can always tell because the grass is so green that it almost has a blue tinge to it.'

I ask him if this matters.

'Not now', he says, as ever unwilling to criticise a fellow farmer. 'But grass generally finds you out in the end.'

'How so?' I ask.

'Long story', he says, after a pause. 'That would be a book in itself.'

But he never notices my new belt, which is a shame, as I purposely tucked my shirt in just so that he would.

13. GRASS-FED COW

Looking back to the future

....

*'A thing is right when it tends to preserve the
integrity, stability and beauty of the biotic
community. It is wrong when it tends otherwise.'*
ALDO LEOPOLD,
A SAND COUNTY ALMANAC

*'Mother Earth never attempts to farm without
livestock; she always raises mixed crops; great pains
are taken to preserve the soil and to prevent erosion;
the mixed vegetable and animal wastes are converted
to humus; there is no waste; the processes of growth
and the processes of decay balance one another; ample
provision is taken to maintain large reserves of fertility;
the greatest care is taken to store the rainfall.'*
SIR ALBERT HOWARD,
AN AGRICULTURAL TESTAMENT

....

Late spring remains cold. Summer is out there somewhere, but she is still concealing herself shyly behind the skirts of the north winds and late-season frosts. Swallows swoop down from the greyness to pick out the flies from around the fresh dung and, apart from the bulls waiting to go to their new homes, the barns are now silent and the farm is well into its new routine. Wherever we go, farmers look up to the sky and mention the weather.

Two weeks after taking our trip to Alton with Prowler, we drive Saturn to his new home with a herd of Sussex cattle some 40 miles away, where, in complete contrast, his role is actually to bulk them out. Through decreasing arteries of roads, lanes, tracks and, eventually, footpaths, we eventually clatter into a steep field containing high hedges and about twenty cows with that burnished dark red that signifies the Sussex breed.

'He'll like this', says John appreciatively, like a parent taking a child to a new school.

Saturn descends the ramp calmly, grazes for a second or two as if it was something he meant to do before leaving home, and then trots obligingly towards the cows, who happen also to be trotting obligingly towards him. And who wouldn't? He is in magnificent shape, here on his new Wealden farm in the wilds of Sussex. His job for the next few years will be to father the cows who will eventually be covered by the pure-bred Wagyu bull to produce the beef animals who, in turn, will grace the tables of fine diners and the kitchens of adventurous cooks.

Wagyu beef has become the beneficiary, or victim, of all the hyperbole that has built up around it, with stories of Mozart being played to the cattle, of giving them rice wine to drink and a diet of pulped olives. Generally, the more extreme stories – and all of those examples are true – refer to the highest-grade Kobe beef which can only be raised in one province in Japan. These days, far more Wagyu is raised outside Japan than in it, especially in Australia and the USA, and the slightly reduced intense marbling that comes from cross-breeding pure-bred bulls with local breeds gives a product that tends to gain in flavour from the grass what it loses in tenderness from slightly less fat. The really expensive stuff, like that £195 a kilo fillet in my local butcher, has been subjected to a harsh grading system, where to gain the coveted A5 status you need to achieve a very high score indeed on the Beef Marbling Standard (BMS) rating. In a western culture that usually prizes big steaks, the trick is to eat half, or less, of what you might normally choose, because an eight-ounce steak with the highest BMS rating of twelve will simply be too much for most human digestions. Like socialism, these days Wagyu beef is what you want it to be.

I buy a small steak at the farm shop, a Denver cut from around the shoulder, and jump back into the Land Rover, asking John what most impresses him about Saturn's new home. The owners' passion, I offer, the welfare, or the sustainable nature of the whole operation?

'The grass', he says after a pause, with the intensity of a pilgrim who has just arrived at the altar of Santiago de Compostela after a 500-mile pilgrimage. 'How in God's name did they pull that off?'

He is lost in his silent thoughts for a while and then, as we drop down the hill into Billingshurst a few minutes later, he adds: 'It's just magnificent.'

For cows, once upon a time it was all about grass. Grass, and the succulent leaves of hedges and low-hanging tree branches. Because the grass and the soil below it are such important components of the cow's history, and its future, it is grass that their lives revolve around.

And with 20% of the earth's vegetation accounted for by grass, you might think that it still should be. After all, at its most simplistic, the soil, the grass and the cow are simply the agents that convert sunshine into protein for us humans to consume, should we choose to. But millions of years of co-evolution between the grass and the cow have recently stuttered to a halt in the blink of an eye, and that has changed everything. We need to think about how this has happened, and why, and what it means.

From our innocent childhood images of Daisy the cow wrapping her long tongue around the stems of a bunch of tall fescue or orchard-grass in the sunlit field, has sprung this new, sometimes dystopian offshoot, in which rainforests are torn down in Brazil so that farmers can grow soy to export to farms around the world and be fed to cattle that are not designed to eat it, so that they can grow quicker and provide a better return on capital employed. Or where subsidised and doctored corn is fed to crowded feedlot cattle to speed up the growth of those nicely marbled steaks, or those price-sensitive burgers, accompanied from time to time by a cocktail of growth hormones and non-therapeutic antibiotics. It's called 'finishing', and it's important because it is our current answer to that old question:

'How do we feed a growing number of people with the growing quantities of beef they want to eat?'*

Because so much of the future of the cow on our planet is wrapped up in how we provide a new answer to that question, we need first to understand a bit more about what grass is, and how this apparent flight away from it happened.

⸺

'Grass', wrote Graham Harvey in his authoritative 2002 book,[1] 'is a reminder that we have a history older than our lives.'

Along with the forests, the deserts and the tundra, grasslands make up one of our four principal terrestrial habitats. Comprising rather more than 10,000 species, they include all flowering plants with a single leaf, and our first records of their existence only go back to between 55 and 60 million years ago, some time after the disappearance of the last dinosaur.[2] Even cynodont, the direct ancestor of the modern cow that we met in Chapter 2, would have been entirely unfamiliar with grass. Without the bright colours of a flower, or deep and tempting

....

* To save a giant statistic-fest in the text, here are the headlines: 21% of all the world's beef is eaten in the USA, 14% in China, 13% in Brazil and 13% in the EU (USDA, 2018). In the last 50 years, global consumption of meat has trebled to 340 million tonnes (Our World in Data, 2019), with the USA topping per-capita annual consumption at 100 kg. In the same timescale, beef consumption has risen from 23.5 million tons in 1960 to 61.5 million tons in 2017 (USDA figures). The main driver of growth in beef consumption is China, which is increasing by 11% annually (Euromeat News item, April 2020). Consumption in the UK is slowly declining.

scents, grasses had to find a suite of different ways of extending their range.

Sometimes, they arrived on the hooves of the tarpans, primitive horses thundering across the land bridge from America to Siberia, and on into Europe, sometimes in the soles of the boots of the homesteaders working their way out west from New England. More typically, though, grasses tend to be wind-pollinated, to be tolerant of drought, and to have the ability to grow and thrive in the least hospitable areas including, most recently, industrial wastelands and the inner cities. Above all, they have been quicker than other plants to seize on any new opportunity and colonise the next place in line.

As with the cows and sheep, so with the grass: man has gradually domesticated it to his own advantage. But plants, contrary to what you may quite naturally think, are not developmentally stupid, and 'as far as they are concerned, we're just one of thousands of animal species that have unconsciously domesticated them'.[3]

In trying to conjure up what our ancient landscapes were actually like, we can often be tempted erroneously down either the 'Robin Hood' route (one big forest), or the 'Stonehenge' route (one big grassy plain). The truth is that no one knows. It was probably neither, and most likely a hotchpotch of scrubland, woods and clearings for meadows. The main architects of the landscape would not have been ploughs, house-builders, road-makers or drainage schemes, as they are now, but the megafauna browsers in the shape of wild or domesticated cattle that had gradually replaced the vast herds of reindeer and even bigger grazers which had earlier roamed the landscape.[4]

Beyond their efforts, the clearings would have been made by a mixture of storms, fires, beetle attacks, flash floods and landslides. To see what our land once looked like, you have to go to the villages of rural Romania, Hungary or Poland, where these ecosystems are still largely intact, or to a rewilded farm. But, even now, we still have about 12 million hectares of grassland left in the UK, and around two billion tons of carbon believed to be sequestered within it.

All grass has an intimate relationship with the soil below it, an exclusive trading partnership that enables each to thrive. Grass is the agent by which essential carbon is taken from the air and fixed into the ground below, and the tiny mycorrhizal fungal strands within the soil pass up the minerals that are essential to the growth of the grass above. Good soil, meaning the best soil that you can work towards in any given stretch of ground, is the very basis of the success of a farm; and the very best of it, we have learned over millennia, comes from the accumulated effects of mixed rotational farming. The good farmer is as attentive to the improvement of their soil as the butcher is to the sharpness of their knives, and the artist to the accuracy of their colour palette.

There is still a great deal about grass that we don't fully understand, but of one thing we can be sure: it has been our constant companion, carpet, larder, bed, playground and hiding place since our ancestor first climbed inquisitively down from their African tree around four million years ago to see what was going on in the surrounding area. Partners in the evolutionary process, grass has been good for us, and it is fair to say that we have been very, very good for grass. Like pigeons and rats, it has learned to enjoy our company. If you were to award a prize for the most influential plants in our history, it would be hard indeed not to give it to the grasses. And if grasses could award prizes for their most useful partner species, we would probably share it with the ruminants.

As the years went by, it wasn't just the farmers who depended on the bounty of grasses for their living. It was the drovers who walked the cattle from the furthest reaches of the kingdom to the southern markets, and the 'cloth makers, clothiers, butchers, shoe makers, saddle makers and workers in horn and bone',[5] the park keepers, the groundsmen and the gardeners. On its varied sward, we have played cricket, football, rugby, baseball, golf and a hundred other sports; we have played make-believe children's games, thrown sticks for the dog and made love. In our own gardens, we have mown it, weeded it, scarified it and occasionally despaired of it. But above all, it is where we have kept and fattened our livestock.

From the cow's point of view, the relationship is a simple one: she asks two things from the grass and the grass requires a couple in return. All that the cow needs is good grazing in the summer to add to anything that can be browsed from the hedgerows and trees, and enough grass left over to provide forage, in the form of silage and hay, for the winter months. The grass needs the cow's angular hooves to aerate the ground below it, trampling its seeds in at the same time, and for her urine and muck to fertilise the soil so that it can thrive on into the future. It helps that only a ruminant can eat grass. This symbiotic relationship, under normal circumstances, works really well. Think back to those 60 million bison on the American prairies in the mid-19th century, and you begin to grasp the ongoing strength of the ecosystem around them. They had an instinctive understanding of when the area they were on had given them enough grazing and, even more important, of when it would be ready to have them back again; just like you and me, grass needs to rest. Knowing that this interval would be shorter in the growing season and longer in the winter, because grass grows to the rhythms of an 'S'-shaped curve, the bison just left longer intervals the colder it got. The land always had enough grass for the bison, and the bison always left it in a condition from which it could quickly regrow.

For centuries, diligent farmers have seen a large part of their job as getting the best they can out of the grass on their land. They have done this by using clover (a legume) within the grass to fix nitrogen into the soil, by spreading muck every now and again as nutrition, and adding lime to keep the pH level to its optimum. They have created herbal leys, a diverse mix of grasses, legumes and wild flowers, to improve the soil health and give the livestock and the forage minerals that they wouldn't get from the grass alone.

Man's recent relationship with grass has been rather more complex, as he has ramped up his appetite for meat beyond nature's capacity to satisfy it unaided. At its simplest, his job was originally to supervise the grazing interval well enough to allow for the grass's regeneration. This could be done from pasture to pasture every few days, or from the valleys to the uplands, seasonally, in a process called transhumance, which is still practised all over the Alps and Pyrenees, and which creates the sweetest butter at the top of the hill, while, at the bottom, hay can be grown and cut for the coming winter. But from the Middle Ages onwards, the farmer has been hell-bent on finding ways to get more out of grass than it is naturally and sustainably able to give. In pursuit of this, he has alternately drained it and flooded it, cropped it to the quick and let it grow and, above all, dumped stuff on it. From potash to guano, from manure to nitrates and a rich list of modern chemicals, he has often been guided by the idea that science, rather than nature, holds the answers. In return, he has kept coming up against the annoying discovery that, in nature, short-term gains generally carry long-term costs.

It's easy to be harshly critical, and we shouldn't; the reality is one of hard graft and lengthy agricultural recessions, in which it is entirely natural to look to innovation to turn things around. Or it is if you are getting it right. High on the chalky South Downs, during a long, cold spring drought, it is hard not to sympathise with a farmer, for example, who is juggling the meagre pickings of one 40-acre field with the equally meagre one next door from which he has to extract a crop of hay before he lets the cattle back on. You can talk of protecting mycorrhizal networks all you like, but if that is all he has got, it is all he has got.

Sometimes it doesn't matter. If animals aren't involved, for example on the 18th green at St Andrews, or at Lord's Cricket Ground, or the lawn in your back garden, there is always a new grass type – and a non-organic treatment for it – to create the perfect effect. But with herbivores, like those bison on the South Dakota plains, it is not so easy, because they and the grass they feed on are just two pieces of a giant and self-regulating ecosystem. Having initially stared out at the rolling westward grasslands and pronounced them a 'desert', the American settlers then quickly did the two worst things that they possibly could: they killed the bison and they tilled the soil. At one stroke, they had broken the magic circle, and it was then only a matter of time before the Dust Bowl of the early 1930s stripped trillions of tons of now unstable topsoil away and rendered 35 million acres of prime farmland unusable. *The Grapes of Wrath* had its seeds in a fundamental misunderstanding, a generation before, of the generosity of nature, and of what lay under the ground.

'The old prairie', said Aldo Leopold, one of the fathers of modern ecology, in 1947, 'lived by the diversity of its plants and animals, all of which were useful because the sum total of their co-operations and competitions achieved continuity. But the wheat farmer was a builder of categories; to him only wheat and oxen were useful. He saw the useless pigeons settle in clouds on his wheat and shortly cleared the skies of them. He saw the chinch bugs take over the stealing job, and fumed because here was a useless thing too small to kill. He failed to see the downward wash of over-wheated loam, laid bare in spring against the pelting rains.'

Because it has evolved to be eaten, the new growth of grass takes place just above the ground, as opposed to most vegetation, where it takes place at the tips. But underneath the ground is where 90% of the activity takes place, and, because it mirrors what is going on up above, if it is overgrazed above, it will be stunted and compacted below. Conversely, if it is alternately grazed and rested to the right interval, being naturally fertilised by the grazer, the roots get longer and stronger which, in turn, helps the grass resist drought and flood long after neighbouring plants have dried up, or been washed away.

An average bit of grass needs to seed itself by mid-summer, and most of what it does is in support of that. What the pioneer farmers of the prairies didn't realise was that, by tilling the soil, they were breaking the strength of the root system that kept the grass – and the topsoil – in place, and 'depriving the prairie of its immortal ally, fire'.[6]* More than that, they were breaking the tiny mycorrhizal networks that were such a vital part of the transfer of nutrients and carbon below the surface. And by killing the bison, they took away the only hope of sustainable regrowth. It turned out that the thick and deep thatch of roots below the grass was, and still is, the stable cornerstone of the land, living in perfect partnership with its grazer-in-chief, something to consider the next time you see a tractor ploughing up a piece of grassland. Especially when you notice that, in many places, there aren't a whole load of gulls following it any more. Gulls follow ploughs because the turned earth exposes a feast of worms for them; when the worms go, so do they. Like all new doctrines, 'minimum till' and 'no till' management seems at times to be a quasi-religion, although most farmers I speak to believe that occasional ploughing can still have its place.

I ask Jonathan Brunyee, head of sustainable farming at FarmED, a not-for-profit agroecological learning farm in the

---

* Fire increases soil fertility by providing valuable nutrients, and it helps to control disease and the numbers of damaging insects.

Cotswolds, what he makes of the current debate. 'We must move to longer and more diverse rotations', he says, 'and minimise soil disturbance. But soil with a healthy structure and good organic matter can cope well with occasional tillage, especially with a shallow plough.' He goes on to explain that the only other reliable method of creating a good seed-bed when going from deep-rooting herbal ley to, say, wheat, is to use the weedkiller glyphosate, which many regenerative farmers would prefer not to. He predicts that there will come a time when the use of laser weeders will allow us to move to a 'no till and no herbicide system', but we are some way off from that. So, for now, the answer will tend to be site-specific, and the key is, as with most new ideas, simply to be wary of the evangelists.

'Although the modern cattle industry all but ignores it', wrote Michael Pollan, in an important article in the *New York Times* in 2002,[7] in which he describes the journey of his own personal cow through the feedlot finishing system, and which sums up much of what we have encountered here, 'the reciprocal relationship between cows and grass is one of nature's underappreciated wonders. For the grasses, the cow maintains their habitat by preventing trees and shrubs from gaining a foothold; the animal also spreads grass seed, planting it with hooves and fertilising it. In exchange for these services, the grasses offer the ruminants a plentiful, exclusive meal. For cows, sheep and other grazers have the unique ability to convert grass – which single stomached creatures like us can't digest – into high quality protein.'

Two decades later, I ask Pollan how much he feels things have changed in America since he wrote that article: 'The system is pretty much unchanged', he replies. 'Still based on corn and pharmaceuticals, I'm afraid.' Where he finds some cause for new optimism, though, is in the small but vibrant network of grass-based beef-raising, which he sees as driven by 'repulsion at the industrial feedlot system and the potential of rotational grazing to sequester carbon'. Hold both those thoughts, as we dig a little deeper into the importance of grass to our story; both may well be central to the cow's future on our planet.

Back in Britain, starting in 1945 with a government that was understandably determined to achieve some sort of food independence after the very real starvation fears of wartime, and going all the way through to the catastrophic European Common Agricultural Policy (CAP), successive farming policies led to just one dominant feature: wheat fields, stretching from horizon to horizon, where once there had been meadows, herbal leys and hedgerows. And chemicals where there had once been hooves, muck and rain. To an extent that our grandparents could never have imagined, mixed farming had given way to monoculture. And the one truism that reappeared time after time, was that the more chemical fertiliser you threw at your land, the lower would be your resulting species diversity. In other words, to maximise the single crop you were growing, whether it was wheat, sugar beet or anything else, you unwittingly ensured that the pyramid of life collapsed below it: from the tiny nematodes in the soil right up to the sparrowhawks that hunted the songbirds that hunted the insects that hunted the smaller insects that fed on them. The astounding thing is not so much that this is still happening, but that it is happening in full possession of the evidence, and in spite of the logic.

If people had listened to Charles Darwin in 1880,[8] rather than to the cacophony of new and exciting science, they might have spent the next 140 years looking at the grass above, and the soil and worms below, in a more holistic way, and disturbing and altering it as little as possible. Thriving soil has dozens of worms in each spade-full, but you won't find that quantity too often these days. Any vegetation, grass included, will struggle if the soil below it is diminished, and the sad fact is that years of ever-increasing quantities of agrochemicals of one sort or another have bleached the living soul of it away.

Just as retired farmer Robert Bridger had been warning all those months ago, it really is about the worms. As the country that invented organised conservation, and that has some of the world's best natural grass-growing and livestock-raising conditions, it's quite an achievement for the UK to come out as one of the most nature-depleted countries on earth 150 years after Darwin's insights, and for the way we farm to be leading the charge that got us there.[9]

But, as we will find out later, in among the carnage of industrial farming, if you cast the net wide enough there is quiet cause for optimism. By way of an example, there has recently been growing enthusiasm for 'regenerative agriculture', a simple and old-fashioned system whereby the soil is constantly improved by the application of five basic principles: not disturbing the soil, keeping the soil surface covered, keeping living roots in the soil, growing a diverse range of crops, and bringing grazing animals back to the land.[10] As with the organic movement years ago, a few farmers talk the talk on this one without ever leaving the farmhouse kitchen, but I found far more who have passionately and diligently taken it on, and are seeing their land slowly become reborn.

Ever since Neolithic man first corralled an aurochs into a thorn shelter on some Mesopotamian hillside 10,000 years ago, supplementary winter feeding has been an issue he has had to tackle. After all, once you stop a highly mobile mob-grazer from moving freely, its instinctive ability to feed itself is clearly going to be diminished, and even prevented.

Grass is seasonal and, once it recedes, it is not as simple as going over the next hill to find some more. As we saw earlier, we need to get away from the idea that the world of the early cattle was one of either rolling grassland or deep forests. The closest we have got, in Britain at least, to recreating the kind of landscapes in which they would probably have been wandering, is Knepp in West Sussex, where nature has been largely left to get on with it for two decades now, in a celebrated exercise in rewilding. Experience there suggests that, in common with the other grazers (pigs and deer), the cattle naturally police the vegetation into a thick scrubland, with occasional trees fighting their way through the years of constant browsing to reach the sky. If you go there, you will find a hidden world of short view lines, open glades and abundant bird and insect life, not wildflower meadows or prairies. In the long history of the cow, the sight of a static chewer of the cud in a large, fenced field is a very new one indeed.

Hay has been around as the principal solution to the problem of winter feed at least since Roman times. 'Only then shall we turn it', wrote the agriculturalist Columella around 60 CE, in recognition of the eternal problem of rain at the wrong time,[11] 'and, when it is dry both sides, we shall bring it together in windrows and bind it up in bundles. And, above all, we shall lose no time in putting it under cover.' Silage (grass cut earlier than hay and then preserved through fermentation) seems to have first appeared in areas of Germany in the late 19th century; more nutritious than hay, and less affected by the vagaries of the weather, it is now an essential weapon in the farmer's armoury, and good for everyone who doesn't happen to be a hare, a field mouse, or a ground-nesting bird. If hay is grass minus water, then silage is fresher grass minus oxygen. On most traditional cattle farms, winter feed is a judicious mix of hay and silage (or haylage, a midway point between the two) bound by the hope that stores of both last until the grass in the meadows is once again ready to receive the cows.

As the demand for beef and dairy products grew, so too did the pressure on farmers to speed up the process and to tinker with the desired end result, such as achieving marbling from a breed whose beef didn't marble naturally, or increasing the yield of milk. This led to the practice of providing cereal-based and other supplements for the herds which, slightly depending on the local geography and background, might be wheat, barley, alfalfa or oily residues from sorghum, oilseed or molasses. So far, so innocent: wheat and barley are types of grass, and alfalfa a member of the pea family (like clover) with which the cow's digestion would be very familiar. The problem, if that is what we accept it is, arises when they are fed maize* (a grain) and soy (which is little more than a protein supplement). The reason why this is important is that a high percentage of what is fed to cattle in finishing feedlots, particularly in the USA, is maize, which is not a natural part of their diet and carries with it a much increased risk of medical problems such as sub-acute acidosis, bloating, gas, liver abscesses, urinary stones and E. coli. Add to this the prevalence of 'placement' antibiotics, which are simply an automatic privilege of arrival in a crowded feedlot, and the inevitable downstream resistance to new ones, and the beef on your plate starts to have rather less to do with natural grass than you might have hoped.

Nowhere on earth is the long-term effect of getting grass management wrong more in evidence than the 7,000-square-mile 'dead zone' where the Mississippi River runs into the Gulf of Mexico. That is where all the fertiliser and concentrated animal waste from the upriver farms in states like Minnesota, Iowa, Illinois and Wisconsin, some of which are 2,000 miles away, are aggregated in a giant, oxygen-starved algal bloom that is easily visible from space.

What feeding maize and soy does to the cow is one thing; what it does to us is quite another. For a start, it sharply alters the balance in the beef, or the milk, of Omega fats, from Omega-3, which is mainly found in green plants and leaves, in favour of Omega-6, which is found in seeds. So what, you might ask? Well, possibly so quite a lot, like the propensity of too much Omega-6 helping to cause heart disease, high blood

---

* 'Corn' in the US and Australia.

pressure, water retention and obesity. Two million years of high levels of Omega-3 from grass-fed animals seems to have suited our species well, at least if you managed to dodge the war, slaughter and famines that travelled alongside our early years. 'You are what you eat, eats', says university lecturer Gillian Butler, repeating the old dietary saw; 'and the split of Omega-3 to -6 these days has skewed heavily in favour of the latter, which is not good.'

There is one more thing to briefly mention, before we leave the feedlot, and that is the doleful connection between the industrialisation of our beef and the disempowerment of smaller farmers.

Nothing in this game is easy but, as we saw in Chapter 9, reducing the number of cattle on earth to the amount that their natural food systems can more or less support appears to have strongly positive arguments for both the cow and its keeper.

A few months before our trip with Saturn, with nature still hunkered down in shades of grey in the cracks of trees and folds of hedges, we start halter-training four young bulls in the bitter cold of the low February sun.

From the four bulls, two will be chosen to go off to a stud farm in Devon where, at £8 a shot, a straw of their semen will be regularly sent off to artificially inseminate some favoured cow. Preparing them to walk peacefully on the halter is part of the deal. Five years, and a thousand or so shots later, the bull will come back, his job done, though probably only for the briefest of stays before entering the food chain. One glance over them, even to an inexperienced eye like mine, is enough to show young animals at the very peak of condition and ambition. If you can really glow with health, then they do. But then, the road ahead of them doesn't look as bleak as all that, if you think about it.

The great thing about halter-training for the casual farm labourer is that it is, by its very nature, sedate and calm, with plenty of pauses and gaps for staring out at the view, eating chocolate or asking questions. Plenty of work on the farm is hard, but this is low-key enough to count as pleasure.

'Do you make an annual grazing plan?' I ask, during a comfortable pause. I have been reading a good deal about theoretical grass management, and I want to learn a bit more about how it is actually done on our own organic fields.

John looks up with the air of a patient teacher who has just been asked, towards the end of a long school day, where babies come from, or how many people James Bond killed in his career.* In gaps like these, he generally prefers to talk about cricket, light aircraft, or the birds flying across his farm.

'Of course', he says. 'Though possibly not exactly like in one of the textbooks.'

'I've got a theory about all this grass business', says Emma, who has overheard the conversation. 'The industrial revolution and mechanisation made it much easier to grow crops for cattle. Prior to that, animals were selected to thrive simply off what

---

* 611 after the first 25 films is the answer, according to Screenrant.com. *Goldeneye* leads with 47.

was around them, however meagre, and only what didn't make the grade for humans got fed to the animals. Suddenly, things were different, and it was possible to finish cattle quicker with cereals and the like that were specially grown for them. And when it was possible, it became desirable, and then unavoidable. From that point on, the whole process got sped up. And more and more land got given over to growing food for livestock, and not humans.'

'We've got 27 fields', says John, explaining why a grazing plan isn't entirely straightforward. 'Not only is each farm different, but each field within the farm is different, and, often, each corner of a field is subtly different from the others. Damp corners, different soil structure, sunshine and shadow, you know, that sort of thing. Added to that, fields can go wrong. Too acidic in this one, which then needs lime, or too mossy in that, which needs harrowing. But year by year, we have come to learn roughly what we have got, or what we are likely to have got, and then we apply certain principles. Number one is that we are organic and can't use synthetic fertilisers. Number two is that we never cut the same field in successive years. Number three is that we rest a field for at least six weeks after the cattle have been on it.'

'Number four', adds Emma, 'we let the sheep tidy it all up over the course of the winter.' I tell her that I rather like the idea of sheep as housekeepers.

We break off to release the fourth bull, Seneca, out of the crush to join his comrades in the yard, and watch him buck and run in his annoyance at the new halter around his head. At one point, he stands on the end of the rope, unable to work out how he has hobbled himself so completely, like a politician being interviewed about his extra-curricular sex life.

'Of the 27 fields, in high summer, we might at any one time have eight with stock on, eight growing grass for hay or silage and eight closed off and simply growing. Principle five', John adds, 'is that grass needs time to recover.'

A farmer has to be a mathematician as well as all the other things. Knowing the total number of bales of silage and hay that he needs for winter forage, and knowing that 30 acres of grass might give him 200 large bales of hay, he is able to do a rudimentary calculation of what space has to be allocated to what activity, and for how long. Understanding this equation generally dictates the size of your herd; getting it right or wrong can be the difference between profit and loss after a long, cold winter. At the end of the day, the grazing plan is the farmer's best guess around a number of principles, and then countless variables. As General Eisenhower pointed out in a rather different context: 'In preparing for battle, I have always found that plans are useless, but that planning is indispensable.'

I will ask the same question of many other farmers over the months and, as with John and Emma, all grazing plans have to be rooted in the reality of the different bits of land you have – high or low, dry or damp, sand or clay – and then adapted to the changing circumstances of weather and events.

'Long ago, when we were a mixed farm, we would also have something like oats – arable – as a fourth category, but not any longer', Emma says.

A decade before, they had foraged the cows on turnips but had sworn never to do it again, as the sodden ground had taken five years to recover from the mauling that the cows had given it when they were let loose on it.

'Three eights are 24', I point out, rather pleased that I have spotted an anomaly in their division of the fields, but not wanting to look like a smart-arse. 'What about the other three?'

John smiles. 'We won't be the only farm in the world that has a couple of fields that you just can't include in any strategy. Too small, too wet or just too ...' He looks around for inspiration, but doesn't find it. 'There are some things that you just can't plan for.'

A few days later, the big news on the farm is that 1025 has achieved a dramatic change in his fortunes. Impressed with photographs of his stocky good looks and his temperament, a breeder of Ruby Red Devons in Somerset has bought him to inject hybrid vigour into his herd. The identifying number, simply a reflection of the lottery of ear-tag distribution, is now a thing of the past, and the beast will leave the farm next week under the proud name of 'Hawkley Red Falcon'. He is now a bull with much to do, and much responsibility ahead of him. For John, this sale means rather more than double the payment that he would get if 1025 had gone into the food chain; for Hawkley Red Falcon himself, it represents that all-important left turn onto the wider road system, rather than a right turn to the A3 and Guildford abattoir, and the Sainsbury's meat counter that beckons from the city beyond.

I am quietly delighted.

14. RESURGENT COW

June

....
*'Plans to protect air and water, wilderness and
wildlife, are in fact plans to protect man.'*
STEWART L. UDALL, US POLITICIAN
....

Following the drought of spring, we have a summer of unremitting rain. Of course we do. That's how farming works.

The corners and gateways of some of the lower-lying fields are quagmires, as we take two young conservation farmers who have come up from the West Country to see the bulls that we have not yet sold. John is ever-wary of little mineral deficiencies creeping up in the animals in conditions like this, and he keeps bags of organic seaweed supplements in the back of the Land Rover just in case. Copper is the one he is concerned about today, but we have dealt with this long before the prospective buyers arrive in the farmyard. The sky is blue for a change, but the sagging elderflowers and flattened chicory tell their own story. Even the dog roses drip. It has been a good spring for ducks, but not much else.

In a way, what follows is a game. John may well have already sold thirteen of the twenty bulls he wants to, but the remainder are good too, and he has a list of people who would probably like to buy them if today's visitors don't. Equally, he likes what these two are trying to do, and I suspect that they know he would be happy to see his bulls on their farm.

'I tend not to haggle', he says to me as an aside. 'They already know what I sell them for; the key is that they get the animals they want. In this case, ones to go to work on their South Devons.'

When we reach the seven young bulls, our visitors are blown away by their calmness.

'Sheeee-it!' says the American, almost under his breath. 'Four of us march into their field, and they don't even bat an eyelid.' They don't. Actually, they look rather bored, like parents at a bad school play.

Their preparation work is good. They have printed off our sheets from the Red Angus Society, and understand exactly what breeding inputs they are looking for, gradually narrowing it down from seven to six (one is too big), to five (one too dark), to four (one a bit 'lively') and finally to three ('a bit closely related to one we've already got'). We get the sense that they want one or two out of numbers 29, 33 and 39 and I can see what they are after. I may not be a stockman, but I've spent enough of the last year discussing the finer points and details of their excellence.

'He'd be nice on the Devons', says the other farmer, of 39. 'Who's the sire?'

'Tiger', replies John without needing to look it up. I find those two syllables reassuring, like someone confirming the wine you are drinking is from a great grower.

'So you had twenty', says the West Country man, smiling faintly. 'You've sold thirteen of them. We don't want the fourteenth. So what's the price for your fifteenth best bull?'

It's a great negotiating line, but all four of us know that it will change precisely nothing. Number 39 will be heading west. And, on this farm, at least, the price is the price.

For now, Anguses like ours, red or otherwise, represent a growing proportion of the British beef industry, accounting for just under one in five of its cattle numbers.[1] Sometimes, as I was about to find out, there is only a very small gap between a thriving breed, and one declining towards extinction.

⎯

'They were simply outclassed by single-purpose breeds', Adam Henson said, as we leaned over a small fence and looked at a pair of Albion cattle. 'And then one day, they were declared extinct.'

Rare breeds run in the Henson blood and have done since the early 1970s, probably a long time before that. 'Simply outclassed by single-purpose breeds' is an epitaph that could be inscribed on the many cattle strains that have gone extinct since Robert Bakewell created the Beef Shorthorn, and it lay behind the long march to a dystopian two-cow future that mercifully never quite happened. Since 1973, when Adam's father, Joe, established his rare breeds farm, followed later by the Rare Breeds Survival Trust, not one breed of cow, sheep, pig, goat or fowl has gone extinct.

As it turned out, those Albions were never quite extinct. Originally a cross between the hardy Welsh Black and the White Dairy Shorthorn, it turned out that there was a man in Cheshire still milking a small herd, and then a few herd records that pointed to others meant that Adam's father was able to get his hands on some, and begin the long process of rebuilding the breed. Cream in colour with what look like faint blue ink stains as a background pattern, they are the living proof that nothing is gone until it is, actually, gone.

'But what really kicked the whole thing off, though', Adam says as we walk up to a different part of his Cotswold rare breeds farm, 'are these guys.'

These were the first White Park cattle that I had ever knowingly seen. An understated but elemental direct link back to the aurochs, they have tramped the woods and parks (hence the name) of England for over 2,000 years. Previously thought to have been brought over by the Romans as a suitable sacrificial offering to the gods of their occupation, they probably actually made it over when there was still a land bridge to Europe, and eventually evolved to be prey animals in the big hunting estates.[2] Not for the wolves and bears that were still out there, but for the local nobility, who chased them down among the forest rides. When the hunting stopped, and the parks fell into decline, so too did the breed. A foot and mouth epidemic in the 1960s wrought further damage on an already fragile population and, for a time, it was almost as if no one could think of a good enough reason to save them. This was just another breed that had been 'outclassed' by its commercial rivals, of no visible use in the brave new world of post-war food production. They were simply a metaphor for all the other livestock breeds that found themselves no longer relevant in the new age of agriculture. To see them on that pasture in the Cotswolds was to see something that was as far away from the vast milk machines that Holstein-Friesians have become as we ourselves are from the ancient Britons. It was a glimpse of a compressed version of part of our island history, and it is not for nothing that the cattle are rented out to add authenticity to period dramas.

Any creature under threat needs an evangelist to speak for it, and in Henson the cows have one of rare persuasive eloquence – rare energy, too. It also helps if you are on prime-time TV (BBC *Countryfile* in Adam's case). The real mission of someone's work is often only slowly revealed and his, I sense, goes beyond the animals to the thousands of children in primary schools who never get to make the connection between what they eat and its origins.

'I went to a school up in Birmingham last year', he explains, 'and most of the kids in the class I spoke to had never seen a sheep. They actually put on extra staff for the day as, in the words of the head teacher, they expected some kind of riot.' But it would always be a 'good riot', he adds of the overwhelming noisy positivity that only a child of a certain age can create.

'So, as much as anything', he says, 'that tiny win is what this is all about.'

I was slightly intoxicated by my encounter with the White Parks, and as we made our way back to the car, I told Adam so.

'You're not the first, and you won't be the last', he said. 'The White Parks have split into a number of localised groups, so you really ought to go up to Chillingham to see the properly wild ones.'

On a warm day in the summer of 1972, the last two Lincolnshire curly-coated pigs on earth made their sad way into the local abattoir, so bringing to an end the 170-year history of that particular breed. That this is, half a century later, still the last British livestock breed to pass into oblivion is due, more than anything else, to the work of the Rare Breeds Survival Trust (RBST).

Cattle breeds, as we have seen, had developed and multiplied over the centuries as a result of a mix of factors, such as ecological and geographical conditions, but also prevailing human needs of the time, such as an increasingly urban lifestyle.[3] Between 1900 and 1973, many breeds of British cattle had disappeared, and others were heading for the same fate, from those Albions and White Parks to Belted Galloways and Dexters and many more. But it was the Old Gloucesters from Joe Henson's own patch that really provided the stimulus to formalise the conservation of the country's native breeds into something a bit less haphazard than mere luck. The Gloucester was the same type of cow as Blossom, who had provided the first smallpox vaccine, and had already been brought close to extinction once by the huge rinderpest outbreak of 1847. Breed societies had existed for many years, and efforts had been made to preserve struggling breeds for a century and a half, but in the act of Joe Henson seeking out and rounding up the last of those Gloucesters, the first protections had been laid down against the long tide of disappearances. Since then, the Trust has been at the forefront of a movement that is actively rolling back the decline of cattle, sheep, goats, pigs and poultry.

'We absolutely don't want to be seen like stamp collectors', says chief executive Christopher Price, pointing out the obvious dangers of saving things just because it feels good emotionally. 'The whole reason that we have been able to be as effective as we have is that just about all these breeds have a strong agricultural use today.' He points out that we are only just starting to realise again the benefits of breeds that are naturally hardy and thrifty, animals that are bred for the landscape they are in, that tend not to rack up high medical bills, but instead live a high-welfare and predominantly outdoor existence. 'At a time when farming is moving away from subsidies and into a more conservation-based approach, what could make more sense than a robust animal grazing its way across its own natural territory?' Price talks of a 'strong sense of place', which I like.

As I had discovered all those months ago on Mary Quicke's Devon pasture, the growth of the artisan food movement, and particularly its retail end, is helping to create demand that enables mainly traditional livestock farmers to supply a highly modern and growing market, and to give those old breeds a commercial, and therefore sustainable, reason for survival. Far from being a museum of nostalgia, a significant number of consumers really appreciate this meat, and will pay the farmer well for it, particularly so in the absence of a vast, insatiable middle man. Without this ready market, the RBST's work would be close to pointless.

'The supermarkets have made occasional efforts to get involved, too', continues Price, when I ask him, 'but the realities of the small-scale nature of the business, and the difficulty of supplying the quantity they need with the consistency that they need, means that it hasn't really worked yet.'

Any thought that the RBST might be little more than a sophisticated petting farm in honour of old livestock dies in front of the cutting-edge work of their gene bank. As an insurance policy against further decline and disease outbreak, the gene bank not only collects, stores and distributes semen from rare breeds but, since 2015, has been doing the same with embryos as well. This safeguards future populations, ensures future genetic diversity, and will eventually enable new and appropriate breeding lines to be established. The conservation of local breeds, 'the ultimate ecosystem service providers', as RBST describes them, can play a vital part in regeneration of rural areas, both economically and in terms of agro-biodiversity, but only if the government supports it. 'When we try to pick out anything by itself', as 19th-century naturalist John Muir said, 'we find it hitched to everything else in the universe', and there is precious little point in raising small regional cattle herds if, for instance, all but the biggest abattoirs have closed down. And lest we forget, these breeds also have a role to play in our cultural life, in our national identity and our heritage.

For a second, I find myself wondering two things. When does a rare breed stop being rare, and what constitutes extinction? I mean, real extinction, like the kind that hit the aurochs, or the Alderney. After all, our cattle story has always been one of adjustment and evolution, of ups and downs, and it is hardly surprising that some are better at it than others.

For the first question, it is relatively straightforward. Breeds like the Belted Galloway and the little Dexter have moved out of the 'rare' category altogether, and are now a common sight all over the British Isles, and not just in their original ranges. It turns out that their ability to make something of nothing on the roughest of ground suits farmers, butchers and conservation bodies alike. Others remain in some sort of peril, six in the 'priority' group, including the Chillingham wild cattle and the Albions, and eight 'at risk'.* 'It's not a question of absolute numbers any more', says Price when I ask him where the various lines are drawn, 'but of general vulnerability to inbreeding, say, or to a disaster like another outbreak of foot and mouth.' Compare and contrast the Friesian (around two million head in the UK)[4] with the Vaynol, a single-location Welsh variant of the White Park, with just eight breeding females in existence in 2019.[5]

Back in 2001, when the foot and mouth epidemic was sweeping its way across the north, with the dark threat of contiguous culls, there was a real chance that the Chillingham herd would be drawn in, and that 700 years of isolation would be brought to a poignant full stop in the smoke of a hurried

....

* Priority list: Albion, Chillingham wild cattle, Dairy Shorthorn,* Gloucester, Northern Dairy Shorthorn, Vaynol. At risk list: British White, Irish Moiled, Lincoln Red,* native Aberdeen Angus, Shetland, traditional Hereford, White Park, Whitebred Shorthorn (* = original population). Beyond this, there are another 21 UK native breeds.

funeral pyre. A nearby MP and enthusiast, Chris Mullins,* successfully lobbied the then Agriculture Secretary to make the herd an exception to the cull, if one had been necessary, on the basis of its extraordinary importance and the fact that it was never intended for the food chain. In the event, the outbreak finally ground to a halt a few miles short, and the herd was saved. These days, a certain degree of rarity would probably excuse a cull in the first place.

The extinction question is a little more nuanced. In the 1920s and 30s when those enthusiastic Nazi Heck brothers were trying to breathe life into the aurochs by 'breeding back' as close as they could get to it, using what was around, to recreate a breed would have been impossible. Now, maybe not. But Christopher Price is adamant that a breed needs to stand on its own four feet to deserve to survive and that, by the same logic, a newly extinct breed should not be resuscitated, even if that were possible. He points out in passing that the UK is in a small minority when it religiously ignores its own livestock animals from biodiversity counts, so the government probably wouldn't notice if they went anyway.

Then there is ancient newness. Six hundred miles north of John's farm, amid the upswellings of the opposing tides on the southern fringes of the Orkney islands, a 'new' breed has arisen without anyone's help, or at least it has according to the *World Dictionary of Livestock*, from the small population of feral cattle on the island of Swona. The island was deserted by

* A trustee of the Chillingham Wild Cattle Association, Chris Mullins told me that he was very much not alone in his intercessions.

its last humans in 1974, leaving a herd of Shorthorn and Angus cows that now make their own breeding decisions, based on collective wisdom, and have 'reverted to an ancestral form after a return to ancestral living conditions'.[6] They graze as a herd, sometimes on seaweed when the winter pickings are scarce, and banish to distant parts of the island bulls that have been superseded. When approached, for example by a human, their instinctive behaviour is to stop grazing, group together and move away.[7] They are checked out once a year from a discreet distance by a visiting vet and, while they might look no more like an aurochs than they did on the day they were abandoned, they are slowly reabsorbing the hierarchies, breeding seasons and classic traits of genuinely wild animals. One of these is to crush underfoot the bones of their fallen comrades, the quicker, so it is thought, to get calcium back into the ground.

These days, the list of cattle breeds is far from static, and new ones are developed regularly. On the farm next door to John's, for example, there is a herd of Stabilisers, a result of composite breeding technology that has brought together four breeds* to 'improve the economic efficiency of suckler cows and the production of high eating quality beef from forage based systems'.[8] While they might not be for the pedigree purists, they have done well for their owners; if they hadn't, they would have come and gone with the autumn rain.

And still we seek out those elusive aurochs. In the depths of a research laboratory in the small Dutch university town of Wageningen, a major project has been under way since 2013

....

* Red Angus, Simmental, Gelbvieh and Hereford.

to do what the Heck brothers couldn't, and breed back to an animal as close to the aurochs as can be done, and then to introduce it in herds of up to 150 animals into a number of rewilded areas of Europe. In an optimistic exercise in which history and science appear to meet around the back, a relic of the distant past has been adjudged to be the supreme tool for a vision of the future.

A few weeks after my visit to Adam, I read that an Aberdeen Angus cow has given birth to a small white female Vaynol calf in Edinburgh, after IVF treatment, at a stroke adding a significant 12% extra to the minuscule breeding population.

Suddenly, the urge to go and see her distant relatives, those wild Chillingham cattle, is irresistible. Maybe they could help me understand where it all started, and hence where it might go.

Up in the very top right corner of England, hard by what is reputed to be the nation's most haunted castle, is where those Chillingham cattle are, and it is where they have been, in complete isolation, since before Charles I had his head removed. Tucked in their home in a wooded valley facing the Cheviot Hills to the west, they are not so much a rare breed as an utterly unique one – and a laser beam shone 500 years back into history. The Chillingham is a White Park cow contained in isolation inside 134 hectares, and one with an extraordinary story.*

....

* As recently as 1872, one was shot at the command of the then Earl of Tankerville, specifically so that it could be displayed in Oxford's Natural History Museum, where you may still find its skeleton.

In almost every detail, the park at Chillingham is a scene that our ancestors might have witnessed, while the Spanish Armada was battering its way through the western storms. These cattle were once regarded as 'super deer', to be eaten at feasts and to be the object of particularly thrilling woodland hunts.

The first thing that strikes you is the colour – 'whiteness among animals carries an aura of magic and mystery'[9] – and their small size. A bit closer to, and you notice their red ears and their horns. Although they originated from husbanded stock, these are cows as evolution intended, and not some Frankenstein creation that produces ten tons of milk a year, or a third of a ton of beef.* To see them on their mixed wood pasture is to return for a moment to how things might have looked in medieval times, admittedly with all the vulnerabilities and uncertainties that go with that. For this is no pastoral idyll. It is a hardscrabble fight for survival through each winter and each disease (they are unvaccinated), rather than the romanticised representations of Landseer, Bewick and Walter Scott. No bull is castrated and the cows calve all year round; fallen cows are buried where they lie, and never enter the food chain. The only thing that stops them being termed completely feral is the occasional hay they are fed in really rough weather. After the bitter winter of 1947, the herd was down to as few as eight cows and five bulls, returning to around 50 beasts for

* Their general mature weight is around 300–400 kg for the bull, and 280 kg for the cow, or around half the weight of current British beef breeds.

the rest of the century before accelerating to today's figure of about 120 once the sheep were cleared off their ground. Up to a quarter of the herd might still die in a tough winter, but that is a wastage rate that can generally be compensated for by the following year's calving.

'The bulls live about nine years, and the cows about twelve', says Ellie Waddington, the warden. We are standing in a small copse watching two bulls nearby edging into a fight. 'Our bulls are more like deer in that respect, constantly asserting them-selves for the right to father the next generation. It's why they don't last as long as the cows.' I ask her how it can be that the effects of cumulative in-breeding don't quickly close down such a small and isolated group.

'It probably should have done', she agrees. 'And in 95% of cases it would have done. But every now and again in nature, instead of the dangerous recessive genes getting more and more concentrated in the herd, it goes the other way, and they are eventually purged out. Which is what has happened here. There may have been some price to pay in fertility, say, but they are basically very healthy. And nature takes over, anyway; weak calves get rejected and die, so the herd is constantly strength-ened.' She explains that there is a small 'reserve' herd kept up in north-east Scotland as an insurance against disaster, and she reminds me of just how close those funeral pyres came in 2001. There's even a frozen herd, lying somewhere as sperm in cryogenic storage. For a moment, it strikes me as a quintes-sentially human achievement that the same species that has worked so tirelessly towards creating the vast meat and milk machines eating soy in feedlots and cavernous barns, has toiled equally hard over the centuries to protect this tiny herd in its original form.

And it matters, if only to remind ourselves from time to time how much we have changed things. Maybe the Chillingham white cows are simply the control species for our endless experimentation with cattle since the days of Robert Bakewell, allowing us to peep back outside the laboratory from time to time and see what it was we started with. Chillingham is clearly not, as is frequently and mistakenly claimed, a rewilding project; it is, instead, a minimally managed herd that gives us a first glimpse in this chapter of the important role of the grazing cow in the maintenance of 'species-rich semi-natural grasslands' and of the multiple conservation benefits that can flow from this free-ranging system.[10]

From our hillside vantage point, the Cheviot Hills lie blue in the morning sun, and the patchwork of forestry blocks, fields and oak woods paint the backdrop in 40 shades of green to the conch-like sound of the little bulls roaring. With such a story, and in such an environment, it is perhaps tempting to romanticise these animals like Sir Walter Scott did, even though to do so would miss the point. Instead, they can show us a way that cows could possibly be again, comfortable within an un-abused body, small enough to calve easily, healthy beyond the reach of the vicious circle of medication and antibiotics, and browsing the tree line as much as grazing the buttercup-laden pasture. Idealistic? Maybe. But at least it's an animal doing what it evolved to do, rather than ingesting an alien diet in an alien place.

We cross a little stream to escape the attentions of the herd's troublemaker, and scramble up to a vantage point behind its alders.

'This is what cows are supposed to be', says Ellie. 'No more or less than that. The cows have small udders, sufficient just for a calf, and you can always just about make out their ribcages. Females don't mount each other,* and there's a 50-50 split in the sexes of calves and bulls. It's a chance to observe un-manipulated herd behaviour.'

Wordlessly, we watch the nearest group grazing swiftly across the contour line of the hill below us.

'Just mimicking nature', we both offer, simultaneously.

Wild Chillingham cattle do not end up in the food chain them-selves, but the future of our rare breeds utterly depends on finding a reliable route to market. Eating a breed, ironically, is the surest way of saving it.

On a little rise above the M5 motorway near Cullompton in Devon, Pipers Farm is one of the modern retail businesses at the heart of this project, using the power of the internet to connect slow food to customers, wherever they may be. Breeds are chosen because they are deemed right, not because they are fashionable, and because they fatten on grass to the natural rhythm of the landscape on which they first evolved.

'We see ourselves as part of the dawn of a new digital rural revolution', says director Peter Greig, when I ask him where he

---

* A sex-drive thing that can indicate to the farmer that the one being mounted is ready for the bull.

draws the line of what they will stock. 'We work with about 40 producers, telling them what qualities we demand, but then giving them the certainty of a price that doesn't go up and down with the market, and a forecast of what we will take from them that goes out three years, in the case of the cattle.' From topside to turkey, goose to gammon, through cheese, bakery, preserves and pet food, they harness the power of an internet platform to create a virtual destination shop with masses of choice. The meat is not cheap, but then it's not designed to be an everyday purchase: a world that is going to need to learn to eat a lot less meat over the next decade might as well forage on the best and least damaging of it.

Back in the 1980s, when he first established the business, Greig had been transfixed by the difference in the cuts, and in the quality of displays, between butchers in France and in Britain. He spent a year on Dartmoor learning how to butcher in a new way, and then established a shop in a street in Exeter that was becoming well known for embryonic artisan food retail.

'Our most important objective', he says, 'was and is giving people pleasure and doing whatever it takes to improve eating quality. Years later, we do the same thing, but now we can also give that opportunity to multiple other farmers.' He talks about the community of their suppliers and how, when Covid first struck, the business became an agency of mutual support to anxious farmers, every bit as much as it was a route to market.

It hasn't all been easy, and it won't be in the future. Farming happens at the command of the seasons; people retire, fashions change and stuff happens. But the exciting thing to me is not just the choice that this kind of business gives to consumers, as this is a world already drowning in choice, so much as the fair and scalable route to a wider market that it presents to the smallest farmer and the oldest breed. Plus, the old argument about a farm shop in Barnstaple not being very useful to a tenant in Balham goes out of the window.

Out at the back, his own Ruby Red Devon cows quietly graze the side of the hill, much as their forerunners might have done in exactly the same place a thousand years ago.

Two days later, in the area of south-west Scotland that Patrick Laurie so beautifully described in his book, *Native*, I finally start to understand what should have been entirely obvious about rare breeds all along.

We are leaning over a fence on the edge of some Forestry Commission land, watching Patrick's little Riggit cattle making their easy way towards us across the confused tangle of bogs and rocks, in answer to his call. The Riggits are an archaic strain of Galloway cattle, identified by their small size and a white stripe running all the way down their spines, broadening at the back end. They are, according to the breed society's website, supreme 'conservation grazers that thrive in all conditions on unimproved pasture and in hill country'. Their thick dual coat, and their typical Galloway skill of finding a good living out of a few blades of grass and thin air, makes them eminently suitable for outwintering. In other words, you put them somewhere and they just get on with it. Low maintenance, low vets' bills and a first-class cut of beef at the end of it. Treated for the most part as a branch of the wider Galloway family, they are not technically a rare breed, and yet numbers insist that they are.

'Round here, it's a toss-up between cow and tree', Patrick explains, 'with the tree just about always winning.' He points out a recently cleared patch of forestry, and mentions an eye-watering profit that it earned for its landlord, in sharp contrast to what his ten cows could earn for him.

'If you're not very careful', he says, 'your local breed eventually just amounts to no more than a picture on an Emma Bridgewater mug, and some old black and white photos.' We mention an article that both of us noticed in the morning's news about the national Gloucester herd having halved from 54 to 27 in the last fourteen years.[11] 'But to let this happen disregards two really important things – the deep connection of specific breeds to the ground they were bred for, and the fact that the right cow on the right bit of hill is a public good.'

I ask him to explain.

'Take this patch', he continues. 'In about 1979, cattle were cleared off the land, ostensibly to protect the golden eagles nesting on Airie Hill. In a classic process of unintended consequences, the birdlife quickly started to disappear: first the golden plover, then the black grouse, then the curlew. Even the eagle population, in whose name the cattle were cleared in the first place, is a shadow of its former self, brought down by a lack of hares, rabbits and red grouse, all heavily depleted by the habitat degradation that follows the withdrawal of farm activity.'

'You see, the magic of the Riggits is that they will eat anything, even the invasive white *sliabh* grass, which no one else will. And by eating it, they keep everything else in balance.' It's a feature of the wider breed that has seen the Belted Galloway – the 'Oreo cow', as it is predictably known in the United States – become the grazer of choice in conservation areas all over Britain, as likely to be spotted in Dorking as in Dumfries. From tough grass to saplings and coppice shoots, a conservation cow is nature's heavy-duty lawnmower.

We look out at the approaching Riggits, bonny but deceptively tough with their little frames and woolly faces, noting that they don't so much walk through the landscape as float across it.

'Eventually, Scottish Natural Heritage saw the point and started to get the cattle back. But it's an agonisingly slow progress, which means the associated wildlife will return agonisingly slowly as well. But at least they're back.'

I think back to what Christopher Price had told me about all these old breeds having a reason to be where they are. Little Dexters for boggy ground, Red Devons for lowland heath and Sussex for chalky downland; for every little ecosystem, a perfect little grazer. Most recently, the National Trust moved cattle back onto the coastal sand dunes at Studland in Dorset for the first time in 90 years, a major part of the armoury in the fight to restore 7,000 hectares of the landscape to how it once was. Meanwhile, in the South Downs National Park, there is an ambitious plan, with the cow at its epicentre, to re-nature an extra 13,000 hectares of land over the next decade. It is what the great ecologist Dick Potts noted time and again, in country after country, with regard to another indicator species: remove the grazers, and you eventually say goodbye to the ground-nesting birds.[12]

In the right place, and at the right time, the right cow is the ultimate biodiversity engineer.

In this most de-natured of all developed countries, that is a very powerful public good, and perhaps this is one of those moments when the past and future, ancient and modern, have the opportunity to meet. Also, at a time when wholesale rewilding is at once popular and problematical, it is striking that these 'ecosystem service providers' can deal with and improve what is out there, just as it is.

PART 3

Tomorrow

15. A SINGLE ROUGH POPPY

August/September

....

'To achieve great things, two things are needed:
a plan, and not quite enough time'
LEONARD BERNSTEIN

'Everyone in the UK should have secure access to
nutritious, sustainable food they can afford, and
nobody should live in a state of household food
insecurity. Food banks and other forms of charitable
food provision should become unnecessary.'
HUNGRY FOR CHANGE, FABIAN SOCIETY REPORT
ON FOOD AND POVERTY, 2015

....

And then there were five.
 As with the British aristocracy, where the Duke of
Norfolk has ended up in Sussex, the Duke of Devonshire in
Derbyshire and the Duke of Sussex in California, so it is with

cows. Our Red Angus bulls from this season have spread far and wide, and not necessarily where you would think.

There's one in Hampshire making South Devons smaller, one in Kent making Sussexes bigger, and one in Derbyshire adding hybrid vigour to Simmentals. One has gone down to the West Country for AI duty, a couple to Dorset to bulk out some conservation grazers, and one we call Harvey will head only ten miles down the road to attend to some sturdy Galloways in the lee of the South Downs. We will keep just the one, and we have already sent the one with the wonky feet up the road to the market.

As my last week on the farm starts, we take the bulls out of their groups and return them to their reluctant bachelor lives. For a few days, we keep them in individual pens in one of the barns, until the urge to fight with each other is reduced.

'Bulls are like combines', says John with a slight shrug, as we move them slowly down towards Brickyard field. 'Bloody busy for a short bit of the year, and utterly useless for the rest of it.' Much like the drones in my beehives, in fact. In sharp contrast to how they were when we threw the doors open for them four months ago, they plod along cheerfully, like students moving between lectures, grazing absent-mindedly on tufts of grass and welcoming the opportunity to browse the overhanging oak and protruding field maple.

It is a day of movement, of glowering skies, purple-headed thistles and clouded heads of sodden yarrow wetting our trousers. This dampest of summers is a reminder, as if we needed one, of the promise of yet another of the evolving climate's unwelcome gifts. Inside the open-sided barn, the huge round bales of hay are safely stacked, thanks to a brief Atlantic high that sat over the Azores just long enough for the heat of the sun to count, and for the harvest to be taken. I tell John that I am struck by the size difference between a few cows in calf that we are moving to a new field and a new group.

'Yup', he agrees. 'And that's the plan. An old hand once said to me that the secret was to breed the qualities that you like the most, personally, but have enough variety to satisfy your customers' many different preferences as well.'

Tilly, the old matriarch, mother of Tiger and grandmother to a decade's-worth of descendants, sidles alongside me, stops and ejects a bounty of rich, runny shit, some of which splashes onto my boot. It is a little rite of passage.

I look down at my wellies and feel strangely at home, just as I am about to leave it. Quite suddenly, I feel an ache of nostalgia, and wonder where she goes from here.

Not Tilly, so much as all of them.

⌇

Where the cow goes from here is, of course, entirely up to us, but back to a field seems like a good start.

In a way, it's been up to us from the moment our ancestors first gathered those few scruffy ruminants in a thorny kraal 10,000 or so years ago, scratched their heads, and then started their Anthropocene gallop towards controlling everyone and everything. In comfort or in cruelty, the cow has become our servant species and, aside from the odd outlier like those Swona cattle, they no longer take their own decisions. Thus we are obliged to make those decisions as good as we possibly can.

Now that there are almost eight billion of us on this planet, or 8,000 times the number that were around when we first domesticated cattle, those decisions have become infinitely more complicated.

You could start by saying that much of what we have done over those last 10,000 years happens to have suited the cow rather well. As a prey animal, we have protected them for the course of their lives; as foragers, we often provide food for them; when they are lame, we cure them; and when we come to kill them, we have generally done so with less cruelty than their natural predators might have done. It's only with our exponentially growing population and its appetite that their de-naturing has become widespread. It's almost as if we got rid of rinderpest and then gave them factory farming in its place.

To the question, 'Do we really need cows any more?' I would, of course, say 'Of course'. Apart from anything, we have killed off just about every other large herbivore and ruminant, so with whose muck are we going to fertilise the land? Besides, it's like asking if we really need cars, or central heating, or fish and chips, in that we'd get by without them, but we'd have to uninvent them first. Cows, and the other ruminants, play a vital role in the evolution and maintenance of the world's eco-systems, bringing a wealth of ecological benefits in their wake; as we have seen, they have the capacity to convert the pasture, which is indigestible to humans and has no other use to us, into nutrient-rich meat and milk; and, for the two and a half million years we have been eating them, they have provided an array of health and developmental benefits to us, particularly in the area of our brains.* But they and their various breeds are also a deep-rooted part of our own culture and our human story – and, anyway, by and large they are nicer than us. Far from kicking them off the grassland, we should be getting them back out there, and quickly.

After that, it is all choices, and it starts with the kind of world we want to live in.

Maybe our start point should be a paper published in 2019 telling us that the cow is doomed, and is now experiencing what it calls its 'final disruption'.[1] Cheap protein technologies, it goes on, will inevitably lead to a situation where 'the current industrialised animal-agriculture model will be replaced by a food as software model, where foods are engineered by scientists at molecular level and uploaded to databases that can be accessed by food designers'. Demand for cow products will have reduced by 70% by 2030 and 90% by 2035, as we welcome in the second domestication of plants and animals, the first of which mastered macro-organisms and the current one of which masters micro-organisms. Get used to new terminology like 'precision fermentation' and 'high throughput screening'. At once vaguely utopian (with far lower emissions, vast tracts of land will be free to re-use) and creepily dystopian (ultra-processed food, computational biology and yet more powerful boardrooms), it is a compelling report that I feel overplays the

* It is generally thought to be the regular protein from a meat-eating diet that has contributed to our brain size, and therefore indirectly to our dominance over all other species.

inevitability. However, it at least sets the challenge: it is as much in the cows' interest to change as it is in ours.

We can't look at one animal in isolation because, if we do, we will just find that animal staring blankly back at us, like a small child in an empty room, waiting for an instruction. The cow is one indivisible piece in a giant jigsaw that contains all of us and every other plant and animal. So the first question is a general one: 'How much is finally enough?', in western lives that are mostly already groaning under the weight of choice. Will we go on believing that the unfettered market has the solution for everything, and that perpetual growth is the only answer? If we will, then it's easy; we just need to go on doing exactly as we have been doing for the last hundred years, finding ways of raising ever more cattle in ever faster timeframes, and consuming their produce with ever more commitment. After all, I am writing as if there is an underlying problem, and not everyone would agree. An institutional shareholder of a fast-food multinational would probably think I was talking gibberish, and be encouraging us to eat twice as much beef as we already do.

But let's say for a moment that I'm more right than wrong. Let's say that we want to keep our cows, but just half of them. If we halve their numbers, which obviously halves their emissions, we need to decide which half goes, and which half stays. Do we do it by country, making no allowance for where is a good place for cattle, and where isn't? Or do we just keep the ones in packed feedlots, and grow them on as quickly as we can, on the basis that they'll be cheap, and that some of the science says that their shorter lives will lead to lower emissions? Or do we work towards abandoning altogether a system where livestock are kept in unnatural conditions, fed on unnatural food and stuffed full of unnatural medications? In other words, do we start to move away from factory farming for ever, and feed them only on grass-based forage, and other stuff humans can't eat? I would say the latter, and not least because the land that currently grows feed for livestock can be returned to nature, or production for humans. Methane has become the totem pole around which activism has been tirelessly dancing for the last twenty years.* If that argument is to go on, then it needs to be in conjunction with the rest of the science, such as methane's relative lifespan compared to CO_2, its role in the natural cycle, and, of course, the wider effects of fossil fuels. How much more useful to actively support farmers in their own efforts to reduce the environmental impact of their livestock? The 'conspiracy' films doing the rounds tend to be bigger on scary sound bites[†] than hard fact, so it is as well for anyone genuinely interested in the consequences of meat to do a little of the homework themselves, and on both sides of the argument. How bad is it for a child to give up a lifetime of well-reared beef just because they have overheard some bad science?

....

* A metaphor that I stole from John Meadley, one of the founders of the Pasture Fed Livestock Association (PFLA), and a tireless source of advice and inspiration.

† The headline-grabbing statistic from *Cowspiracy*, for example, was that animal agriculture was responsible for 51% of greenhouse gas emissions. This was the finding of one extreme, non-peer-reviewed piece of research, and was quietly revised down to the UN FAO's 18% in a later tweet by the film-makers, by which time the truth hadn't even got its boots on.

Because biodiversity doesn't have an easily measurable financial value, it has been tempting until recently to think that its importance to the human race is in some way diminished. For over half a century before that, the hedges were ripped up and the fields became ever-larger wildlife deserts with ever-decreasing margins, until, in the end, a single kestrel became an event, and a cornflower a cause for celebration. In the last few decades, though, there has been a growing awareness of biodiversity loss as probably the greatest of all the threats to life on earth, and of the cow's central role in reversing it, if allowed. These days, on all but the most industrialised farming operations, species protection is starting to become part of the routine.

Whatever the evidence, and it is everywhere, the signs are not there yet that we fully understand the link between good food and good health, and that the less processed food is, the better for us it will always be. All major diets have benefits, just as all have associated costs, so the least we can do is to learn as much as we can, and try to be broadly tolerant of people who eat differently from us. And should our food be as cheap as it possibly can, or should we pay the real, unsubsidised price for it, and encourage its producers to find ways of making it ever better, and to become better rewarded in doing so? We need to give up for ever the idea that it is inevitable that the rich will always eat better, more nutritious food than the poor, just because that is how the law of the jungle works. Are we prepared for the imagination and effort that will be involved to abolish food poverty? The questions ripple out far beyond the pasture.

Cattle are looked after by farmers, and we need people to enjoy farming again, and to want to get into the profession. We therefore have to make it easier for new entrants to farming, particularly young ones, with trailers full of optimism and new thinking. Are we happy to see a profession that is ageing before our eyes, and consolidating into ever bigger units every time a farmer retires without a succession plan? As the old system of EU Common Agricultural Policy subsidies is replaced by hybrid schemes around the four nations of the United Kingdom, it is also probably worth remembering that farms are where our food comes from, and that 42% of all farms currently operate at a loss without direct payments.* And finally, do we want to go on isolating the profit from our food, ever further from its source and ever deeper into a few efficient and value-driven boardrooms? Or do we feel a nagging worry that having 90% of our food controlled by eight companies implies a certain vulnerability on our part, and only the faintest illusion of real choice?

With respect to all that went before in this book, let us say that we *would* like more of that choice and that we *would* like to strive for the highest-quality food possible, pay an honest price for it, be imaginative enough to at least try to make it available to everyone, and then all counterintuitively try to eat a bit less of it; furthermore, that we would like those cows that are left to be raised close to their natural state, eating largely grass and grass-related forage, leading largely unmedicated

----

* National Audit Office (NAO), 2019. You might add that 16% of farms lost money even *with* direct payments.

lives, crossing oceans as little as possible, enjoying high welfare, and helping to engineer the biodiversity around them.

This was not originally intended as an overtly political book, far from it. But, as Mary Quicke said to me on her Devon pasture, we ought to re-learn that buying food should be an intensely political action. It has only not been so since the rich west first started bursting out of its jeans at the rate of one extra inch on the waistline each decade,[2] and couldn't remember what being hungry was like – apart, of course, from the ones who had to face hunger every day. The cow is food, so this book is entitled to enter that debate. Also, for a country so blessed with near-perfect pastoral conditions to be importing twice the tonnage of beef than it exports,[3] perhaps we should be taking more of an interest in our own cows. Read the National Food Strategy[4] if you don't think our food systems are screwed up. From pesticide over-use to ammonia emissions, from biodiversity loss to oceans empty of entire fish species, we are simply producing the wrong food, in the wrong places and in the wrong way, in vast quantities, and then wasting around a third of it. If that sounds like a good system to you, you are easily pleased. Nearly 70% of our adult population is overweight, leading to an epidemic of high blood pressure, diabetes and any amount of wear and tear on our bones and muscles; all this, and we still spend seven times as much on weight-loss surgery as we do on promoting healthy eating. Who wouldn't want to rock a boat that lurched along like that?

We are also taking what the farmers produce and then often over-processing any goodness out of it. 'The UK is awash with food', says a leading food scientist, 'but from modes of production, processing and packaging which are unsustainable ecologically and socially.'[5] We crow about how many extra years we all live these days, but are strangely silent on how many more of them have become years lived under the shadow of disability. Blaming the cow for the effects of a 50-year love affair with salt and sugar is like blaming climate change on just one country. To hell with not rocking the boat.

So, if we don't want blanket trade deals to be put above our own hard-won quality and welfare standards, for example, we have to do more than moan about it, and instead not vote in politicians who will enable it. We should apply pressure on them to put taxes on foods that damage people and the environment, to make clear product labelling mandatory, and to make the polluter pay directly for the mess they make, and not the taxpayer. The idea that the introduction of a meat tax will do anything other than increase imports of cheap beef at the expense of high-welfare, sustainable (and therefore pricier) British farmers, is ludicrous, unless it is accompanied by rigorous import controls. Which it won't be. If they wanted to, the government could lead on democratising food, starting with real support for the remaining small abattoirs, so let's make them want to. We should demand that food education is introduced back to primary schools, so that children are allowed to enter that magical world of food early enough to usefully colour their lives, and then we might even introduce a Natural History GCSE for secondary schools. We would be shamed into action until the day that rich and poor can eat roughly the same quality of food, perhaps hypothecating the proceeds of those salt and sugar taxes to a scheme of green vouchers. It might help if we thought that progress was a society that all ate well, rather than a small proportion of it eating mangoes delivered out of the belly of an intercontinental aeroplane. We have accidentally surrendered our food democracy to the financial sector, for good and ill, and the industrialised cow is paying part of the price. We should seize it back.

Finally, we need to have the patience and imagination to understand that food production and nature can and should co-exist – as they always used to – effectively enough to feed all of us. Systematically removing nature from our farming is probably the worst thing that the last 50 years of 20th-century policy, science and subsidy did to us. In the last twenty years or so, the worm has been turning, be it ever so slowly. Somewhere out there in those huge intellectual spaces between intensive agriculture and complete rewilding is a sweet spot that produces an abundance of food within corridors of rich biodiversity. Call it re-naturing.

In the free world, politicians and corporations can only do in the long term what we make them do, or allow them to, so the future for the cow depends principally on us as individuals.

First, I need to take responsibility for my own food choices, learn about the stuff I put into my body, and understand its real cost beyond mere cash and indigestion. Tolerance of other people's diets would be good, while I am about it. Then, because I choose to eat beef, I must make sure it is genuinely grass-fed, high-welfare, and as local as possible. In other words, find a butcher I can trust. Doing the maths backwards, I should limit my beef habit to maybe twenty times a year, which includes the sneaky railway station burger just as much as it does the Sunday roast. I should avoid beef that has travelled, or whose food has travelled, across continents to get to me, and do the same to meals that arrive through my car window. I should continue to buy cuts from the whole cow, and not just the top back quarter, and to embrace slow cooking. I must consciously reduce my food waste; in the rich world, a third of our food goes into landfill or down the sink – which, in the case of the cow, is simply an insult. In terms of portion sizes, some shops are better than others, and it pays to shop around; loyalty schemes are designed to monetise my custom, not make me happier or richer; I can sign up to as many as I like, but then be as disloyal as I need to. Where I can, I should support farm shops and small artisan businesses: they are generally, if not always, better for the farmer and the environment.

Equally, I need to be alert to the genuine nuances and contradictions around the cow, starting with the admission that my meat habit has a real cost to the planet, and more than that of a vegetarian, somewhere within the hierarchy of all the other costs; a sustainable food system is another reason why I should reduce my meat consumption by at least a half. I need to accept that our supermarkets, however uncomfortable I may be with the power they wield, often brutally, provide millions of us with a reliable and affordable source of the food that keeps us alive; that fast food in moderation is still a positive pleasure, and that regenerative farming is only good so long as it is not used as an excuse for having even more livestock, rather than less. Neutering thousands of wild horses just so that you can shove more cattle out on the grassy ranges of Oregon is trashing biodiversity, rather than enhancing farming. In food, as in life, there is far more that should unite than divide us, and meat-eaters will never be taken seriously so long as enough of them use the word 'vegan' as an insult rather than a genuine dietary choice. For the time being, as the Archbishop of Canterbury once said, we have all forgotten how to disagree constructively.

Happily, there are signs that it is starting to change, if you look under enough stones.

In eighteen months on and around cattle farms, I found an industry at once scared for its future and yet alive with ideas and experiments, not to mention good practice. Some of these experiments, such as the mitigation of emissions with red sea-weed, are rooted deep in bioscience. Some, like regenerative farming, are simply a restatement of practices that have worked since the dawn of time. Many farmers are actively questioning the wisdom of making herd sizes bigger, just so that they can cling on in the brutal supply game that ends up in your super-market chiller. They are also starting to question the traditional routes to market, and are building their own brands and taking their own risks.

If you look hard enough, you can see the signs of people starting to take back a bit of control. A young self-employed farmer with an Oxfordshire micro-dairy featuring just three Austrian Gelbvieh cows, enabled by a supportive landowner to sell his 30 litres of surplus milk a day to his discerning consumers; a tiny new butchery on a remote Scottish farm that produces a perfectly integrated digital route for their beef into an appreciative local market; the Devon artisan food cooperative that, together, allows its members to reach a far wider audience than they ever could on their own; a peri-urban farm on the misty, industrial fringes of the Thames estuary; those little Riggits wandering back onto the nature reserve in Galloway to kick-start the return of proper biodiversity; a farm in West Wales that is becoming a price-maker, rather than a price-taker, by growing a new brand of bottled milkshakes; that mobile abattoir deep in the Cotswolds. There is room for scale, too, as there has to be, and plenty of farms with 400 or 500 cows have welfare and quality that rival the smaller operations. Arla, the huge dairy cooperative, is leading the charge to make the UK the dairy-producing country with the lowest carbon footprint on earth, and seems to be succeeding. Small doesn't need to be beautiful, any more than large has to be bad; the business of feeding 67 million people cannot afford to be precious and nostalgic.

While the signs of our excesses are still everywhere, the marks of abuse on our bruised planet have ignited a widespread and vibrant debate about sustainability in the way we farm. Regenerative agriculture, grass-feeding, rewilding, re-naturing have all started to move from cutting edge to mainstream – bright new thinking, though much of it rooted in ancient agricultural practice.

One evening, towards the end of my journey, I went to a meeting in a Sussex barn high up on the South Downs in which 30 local farmers and landowners were plotting to create a cluster of rewilded corridors that will stretch from Gatwick south to the sea, and then along the coast to Chichester, fully 40 miles of nature with the cow rightfully at the heart of it.

When the meeting was over, I walked back to where I had left my car, cutting through a conservation headland in the half-light, and found, ragged and bright in the evening pathway, a tiny rough poppy. To me it felt like a symbol for a world that is slowly reawakening, and also a vanishingly rare survivor from the seedbank within those old arable chalklands. Poppies don't want peace and quiet; they want disturbance. And then, generally, nature bounces back if you let it.

And somewhere deep in a Dutch laboratory, that aurochs is slowly coming to life again, in a space-age assertion that what worked for the planet a quarter of a million years ago, still works now.

To go forward, sometimes we just need to start by looking back.

EPILOGUE
A Field in Devon

September

....

'Despite all our accomplishments,
we owe our existence to a six-inch layer
of topsoil and the fact that it rains.'
PAUL HARVEY

....

A few weeks later, on a low hill overlooking Dartmoor, and to the muted soundtrack of faraway stock doves and soft, soft rain, I notice a life-sized plastic Friesian cow on the lawn of a large Victorian manor house. From behind it comes the unmistakable noise of children enjoying themselves.

I am at Nethercott, one of three farms established by the author Michael Morpurgo and his wife, Clare, as part of their 'Farms for City Children' charity, which enables kids from disadvantaged urban areas to experience 'working together in the heart of the British countryside'.[1] They come here one school at a time, three or four teachers and 40 children, and witness the alchemy that connects farm with fork. That cow is the only fake thing I'll see all morning.

Because it's human nature, I follow the sound of happiness. I walk past a productive walled garden, past a group of loose brick composters and a greenhouse full of tomatoes and squashes, and eventually see about a dozen children, ten or eleven years old, dressed in blue waterproof suits and picking runner beans for their lunch. There is nothing complex about their experience, or fake about their engagement; from a corner of London that we tend to hear about only in relation to gangland violence, they are simply immersing themselves for a week into the magical world of where their food comes from. Deprived of screens of any sort, they are looking after livestock, gathering eggs, harvesting vegetables, making cream, weeding ground and eating together. From the complexity of putting eggs under a hatching lamp to the simplicity of wolfing down a couple of blackberries that happen to be overhanging the path, they often start a relationship with the place that lasts for decades, and one with food that lasts for life. Indeed, some of this week's guests are the children of parents who went through the same experience 30 years before. If it all sounds idyllic, that's probably because it is.

Another group were out on the neighbouring farm, working with the Limousin and Charolais cattle.

'It's very much not some glorified petting farm', says Tim Rose, the director. 'Part of the process will be explaining to them that death is an essential part of the process of bringing that burger to their plate, and that the muck of the cow contributes to the growing of the grass.'

'We had a boy here last year', he continues, 'whose teas for the last three years had consisted of two shredded wheat.

Nothing more. Can you imagine what that week stirred in his brain?' He is right, of course. My experience as a parent is that, with children, you simply ignite the pilot light, and their natural curiosity will do the rest.

If there is a metaphor for the ignorance with which we have chosen to burden our children in the matter of food, then maybe it is the girl who rushed excitedly into the yard a while ago, clutching a basket of freshly laid eggs. 'There's something wrong with them', she told a teacher. 'They haven't got numbers on.' Extreme, maybe; exaggerated in the telling, possibly, but it neatly encapsulates the way that we have allowed our food to become just another industrial process in a world full of industrial processes. By placing ourselves above and apart from the nature that sustains us, we have too often turned our eyes away from the central role of food in our lives. It could be so much better.

Long after I have gone eastwards and home, those children will sit down to their evening meal. Whatever their choice of diet, there is the right fresh and unprocessed food for them, and just about all of it will have come from within a couple of hundred metres of where they are sitting: beans, burgers or bantams' eggs, they have seen the cane, cow or chicken that it came from. And above all they will eat it together, in an ancient ritual of sharing pleasure that some of them will be doing almost for the first time.

The future of cattle, and of our relationship with them, will be decided by government ministers, negotiators, scientists, farmers, retailers, campaigners and, above all, consumers, just as it always has been, every one of them at some stage in the past an eleven year-old child who either got, or didn't get, an opportunity to pick runner beans and look at livestock.

That may be the secret to how we start loving the cow again.

RTMG
September 2021

BIBLIOGRAPHY

Chillingham: Its Cattle, Castle and Church, Paul Bahn,
    Fonthill, 2016
Practical Cattle Farming, Kat Bazeley and Alastair Hayton,
    Crowood, 2007
What Are People For?, Wendell Berry, Counterpoint, 1990
The World-Ending Fire, Wendell Berry, Penguin, 2017

Silent Spring, Rachel Carson, Houghton Mifflin, 1962
The Cow Book, John Connell, Granta, 2016
A Short History of the World According to Sheep, Sally
    Coulthard, Head of Zeus, 2020
Britain Begins, Barry Cunliffe, Oxford University Press, 2012

The Economics of Biodiversity, Dasgupta report, 2021
Guns, Germs and Steel, Jared Diamond, Vintage, 1997

Invasive Aliens, Dan Eatherley, Collins, 2019

Meat: A Benign Extravagance, Simon Fairlie, Permanent
    Publications, 2010
Livestock's Long Shadow, FAO (UN) report, 2006
Islands of Abandonment, Cal Flyn, Collins, 2021
The Bull, Allan Fraser, Osprey, 1972
Raising Steaks, Betty Fussell, Orlando, 2008

The Aurochs: Born to be Wild, Ronald Goderie et al.,
    Roodbont Publishing, 2013
Thinking in Pictures, Temple Grandin, Bloomsbury, 2006

Bibliography

The Forgiveness of Nature, Graham Harvey, Vintage, 2002

Grass-Fed Nation, Graham Harvey, Icon Books, 2016

Green and Prosperous Land, Dieter Helm, Collins, 2020

Death in the Afternoon, Ernest Hemingway, Penguin, 1939

A Breed Apart, Adam Henson, Penguin, 2019

Meat Logic: Why Do We Eat Animals?, Charles Horn,
    CreateSpace, 2014

Rewilding, Paul Jepson and Cain Blythe, Icon Books, 2020

On Bullfighting, A.L. Kennedy, Penguin, 1999

Feeding Britain: Our Food Problems and How to Fix Them,
    Tim Lang, Pelican, 2021

Native: Life in a Vanishing Landscape, Patrick Laurie, Birlinn,
    2021

A Sand County Almanac, Aldo Leopold, Penguin, 1948

The Dead Zone, Philip Lymbery, Bloomsbury, 2018

Farmageddon, Philip Lymbery, Bloomsbury, 2015

Orchard: A Year in England's Eden, Benedict Macdonald and
    Nicholas Gates, Collins, 2021

Rebirding, Benedict Macdonald, Pelagic, 2019

End of the Megafauna, Ross D.E. MacPhee, Norton, 2018

Feral, George Monbiot, Penguin, 2014

Humans: A Brief History of How We F*cked It All Up, Tom
    Phillips, Wildfire, 2018

Food Rules, Michael Pollan, Penguin, 2010

The Omnivore's Dilemma, Michael Pollan, Bloomsbury, 2006

Partridges, G.R. Potts, HarperCollins, 2012

The Illustrated History of the Countryside, Oliver Rackham,
    Weidenfeld & Nicolson, 1986

English Pastoral, James Rebanks, Penguin, 2020
The Shepherd's Life, James Rebanks, Penguin, 2015
Beef: The Untold Story of How Milk, Meat, and Muscle Shaped the World, Andrew Rimas and Evan Fraser, Morrow, 2008
Sacred Cow: The Case for (Better) Meat, Diana Rodgers and Robb Wolf, Benbella, 2020

The Good Book of Human Nature, Carel van Schaik and Kai Michel, Basic Books, 2016
Fast Food Nation, Eric Schlosser, Penguin, 2002
Cows Save the Planet, Judith Schwartz, Chelsea Green Publishing, 2013
The Diet Myth, Tim Spector, Weidenfeld & Nicolson, 2016

The Grazing Animal, J.F.H. Thomas, Faber, 1949
The Drovers, Shirley Toulson, Shire Books, 2011
Wilding: The Return of Nature to a British Farm, Isabella Tree, Picador, 2018

Cow Care in Hindu Animal Ethics, Kenneth Valpey, Palgrave Macmillan, 2020
The Holy Bible, Various

The Angry Chef, Anthony Warner, Oneworld, 2017
Cattle: An Informal Social History, Laurie Winn Carlson, Ivan R. Dee, 2001

The Secret Life of Cows, Rosamund Young, Faber, 2017

ACKNOWLEDGEMENTS

The 'cow' community, for want of a better term, is one that has probably felt isolated, recently. When I began this journey, I found a general suspicion about the motives of an outsider coming in to write about a subject that has only found itself controversial in the last fraction of its history. The more I went on, the more I found myself entering a rabbit warren of introductions to warm-hearted and generous people who, from whatever part of the story and the debate, were genuinely passionate about the subject and its challenges. Sadly, I will have missed out many, but I am profoundly grateful to all of them for their constructive help, whether they are on the list below or not. Also, farming tends to be a family business, so if I only happen to have mentioned one person from a particular farm, it nearly always includes others.

Robert and Sophie
  Whitcombe
James Renwick
Robert Bridger
Arthur Crutchley
Keith Baxter
Mary Quicke
Shon Sprackling
Sam Beard
Lee Pay

Adam Henson
Richard Perkins
Graham Harvey
Patrick Laurie
Jeremy Way
Edmund Sutcliffe
Ross Wingfield
Tim Rose
Jim Rowe
Grahame Kittle

Emma Ridge

Charlie and Hazel Flindt

Professor Stephen Hall

Simon Doherty

John Bragg

Christopher Price

Chris Mullins

Oliver Hemsley

Amelia Lawrence

Wolfram Lohr

Kenneth Valpey

Philip Lymbery

John Meadley

Ellie Waddington

Denise Walton and family

Lindsay Whistance

Andy Gray

Satish Kumar

Guy Singh-Watson

Paul Stevenson

Ian Wilkinson

Jonathan Brunyee

James Joicey

Peter and Henri Greig

Paddy Hoare and Jane Parker

John Wilson LVO

Andrew Parr

Kat and Peter Bazeley

Hallam Duckworth

Gillian Butler

Hannah Davis

Dr Tara Garnett

Rosamund Young

Monique Stone

Aarti Bhogaita

Andrew Lee

George Cusworth

Simon Fairlie

Penny Franklyn

Richard Benyon

Richard Goring

James Foottit

Michael Pollan

APPENDIX 1

Alex's Beef Shin Ragù Recipe

Beef shin ragù
(for 6 people)

Ingredients

~250g pancetta
1–2 large carrots (finely diced)
1–2 large celery sticks (finely diced)
1–2 large onions (finely diced)
2 garlic cloves (finely diced/crushed)
600–800g beef shin (cubed)
Glass and a bit of red wine
400g tin of tomatoes
1 tablespoon tomato paste
150g whole milk
1 bay leaf

3 sage leaves (finely chopped)
Sprig of rosemary (leaves stripped, finely chopped)
Sprig of thyme (leaves stripped, finely chopped)
½–1 teaspoon cayenne pepper
½ teaspoon ground nutmeg (fresh if possible)
2 teaspoons ground coriander
1 square of dark chocolate
Salt
Olive/vegetable oil

To serve

625–750g (1.25–1.5 packs) good-quality spaghetti
Grated Parmigiano Reggiano
Simple salad

Recipe

1. Stick the pancetta in a big sauté pan on low heat until the fat renders out – maybe 10–15 minutes.

2. While bacon is rendering, finely chop all the veg (carrot, celery, onion, garlic) and add it to the pan to soften for about 10 minutes, stirring occasionally.

3. While the veg is softening, cut beef into cubes. Remove as much gristle as you can – this becomes annoying after a few hours of cooking if you haven't done it at the start. The smaller the beef chunks are, the richer and smoother the pasta will be at the end.

4. Once the vegetable mixture is soft and starting to become cohesive, add the beef, along with a big pinch of salt and your herbs and spices. If the mixture looks dry, give it a swig of oil.

5. Add the wine, and once it has mostly evaporated add the tomatoes, breaking them up if needed. At this point you could add a few more diced fresh tomatoes if the mixture doesn't look tomatoey enough, and cook them down for a few minutes.

6. Add the tomato paste, half the milk and the chunk of chocolate (for a deeper richness). Stir and turn the heat down very low.

7. Simmer for as long as you want – six hours or more is good – adding a splash of milk or water when it looks dry.

8. 10 minutes before eating, turn the heat off (to allow the sauce to cool slightly and absorb its own juices), then prepare the salad and stick on a pan of boiling water (with a small handful of salt). Cook the spaghetti for 5 or 6 minutes, then taste every minute – it should be soft but still have very slight bite in the middle. Make sure you save a mug of pasta water.

9. To serve, mix half the ragù into the pasta and add pasta water, stirring and adding until it becomes glossy. Plate up and spoon the other half of the sauce onto the tops of the pasta servings. Grate parmesan and serve with salad.

NOTES

Prologue
1. www.beef2live.com
2. *Cow Care in Hindu Animal Ethics*, Kenneth Valpey, Palgrave Macmillan, 2020.
3. www.worldhunger.org, 2016.
4. World Health Organization (WHO) Fact Sheet.
5. 'Cooking up a Storm: Food, greenhouse gas emissions and our changing climate', Tara Garnett, Food Climate Research Network, 2008.
6. *Green and Prosperous Land*, Dieter Helm, Collins, 2019.
7. Office for National Statistics.
8. Dr Tim Leunig, London School of Economics, Adviser to Departments of Education and Environment, February 2020.
9. *Feeding Britain*, Tim Lang, Pelican, 2021.
10. 'How Mental Systems Believe', Daniel T. Gilbert, University of Texas paper, 1991.
11. *The Cow Book*, John Connell, Granta, 2016.

Chapter 1
1. 'Even Toed Ungulates', *Encyclopaedia of Mammals*.
2. *Rewilding*, Paul Jepson and Cain Blythe, Icon Books, 2020.
3. *End of the Megafauna*, Ross D.E. MacPhee, Norton, 2018.
4. 'Palaeopopulations of Late Pleistocene Top Predators in Europe', Cajus G. Diedrich, *Paleontology Journal*, Volume 2014.
5. *The Aurochs: Born to be Wild*, Ronald Goderie et al., Roodbont Publishing, 2013.
6. 'The role of brain size on mammalian population densities', Manuela González-Suárez, *Journal of Animal Ecology*, December 2020.
7. *Feral*, George Monbiot, Penguin, 2013.

Chapter 2
1. 'Where the Wild Things Went', article in *The Land*, Issue 24, 2019.
2. *A Short History of the World According to Sheep*, Sally Coulthard, Head of Zeus, 2020.
3. *Cattle: An Informal Social History*, Laurie Winn Carlson, Ivan R. Dee, 2001.
4. *The Diet Myth*, Tim Spector, Weidenfeld & Nicolson, 2016.
5. *A History of Domesticated Animals*, Frederick Zeuner, Harper & Row, 1963.

Chapter 3
1. *Orchard*, Benedict Macdonald and Nicholas Gates, William Collins, 2020.
2. *Britain Begins*, Barry Cunliffe, Oxford University Press, 2012.
3. www.ancient.eu
4. 'Neolithic explanations revisited: modelling the arrival and spread of domesticated cattle into Neolithic Britain', Cummings et al., *Environmental Archaeology*, October 2018.
5. 'The state of the world's animal genetic resources for food and agriculture', Barbara Rischkowsky and Dafydd Pilling, FAO Commission on Genetic Resources for Food and Agriculture, 2007.
6. *Cattle: An Informal Social History*, Laurie Winn Carlson, Ivan R. Dee, 2001.
7. *A Breed Apart*, Adam Henson, Penguin, 2019.
8. 'The ecological niche of the aurochs', The Breeding Back Blog, Daniel Foidl, February 27th, 2021.
9. *Invasive Aliens*, Dan Eatherley, Collins, 2019.
10. *Feral*, George Monbiot, Penguin, 2013.
11. 'Livestock and animal husbandry in early Medieval England', Terry O'Connor, *Quaternary International*, 30, 2013.
12. *The Illustrated History of the Countryside*, Oliver Rackham, Weidenfeld & Nicolson, 1986.
13. 'The Animals of Cottage and Castle: Cows, Bulls and Oxen', Katherine Ashe, EHFA, December 2013.
14. Rackham, op. cit., 1986.
15. *Drovers' Dogs*, Verity Collins, WSN, 2005.
16. 'The Origin of Red Angus', The Red Angus Society of Australia website.

Chapter 4

1. Beef Market Central article, September 2020.
2. *Beef: The Untold Story of How Milk, Meat, and Muscle Shaped the World*, Andrew Rimas and Evan Fraser, Morrow, 2008.
3. 'Robert Bakewell (1725–1795) of Dishley: farmer and livestock improver', David L. Wykes, article in *British Agricultural Historical Society*, 2004.
4. *Guardian* article, April 17th, 2019.
5. National Agricultural Statistics Service, USDA, 2010.
6. Compassion in World Farming (CIWF) briefing sheet.
7. Defra statistics, published March 2019.
8. *Journal of Applied Ecology*, Volume 39, Issue 1, June 2002.
9. House of Commons Library, Briefing Paper 3339, June 2019.

Chapter 5

1. 'A brief history of milk', Homestead.org
2. *Till the Cows Come Home*, Philip Walling, Atlantic Books, 2018.
3. *Grass Fed Nation*, Graham Harvey, Icon Books, 2016.
4. Walling, op. cit., 2018.
5. BBC series, *Mud, Sweat and Tractors* ('Milk' episode), 2009.
6. Agriculture and Horticulture Development Board (AHDB), June 2021.
7. House of Commons Report, 2004.
8. AHDB report, 2021.
9. Statista, 2019.
10. Eurostat, 2019.
11. *Times* article, February 27th, 2021.
12. Briefing 3692, Institute of Agricultural Management, 2021.
13. *Feeding Britain*, Tim Lang, Pelican, 2021.
14. 'How to fight desertification and reverse climate change', Allan Savory, Ted Talk, 2013.

Chapter 6

1. National Animal Disease Information Service (NADIS) website.
2. Agriculture and Horticulture Development Board (anecdotal; *Farming Today*, BBC, March 17th, 2021).
3. *Oxford English Dictionary*.

4. 'Close-up on the meat we eat', BEUC (European Bureau of Consumers' Unions) report, November 2015. Freely available and worth a read.
5. Consortium for Labelling for the Environment, Animal Welfare and Regenerative Farming, www.pastureforlife.org
6. ADHB report, 2020.
7. Kantar Worldpanel.
8. Statista Food and Nutrition report, 2020.
9. *Guardian*, March 22nd, 2016.
10. Average Farm Business Income Survey, Defra, 2021.
11. *English Pastoral*, James Rebanks, Penguin, 2020.
12. 'Which countries spend the most on food', World Economic Forum Report, 2015.
13. 'Share of food expenditure in gross disposable income', Statista, October 2015.
14. 'Household consumer spending by segment in Germany', Statista, 2019.
15. *The Omnivore's Dilemma*, Michael Pollan, Bloomsbury, 2006.
16. 'The Hidden Costs of UK Food', Sustainable Food Trust Report, 2019.

Chapter 7

1. www.gardenorganic.org.uk
2. *Serengeti Rules*, Sean B. Carroll, Google Books, 2016.
3. *Beef: The Untold Story of How Milk, Meat, and Muscle Shaped the World*, Andrew Rimas and Evan Fraser, Morrow, 2008.
4. *Guns, Germs and Steel*, Jared Diamond, Vintage, 1997.
5. *The Good Book of Human Nature*, Carel van Schaik and Kai Michel, Basic Books, 2016.
6. *Farmers Guardian* anniversary report, March 12th, 2021.
7. *The Shepherd's Life*, James Rebanks, Penguin, 2015.
8. 'What We Didn't Learn From Foot and Mouth', *Unherd* article by John Lewis-Stempel, February 2021.
9. 'Foot and Mouth Disease: Lessons to be Learned', Inquiry report, 2002.
10. Health and Safety Executive, initial report on potential breaches to biosecurity at the Pirbright site, August 2007.

11. World Organisation for Animal Health (OIE).
12. *The Secret Life of Cows*, Rosamund Young, Faber, 2017.
13. *Farmers Weekly* article, May 2020.
14. Antibiotic Research UK paper, June 8th, 2020.
15. 'Maximum Growth: Whatever the Cost', paper by Sustainable Food Trust, 2020.
16. *The Forgiveness of Nature*, Graham Harvey, Vintage, 2002.
17. 'Health Risks and Benefits of Urban and Peri-Urban Agriculture and Livestock in sub-Saharan Africa', Ana Boischio et al., paper for International Development Research Centre, August 2006.
18. *Feeding Britain*, Tim Lang, Pelican, 2021.

Chapter 8
1. www.mcdonalds.com
2. *Fast Food Nation*, Eric Schlosser, Penguin, 2002.
3. Ibid.
4. *New York Times* article, January 27th, 2022.
5. *Green and Prosperous Land*, Dieter Helm, Collins, 2019.
6. *The World-Ending Fire*, Wendell Berry, Allen Lane, 2017.
7. 'Tesco's deforestation claims are misleading the public', Greenpeace article, August 2020.
8. 'Tesco urged to ditch meat company over alleged links to Amazon deforestation', *Guardian* article, August 5th, 2020.
9. 'The Tragedy of the Commons', Garrett Hardin, paper in *Science*, December 13th, 1968.
10. *Table Talk*, A.A. Gill, Phoenix, 2007.

Chapter 9
1. *Sacred Cow*, Diana Rodgers and Robb Wolf, Benbella, 2020.
2. *Ecowatch* article, May 2018.
3. *Guardian* article, May 21st, 2018.
4. 'Water resources, agriculture, the environment and society', Pimentel et al., *Bioscience*, February 1997.
5. *Meat: A Benign Extravagance*, Simon Fairlie, Permanent Publications, 2010.
6. *Food Rules: An Eater's Manual*, Michael Pollan, Penguin, 2009.

7. 'Forage-fed cattle point the way forward for beef?', Gillian Butler et al., paper for Future Foods, 2021.

8. *The Angry Chef*, Anthony Warner, Oneworld, 2017.

9. 'In the Service of All that Lives: Gandhi's Vision of Engaged Nonviolent Animal Care', Kenneth Valpey, paper for *Animal Theologians*, 2020.

10. 'Global methane levels soar to record high', article in Nature.com by Quirin Schiermeier, July 14th, 2020.

11. 'Overview of Greenhouse Gases', US Environmental Protection Agency report, 2018.

12. Article in *The Times*, March 18th, 2021.

13. 'Role of livestock in carbon dioxide, methane and nitrous oxide emissions', *Livestock's Long Shadow*, FAO report, 2006.

14. Article in *Australian Farm Weekly*, January 29th, 2021.

15. 'Cooking up a Storm: Food, greenhouse gas emissions and our changing climate', Tara Garnett, Food Climate Research Network, 2008.

16. *The World-Ending Fire*, Wendell Berry, Allen Lane, 2017.

17. 'Perspectives for Parking Policy', Bates and Liebling, RAC Foundation, 2012.

18. 'Including carbon emissions from deforestation in the carbon footprint of Brazilian beef', Cederberg et al., paper for *Environmental Science and Technology*, January 2011.

19. 'Will Defra's plans for farming make things better or worse?', Richard Young, Sustainable Food Trust article, December 2020.

20. 'Meat company faces heat over "cattle laundering" in Amazon supply chain', *Guardian*, February 20th, 2020.

21. 'We're Living in a Golden Age of Greenwash', article on dishonest PR, Greenpeace, June 2021.

22. *Livestock's Long Shadow*, UN FAO report, 2006.

23. 'Beef Production is Killing the Amazon Rainforest', One Green Planet report, 2014.

24. Rainforest Action Network.

25. 'Impacts of feeding less food-competing feedstuffs to livestock on global food system sustainability', Schader et al., paper for Royal Society, 2015.

26. EAT–Lancet Commission report on 'Food, Planet, Health'.

Chapter 10

1. *Beef: The Untold Story of How Milk, Meat, and Muscle Shaped the World*, Andrew Rimas and Evan Fraser, Morrow, 2008.
2. 'Some Characteristics of Hinduism as a Religion', Professor Hervey D. Griswold, Christian College, Lahore, 1912.
3. *Times* article, February 24th, 2021.
4. *Death in the Afternoon*, Ernest Hemingway, Penguin, 1939.
5. *Spain*, Jan Morris, Faber, 2008.
6. *On Bullfighting*, A.L. Kennedy, Penguin, 1999.
7. YouGov survey for HuffPost from May 2020.
8. *Feral*, George Monbiot, Penguin, 2013.
9. *Modern Farmer* article, September 2013.

Chapter 11

1. 'Patterns of smallpox mortality in London over three centuries', Krylova et al., *PLOS Biology*, September 2019.
2. British Society for Immunology website article (undated).
3. Global Animal Health Association newsletter.
4. World Health Organization (WHO) bulletin, November 30th, 2020.
5. Article in Antimicrobial Resistance Centre publication (LSHTM), June 3rd, 2020.
6. Centers for Disease Control and Prevention website.
7. *Meat: A Benign Extravagance*, Simon Fairlie, Permanent Publications, 2010.

Chapter 12

1. *The Leather Dictionary*.
2. Heritage Craft Association website.
3. *Color: A Course in Mastering the Art of Mixing Colors*, Betty Edwards, TarcherPerigee, 2004.
4. Sustainable Food Trust, Campaign for Local Abattoirs, 2018.
5. 'Genetic link between cattle temperament and autism in humans', *Science Daily* (Australia), August 2020.
6. National Craft Butchers Survey, 2021.

Chapter 13

1. *The Forgiveness of Nature: The Story of Grass*, Graham Harvey, Vintage, 2002.
2. 'Evolutionary History of the Grasses', E. Kellogg, ASPB paper, March 2001.
3. *Guns, Germs and Steel*, Jared Diamond, Vintage, 1997.
4. *Britain Begins*, Barry Cunliffe, Oxford University Press, 2012.
5. Harvey, op. cit., 2002.
6. *A Sand County Almanac*, Aldo Leopold, Penguin, 1948.
7. 'Power Steer', article for *New York Times Magazine*, Michael Pollan, March 31st, 2002.
8. *The Formation of Vegetable Mould through the Action of Worms*, Charles Darwin, John Murray, 1881.
9. Local Biodiversity Intactness Index, data.nhm.ac.uk/dataset/bii-bte
10. www.groundswellag.com
11. Columella, *De Re Rustica*, 2.18.

Chapter 14

1. *Farming UK* article, June 28th, 2019.
2. 'Revisiting demographic processes in cattle with genome-wide population genetic analysis', Orozco-terWengel et al., *Frontiers in Genetics*, 2015.
3. 'Livestock diversity as interface between people, landscapes and nature', Hall, British Ecological Society paper, 2019.
4. Defra website.
5. www.rbst.org.uk
6. *Islands of Abandonment*, Cal Flyn, Collins, 2021.
7. 'Feral Cattle of Swona, Orkney Islands', Hall et al., article for *Mammal Review*, 1986.
8. Stabiliser Cattle Company handbook, May 2009.
9. *Chillingham: Its Cattle, Castle and Church*, Paul Bahn et al., Fonthill, 2016.
10. 'The use of cattle *Bos taurus* for restoring and maintaining Holarctic landscapes', Hall, paper for *Ecology and Evolution*, 2019.
11. BBC Online article, June 28th, 2021.
12. *Partridges*, G.R. Potts, HarperCollins, 2012.

Chapter 15

1. 'Rethinking Food and Agriculture, 2020–2030', Tubb and Seba, www.rethinkx.com
2. *The Diet Myth*, Tim Spector, Weidenfeld & Nicolson, 2016.
3. Agriculture and Horticulture Development Board (AHDB) figures for 2020. 242,828 tons imported against 119,385 tons exported.
4. www.nationalfoodstrategy.org
5. *Feeding Britain*, Tim Lang, Pelican, 2021.

Epilogue

1. Farms For City Children website: www.farmsforcitychildren.org

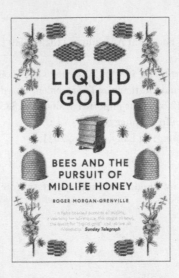

After a chance meeting in the pub, Roger Morgan-Grenville – entering his late fifties with some trepidation – and his much younger friend Duncan decide to take up beekeeping. Their enthusiasm matched only by their ignorance, they are pitched into an arcane world, emerging two years later with a new-found understanding of nature and a respect for the honeybee and the threats it faces.

Wryly humorous and surprisingly moving, *Liquid Gold* is the story of an unlikely friendship. It is also an uplifting account of the author's own midlife journey: coming to terms with an empty nest, getting older, and finding solace in learning something new.

'A great book ... humorous, sensitive and full of wisdom' Chris Stewart, author of *Driving Over Lemons*

'A light-hearted account of midlife, a yearning for adventure, the plight of bees, the quest for "liquid gold" and, above all, friendship.' *Sunday Telegraph*

'*Liquid Gold* is a book that ignites joy and warmth' Mary Colwell, author of *Curlew Moon*

**ISBN 978-178578-714-0 (paperback) /
ISBN 978-178578-606-8 (ebook)**

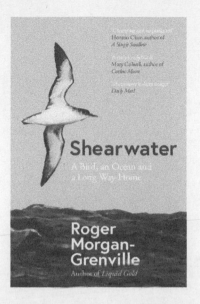